The Contempt Power

The Contempt Power

Ronald L. Goldfarb

Columbia University Press
New York and London 1963

Ronald L. Goldfarb, of the Attorney General's Organized Crime and Racketeering Section in the Department of Justice, is a member of the New York and California Bars and the Bar of the United States Supreme Court.

I dedicate this book to
my Mother and Father

Acknowledgments

This book is a result of three years of work, which began and ended at the Yale Law School. While a candidate for a Master of Laws degree in 1960, and at the suggestion of Professor Richard Donnelly, I wrote two articles (one with Professor Donnelly) which dealt with one aspect of the contempt power. My research made me aware of certain things: that, though the impact of the contempt power was far-reaching, the subject was academically neglected; that this was not simply a technical legal device, but a legal power with deep and broad ramifications; that serious work on this subject would be interesting, and might be useful.

As my work developed and separate articles resulted from time to time, the inclination often arose to stray into tangential areas which crucially bore upon any discussion of the main subject. The character of the contempt power itself is no more interesting than the diverse problems it provokes. So, at once, I tried to include and exclude, with little more to guide me than a personal evaluation of the pertinency and weight of any matter upon the main questions to which answers were ultimately sought. This, I suppose, is both the responsibility and the license of the writer.

The content of this subject often tended toward technicality. Yet, I felt that the extra-legal significance of the subject warranted an attempt to reach a broader audience than the legal world. In trying to straddle two horses, I hope I have not toppled from both. For I hope that this book will be of interest to others than lawyers; yet I undertook to formulate it in a way which would be of use to my profession. If there is a style between specialty and catholicity, this is what I sought.

A substantial part of the time I spent working on this book was encouraged and endorsed by the Arthur Garfield Hays Program at N.Y.U. Law School. For no other consideration than the faith that something good might come from my work, and, if so, that they would have been a part, the administrators of this program gave me assistance which made my work more pleasant and realizable. For this I am indebted to Dean Niles and many others of the faculty and administrative staff of the law school. Most especially and singularly do I wish to thank Professor Paul Oberst, who as director of the program and my chief friend and critic was helpful in so many ways. That his advice and talent must be reflected in any worthwhile parts of this book is the bounty of the reader. That I have had his association and friendship is a privilege for which I am grateful. The Hays program sponsored the work of Bernard Mindich, who assisted me in a research capacity in the months I worked at N.Y.U. He did an excellent and noteworthy job. His research and memoranda in the area of administrative contempt powers resulted in great measure in Chapter III of this book. His should be the greatest credit for that section. His advice and friendship were sources of continuous encouragement, and I look forward to his personal accomplishments.

I am also grateful to the individuals of the Washington University, Syracuse University, and Michigan University Law Reviews whose publications of parts of the book accelerated the physical perfection of my ultimate manuscript.

After months of completing, editing, and worrying in spare minutes, while working for the Department of Justice, I returned, if only in spirit, to the Yale Law School. In submitting this book as my doctoral thesis, I was subjected to the criticism of Professors Pollak, Rodell, and Donnelly of the Yale Law faculty. Their advice was helpful, and their considerations were encouraging. I send special thanks to Fred Rodell for helping me learn how to write, and for encouraging the publication of this book.

At last, to my wife, my thanks again for incalculable help, patience, and good will.

I have added this section, though I had always questioned the worthwhileness of such an indulgence. Not until I had the experience of writing a book, did I appreciate either the total obsession and involvement necessary on the part of an author or the dependency he must have upon the counsel and good will and assistance of others. While on the one hand I shall feel an emptiness now that my work on this book is all done, on the other I shall be the more fulfilled for having had all the help and consort which these others have given. It would be unkind, if not dishonest, to omit mentioning this, or to deny sharing whatever credit may come. Of course, the views expressed and the responsibility for them are mine alone.

RONALD L. GOLDFARB

Alexandria, Virginia (1963)

Contents

King:	How might a prince of my great hopes forget
	So great indignities you laid upon me!
	What! rate, rebuke, and roughly send to prison
	The immediate heir of England! Was this easy?
	May this be wash'd in Lethe, and forgotten?
Chief Justice:	I then did use the person of your father;
	The image of his power lay then in me:
	And, in the administration of his law,
	Whiles I was busy for the commonwealth,
	Your highness pleased to forget my place,
	And majesty and power of law and justice,
	The image of the King whom I presented,
	And struck me in my very seat of judgment;
	Whereupon, as an offender to your father,
	I gave bold way to my authority,
	And did commit you. If the deed were ill,
	Be you contented, wearing now the garland,
	To have a son set your decrees at naught,
	To pluck down justice from your awful bench,
	To trip the course of law and blunt the sword
	That guards the peace and safety of your person;
	Nay, more, to spurn at your most royal image,
	And mock your workings in a second body.
	Question your royal thoughts, make the case yours;
	Be now the father, and propose a son;
	Hear your own dignity so much profan'd
	See your most dreadful laws so loosely slighted,
	Behold yourself so by a son disdain'd;
	And then imagine me taking your part,
	And, in your power, softly silencing your son:
	After this cold considerance, sentence me;
	And, as you are a King, speak in your state
	What I have done that misbecame my place,
	My person, or my liege's sovereignty.
King:	You are right, justice, and you weigh this well;
	Therefore still bear the balance and the sword:
	And I do wish your honors may increase

Till you do live to see a son of mine
Offend you, and obey you, as I did.
So shall I speak my father's words
Happy am I, that have a man so bold,
That dares do justice on my proper son;
And not less happy, having such a son,
That would deliver up his greatness so
Into the hands of justice. You did commit me:
For which I do commit into your hand
The unstain'd sword that you have us'd to bear;
With this remembrance,—that you use the same
With the like bold, just and impartial spirit
As you have done 'gainst me.

Henry IV, Part 2, Act 5, Scene 2

The Contempt Power

CHAPTER I

The History of the Contempt Power

Contempt can be generally defined as an act of disobedience or disrespect toward a judicial or legislative body of government, or interference with its orderly process, for which a summary punishment is usually exacted. In a broader, more general view, it is a power assumed by governmental bodies to coerce cooperation, and punish criticism or interference, even of a causally indirect nature. In legal literature, it has been categorized, subclassified, and scholastically dignified by division into varying shades—each covering some particular aspect of the general power, respectively governed by a particular set of procedures. So, the texts separate retributive or criminal contempts from merely coercive or civil contempts: those directly offensive from those only constructively contemptuous; those affecting the judiciary and others the legislature. The implementation of this power has taken place predominantly in England and America, and has recently been accelerated into a continuingly greater role in the United States.

The legal literature of the common law is replete with references to the contempt power. It occupies so accepted a place in Anglo-American law that any questions that have been raised are less addressed to whether the power should exist than to what extent it can be exercised and what are its limitations. But, indeed, to the lawyer from a non-common-law country the contempt power is a legal technique which is not only unnecessary to a working legal system, but also violative of basic philosophical approaches to the relations between government bodies and people.[1] Neither Latin American nor European civil law legal systems use any device of the nature or proportions of our contempt power. While critics of these systems may make preferential comparisons, so long as these countries keep well within anarchy on the one hand and totalitarianism on the other, there is room to question whether indeed this power is as necessary and essential as our decision-makers suggest.

Cases in England and the United States which treat the contempt power all assume that the order of society's affairs dictates that this power is inherent in the very nature of governmental bodies, and that all individuals figuratively sacrifice some portion of their civil liberties to this needed expedient when they adopt their social contract. Civil lawyers have voiced the fear that such a concession would allow governmental arbitrariness. Though these countries recognize to some extent the propriety of punishment for past acts (some criminal contempts), they recoil at the suggestion of punishment for the purpose of coercing an individual to act in a certain way in the future (civil contempt). Though criminal contempts are sometimes accepted in civil law systems (if limited and under different labels), these legal systems draw a distinction between punishment as a willed consequence of human behavior, and contempt as a means of coercing the commission of certain desired acts. This difference of approach in the use of a power like contempt underscores an anomalous difference in the recognition of individual values in the ideology of a system of law. For example, it has been pointed out that the magnitude of the coercive penalty in civil contempts is measured by the resistance to be overcome rather than the gravity of what has been done. Though all societies punish people for what they have done, only the common law punishes man "in order to do violence to his incoercible freedom to do or not to do something." [2] Moreover, the injury which caused the contempt proceedings is often incapable of reparation, deterrence, repentance, or reformation, which goals are often secondary to personal punishment. The sanction is aimed at a resisting will.

Anglophiles will jump to the argument that theirs is not a system directed by ideologies of individuality. They are correct. Yet, it takes some straining of reason to include the contempt power within the best characteristics of Anglo-American, freedom-conscious law. And even assuming the value of this power device in a legal system such as ours, it is still another question whether it ought to be exercised either in the procedural manner or to the quantitative extent that it is now. The summary and comparatively unlimited exercise of the power compounds the danger to individual freedom which its mere existence implies. More subtle, intangible social results are liable to derive from this latter aspect.

The American ideology is one based upon recognition of the rights and liberties of the individual. This concept was ensured by the architects of our government when they created this republic, one in which all men are, at least philosophically, sovereign, while government is but the vehicle of their sovereignty. The manifestation of this dream was encouraged by bitter memories of monarchial experience—the hope was for individual liberation. How can it then be that man can be contumacious to a sovereign which is, theoretically at least, the ultimate extension of himself; or inversely, should government, created by, of, and for man be allowed to punish the exercise of the will of its constituent self? This issue was dealt with by a Mississippi court in 1858. Discussing the rationale for the contempt of court power, that court suggested a converse answer to the above question. Drawing a distinction between a wrongdoing *person*, and the sovereign *people*, the court suggested:

In this country, all courts derive their authority from the people, and hold it in trust for their security and benefit. In this state, all judges are elected by the people, and hold their authority, in a double sense, directly from them; the power they exercise is but the authority of the people themselves, exercised through courts as their agents. It is the authority and laws emanating from the people, which the judges sit to exercise and enforce. Contempt against these courts, in the administration of their laws, are insults offered to the authority of the people themselves, and not to the humble agents of the law, whom they employ in the conduct of their government.[3]

And so respected a judge as Chancellor Kent has agreed that the contempt power was given to the courts in trust for the public. Respect for courts, which are ordained to administer the laws which are necessary to the good order of society, is as necessary as respect for the laws themselves.

Even assuming the political propriety of the contempt power, is the summary contempt procedure, by which the contemnor is tried, sometimes by the offended party, often without jury, counsel, and ordinary appeal, either right or reasonable? Is this scheme of governmental power consistent with our constitutional principles of jury trial, self-incrimination, nonexcessive punishments, free press and speech, double jeopardy, and fair trial?

Aside from contemporary, mid-twentieth century conflicts, can the contempt power be traced to a proper historical foundation? Or was the comment, made some time ago by one student of the problem, correct that this criminal, arbitrary power is less unassailable than unquestioned historically, though it is "foreign to the whole spirit of Anglo-American jurisprudence"? [4]

In dealing with legal problems, Americans are faced with what are often the paradoxes and anomalies of the common law. These rules of law, so long-stated and often expedient, seem to be ensconced in a sacrosanctity of age and prestige, which can be deceiving. Then is it when scholarship needs to combine with fortitude to focus a truer vision on contemporary values. Historical assessment casts serious doubts upon historical rationales for the contempt power, as we shall see.

Are the rationales, other than historical precedence, offered in defense of the contempt power apropos of American political relationships? Need courts and congresses have this power in order to operate efficiently, or at all? If so, is there an alternative more suited to expedience, as well as political propriety? These rationales, too, are ripe for appraisal, and will be discussed.

Though the subject of contempt has occupied an increasingly more common role in the newspapers, and in the political comments and writings of recent times, the subject is one that has long been with students of Anglo-American law, and government. Its prestige has vacillated. Throughout different times in history, both in the United States and in England, it has been used in ways that have provoked great public interest. Depending upon the time and situation, its function as a manifestation of governmental power over individuals has provoked praise, and demands for its exercise, as it has condemnation and criticism.

In fact, the contempt power is less a technical procedural, legal device than a volatile, focal point of significant and timely political issues. Throughout our history contempt has been the vehicle for deciding a variety of dramatic and significant social problems.

Both in Shakespeare's *Henry IV*, Part 2,[5] and in *The Lives of the Chief Justices of England*,[6] one can read of the escapades of ruddy Prince Hal, later to become Henry V of England, and his notorious brush with the law of contempt. When Hal was the Prince of Wales, one of his servants was arrested for committing a felony. Upon his servant's arraignment at the King's Bench, the prince appeared in a rage, and demanded that his man be let free. Chief Justice Gascoigne delicately but firmly ruled that the laws of the realm must be met, and that if the prince wished his servant to be pardoned he should secure this from the king, his father. The prince tried physically to take the servant away, whereupon Gascoigne ordered him again to behave. When the prince raged (and some say he even struck Gascoigne) the judge reminded his prince that he kept the peace of the king to whom even Hal owed allegiance, and suggested that Hal set a good example. When Hal did not heed this advice, he was sentenced for contempt, and committed to the King's Bench prison until the king's pleasure could be known. People speculated whether this would be the end of Gascoigne's career. It developed that the king was pleased, and rejoiced that he had both a judge who dared to minister justice to his son, and a son who obeyed him (if reluctantly).[7]

Centuries later another historical *cause célèbre* involved the use of the contempt power.[8] Major General Andrew Jackson, in command of the city of New Orleans in 1814, heard rumors that the state legislature was thinking of capitulating to the British. Not knowing that the war was actually over, and that peace had been declared by treaty, Jackson was suspicious of the French volunteer troops who had been leaving the ranks. He ordered them out of the city. Lewis Louallier wrote an article in the local press critical of General Jackson's conduct. Jackson ordered his arrest and imprisonment. Louallier then brought habeas corpus proceedings before Judge Hall of the district court. The judge granted his release. Jackson went into another rage, and arrested Hall. Then, the United States District Attorney brought habeas corpus proceedings for release of Judge Hall, and it was granted. He joined Hall and Louallier in prison. After many judicial and political machinations all parties were released, and Jackson learned that the war was over. The United States Attorney then appeared before Judge Hall and moved for General Jackson's punishment for contempt. Jackson, shifting tactics, and under the good advisement of his attorney, argued the inequities of contempt. He asserted that the summary power of contempt violated his rights under the Fifth and Sixth Amendments. He ingeniously argued that the necessity which allowed circumvention of constitutional privileges in contempt cases was a lesser one than the necessity which prompted his conduct. He had ordered martial law because it was necessary for the preservation of the whole country. Nonetheless he was found guilty of contempt and fined $1,000. It has been reported that the memory of this incident plagued Jackson until long after his later ascendency to the presidency.[9] Finally, a year before his death, he successfully implored a congressional representative to bring a bill before Congress to repay the $1,000 to him, and vindicate his honor. This was eventually done.

Until the mid-twentieth century, the contempt power was the testing ground for the power of the press with respect to its privilege of contemporaneous comment about courts and trials. Although today the American press is relatively free to report, in England the publishing world still knows the strict and sometimes severe sanction of the contempt power. This interesting and challenging subject will be covered in Chapter III.

During the early part of the twentieth century labor's struggle for economic equality was the most dramatic and socially vital domestic issue in America. During this time disputes both legal and otherwise were frequent and provoked the attention of the nation. The labor injunction was frequently resorted to, and many issues were resolved in the context of contempt proceedings for violations of these injunctions. The contempt involving John L. Lewis and the United Mine Workers was, of course, the most renowned of these cases.

More recently, the various press media have abounded with details of vexed officials and assertive individuals, and their battles with the contempt power. The era of the congressional committees, more than anything else, has brought pervasive application of the contempt power. The conflicts which have been aroused as a consequence of this have been many and severe. How far government can go has been one of the most vital questions of our middle twentieth century.

The McCarthy era of congressional investigations into subversion and communism captured the attention and emotions of much of the world. Somewhat lost in the exciting and dramatic political arguments centering on this subject was the fact that without a congressional contempt power much of this struggle would not have come to pass. And it was not until this time, and the subsequent investigations into organized crime and racketeering which soon followed, that the Congress exercised its investigative powers with any frequency or as much public interest or attention. The Hollywood Ten and a number of the disenchanted liberals of the 1930s whose artistic restlessness had led them to improvident political action or associations were paraded through Congress and into national headlines and debate. The right of government to pry into people's past associations and otherwise private associations was questioned by famous artists like Arthur Miller in the context of highly publicized and emotional contempt proceedings.

Somewhat less appealing were the moguls of the rackets who came under national scrutiny during the 1950s when state and federal investigating committees, grand juries, and congressional committees began a drive against nationally syndicated crime. Here again the contempt power was frequently resorted to in the legal battles between these individuals and government investigatory bodies.

In the civil rights battles of the late 1950s and early 1960s, the contempt power has also served a versatile function. Contempt procedures were included as a part of the 1957 Civil Rights Acts. And of course the contempt proceedings against Governor Barnett of Mississippi arising out of the celebrated integration of the University of Mississippi was at least in notoriety the contempt case of the century—if not the case of the century.

Interestingly, one can speculate that many of the liberals who deplored the congressional contempt convictions in some of the Communist cases undoubtedly applauded the contempt convictions in the race riot cases such as the contempt conviction of John Kaspar, the avid segregationist leader in the Tennessee school riots.

Perhaps, this accommodating nature of the contempt power, by which it can be used in ways which appeal emotionally to large groups, yet boomerang against its appreciators to the satisfaction of their critics, has been one of the reasons for its long acceptance in the face of periodic and sometimes severe criticism.

The legal problem is then one with deep philosophical undertones, far-reaching political implications, and, as we shall see, historical inconsistencies. The fact that its status and value have been scantily and infrequently analyzed is but one of the reasons for this book. But, because its position and its acceptance as an American governmental power vehicle raises deep and probing problems, their exposure, if not their solution, must be still another goal. Because of the ramifications which these problems provoke, and the possible conflict between contempt and the basic American ideology of individual freedom, some analysis and study was forthcoming. The purpose of this book is to examine the history, varieties, and implications of the power of contempt of court and Congress and other governmental bodies, to describe its birth, growth, and maturation, and its conflicts with American notions of constitutional law.

Contempt of Court

The power of courts to punish contempts is one which wends historically back to the early days of England and the crown. A product of the days of kingly rule, it began as a natural vehicle for assuring the efficiency and dignity of, and respect for the

governing sovereign. Viewed as a legal doctrine which was articulated and immersed in the common law, it is generally a product
of Anglo-American society.

Those informal groups which ruled the primitive associations
of men undoubtedly looked to some pagan, religious, or divine
and natural right to enforce their systems. There is some evidence
that schemes akin to contempt were at least thought of in more
antiquated societies. The writings of Emperor Justinian refer to
certain judicial punishing powers which were conceded to be
necessary means of official force, and which resemble contempt.[10]
The Codes of Canon Law, the religious rules of the Roman Popes,
contain sections which deal with disciplinary or penal powers
akin to judicial contempt as we now know it.[11] Maitland referred
to these sources as influences upon the original equity jurisdiction
of the king's chancellors, whose judicial culture was inspired by
the canon law.[12] One author reported that the Theodosian Code
considered the subject of contempt of a governmental authority,
and concluded that it should not be punishable; "for if it arose
from madness, it was to be pitied; if from levity, to be despised;
and if from malice, to be forgiven." [13] Such Taoistic reasoning,
if not practical in the complex societies of our age, at least recognizes that respect by compulsion may be a contradiction in terms,
and the least ideal means to a free, libertarian government.[14] Respect can be more firmly based upon moral rightness than artificial might.[15]

With the multimillenary growth of organized societies, the
sophistication of governing systems, and the intercomplexity of
the relationships between sovereigns and men, some power force
within a rule-of-law scheme became necessary to replace the cave-
man's club as a means of enforcing obedience and respect.
Though centuries later men were to accept the self-righting
process, recommended by the writings of men like Locke and
Milton, as the more democratic way to resolve individual-govern-

mental conflict,[16] the contempt power was more suited to the early English rulers and their style of government. And the law of contempt is not the law of men, it is the law of kings. It is not law which representative legislators responsibly reflecting the *vox populi* originally wrote, but is rather evolved from the divine law of kings, and its aspects of obedience, cooperation, and respect toward government bodies. Though this is not the only source of the power, it is the seed from which the power grew, if later adopted and cultivated by men not adverse to its exercise. Later institutions agreeably accepted it, less as adjuncts to the king than to protect their own dignity and supremacy.

The idea that the headman must be obeyed, at the risk of committing unnatural and punishable offense, cannot be traced with scientific exactness to a precise moment and place. It is agreed though that authority for that premise can be traced in part to ancient concepts of government, both secular and religious. The idea that obedience to divine commands was good and disobedience sinful has been traced to the assertions of the early popes, as well as the emperors.[17] It was probably not new with them. In enjoining obedience to civil government, resort was often had to the Scripture. Early in English history the king was called the Vicar of God.[18] With the rise of the feudal system in England, accompanying the pre-eminence of royal power after the Norman Conquest, there developed manifestations of the idea of the complete ownership, authority, and power of the king.[19] This was but another, though not different, step from the sanctity of the medicine man, the priestly character of primitive royalty, and the Christian concepts of obedience—starting in Christian history with papal obedience and bridging Middle Age centuries of monarchistic, secular governments.[20]

The contempt power is understandable when seen through the perspectives of its age of inception, an age of alleged divinely ordained monarchies, ruled by a king totally invested with all sovereign legal powers and accountable only to God. Under any circumstances resistance to the king was a sin which would bring damnation.[21]

As society became more diverse and extensive, the English kings found it necessary to have their kingly governmental powers exercised by representatives. The courts of early England acted for the king throughout the realm. And their exercise of contempt powers derived from a presumed contempt of the king's authority.[22] Violation of their writ or disobedience to their officers violated the peace and flouted the king they represented. Though the king acted through others, in a mystical way he was presumed to be present and subject to being contemned.[23]

The contempt power of the equity courts had a similar origin. The equity chancellor dispensed justice in the place of the king, and his orders obtained their validity because of the use of the great seal, disobedience of which was considered a grievous contempt of the king.[24] Since the lord chancellor had no individual power, he used the king's seal as a basis for his own judicial power. "The decree of his court derived its force from the fact that it was granted by the keeper of the King's seal, and was executed by means of a writ sealed with that seal." Disobedience of the king's seal was contempt of the king, much as contempt of a manorial court was contempt of the lord of the court, and contempt of a maritime court was contempt of the admiral of that court.[25]

This engraftment, from a power of the courts as adjuncts of the king to one inherent in the courts themselves, was described in the decision of an Irish judge in 1813.[26] The process of attachment, he reported, was one used by the judges of the Aula Regis, by which those who interfered with the king's peace were brought before the court and punished. Derived from Norman law, it was resorted to "because disobedience of their orders was a contempt of the King himself whose ministers they were. . . .

By the Norman law it was established that nothing could be done but by the King's writ." [27] So, the origin of the courts' power was from this presumed contempt of the king's authority. Under the Norman kings, an offender's personal property was forfeited to the king's mercy. Later, this was changed to a fine, which in turn was later refined into a procedure whereby the offender was imprisoned until the fine was paid.[28] This is akin to the current practices with contempt. For civil contempt, the offender is imprisoned until he purges his act of contempt. Originally, contempt of Congress was used merely to coerce cooperation, at which time the imprisonment ended. For criminal contempt, the offender of today may be fined or imprisoned, or both, and nonconditionally.

Gradually, any questions about the right of the judiciary to punish disobedience, obstruction, or disrespect (and they were few) were answered with the claim that this was an inherent right of English courts. Necessity then became with maturity the mother of this claimed innate, natural right of courts. The natural inclination to claim this power as one innate in judicial institutions was but one step in the rise in power of the courts, and later the Parliament, in England. The king had pointed the way. But, the subsequent increase in the use of the sealed writ by private parties, to secure their personal judicial rights, dissolved the dread symbol of sovereign power which originally issued from this process.[29] Gradually, this procedure became but a part of the court's machinery for administering justice between private parties—a step in the judicial, as opposed to the executive process.

The roots of English law, from which the contemporary contempt doctrine sprouts, are thin but deep in history. Sir John Fox trod through the complex and voluminous writings appropriate to this subject and presented his results in a series of articles in the *Law Quarterly Reviews* of 1908, 1909, 1920, 1921, 1922 and

1924.[30] Citing Pollock and Maitland, he probed the histories of English law to find that contempt was extant as far back as the tenth century in England.[31] The theory then offered for its being was that the law became irritated by contumacy, and instead of saying to the contemnor "I don't care," it set its will against his will, and ordered him. This theory was rationalized in Bracton's *De Legibus* on the ground that there is no greater crime than contempt, because all within the realm ought to obey the king and be part of his peace.[32] Here we see the true assumption by courts of a power originally based upon their peculiar position as adjuncts to the king, and administrators of his will. This is a characteristic no longer prevalent in England, and never accepted in America. Yet, this assumption seeped into a court frame-of-reference, and has welled and risen, not as a force rooted in kingly relations but as a necessary and inherent characteristic of courts independently. He wrote:

Thus from the earliest laws of the kingdom, through the records of the Curia Regis and the Parliament, the Year Books, and the first treatises on law, the development of "contempt" in the legal sense can be traced until by the fourteenth century the principles upon which punishment is inflicted to restrain disobedience to the commands of the King and his courts as well as other acts which tend to obstruct the course of justice, have become firmly established.[33]

Paring the facts from the legend, Sir John further particularized that the idea that every contempt of court was considered indirectly a contempt of the king is corroborated even by the wording of the writ applied in contempt cases. It read a contempt had been "committed against us"—us being the court and its king. More particularization would border on the picayune.

In the thirteenth century, contempt action was taken for such acts as default or misfeasance of parties, assaults and disturbances in court, insults to judges, and misconduct by officers of the law. However, in all the cases reported, contempt was treated procedurally "in the ordinary course of the law." [34] Summary punishment was meted out only where the accused person confessed his guilt. Then a jury trial was unnecessary. Further collating the cases, he reported that until the fifteenth century innumerable contempts "which would have been dealt with by summary process in the 18th century were being tried . . . in the ordinary course of law." [35] A Scottish jurist traced the cases up to the time of Henry V, and concluded that criminal contempt cases in the King's Bench until that time were dealt with by procedures not summary.[36] With the Star Chamber came nonjury procedures, and the treatment of contempt by interrogatories of the court. This latter procedure was cited by Justice Wilmot in the *Almon* case as the nub of due process, far better than capricious juries. Yet with the abolition of the Star Chamber,[37] it was legislated that all matters theretofore handled by that court would be treated "by the common law of the land and in the ordinary course of justice. . . ." [38] Summary process was exercised only in limited cases where it was deemed appropriate because of the immediacy and physical relation of the contemptuous act to the courts.

Justice was as strict as it was swift. In a case in 1631, a man threw a brickbat at the Chief Justice after being convicted of a felony. Though he missed the judge, his right hand was cut off and fixed to the gibbet, and he was immediately hanged in the presence of the court.[39] It was said that such misconduct must be summarily punished by courts because without this power of punishment they could not perform, and the kingdom would stand still if "justice" was not immediate—and, of course, custom and necessity called for it. Other contempts were punishable, but only in the ordinary nonsummary course of the law. It was not until the time of Blackstone and the eighteenth-century writers that contempt was summarily punished, without question as to where it was committed. Before then, those contempts which were summarily punished were committed in the face of the court (*in facie curiae*). The very view of the court was considered to supply a basis for the conviction.[40]

Blackstone was a friend of Justice Wilmot, the author of the *Almon* case; and an analysis of this case explains the sudden change in the then current law of contempt, and its impact on the future. The legal status of contempt of court was given not only enunciation but also an authoritative and pervasive application in this much criticized but more quoted decision which, though decided in 1764, was not published except posthumously in 1802 in the notes of Justice Wilmot, the author of the opinion.[41] Before this case, it was accepted that orders of a court were not to be disobeyed, and that acts hindering the administration of justice were punishable. Statutes were extant which allowed private redress for the scandalizing of governmental figures—*scandalum magnatum*.[42] But Justice Wilmot, in *Rex v. Almon*, extended the then contemporary contempt doctrine and gave the world an opinion full of dicta which was later seized upon, quoted and requoted, and made sacrosanct, until years later when discerning scholars found and pointed out his error.[43] His doctrine now lives, a venerable product of stare decisis and years of acceptance, though somewhat limp from recent criticism.

Almon was a bookseller who was tried in 1765 for publishing an alleged libel about Lord Mansfield. Justice Wilmot, who wrote an opinion which held Almon in contempt for the article, had been elevated to his position by a Cabinet which was under the strong influence of Lord Mansfield. It is reported that he deemed criticism of the Lord as bordering on sacrilege.[44] One of the charges Almon had made against Lord Mansfield related to a court action involving a person named Wilkes. When Justice Wilmot's judgment granting an attachment against Almon was about to be delivered, it was discovered that it referred, by some error or confusion, to *The King v. Wilkes*, instead of *The King v. Almon.* Then, it has been written: "Mr. Justice Wilmot urged the defendant's counsel, Sergeant Glynn, 'as a gentleman' to consent to an amendment, to which Sergeant replied that as 'a man of honor' he could not." [45]

The action was abandoned and the opinion was never delivered. In 1802, Justice Wilmot's son published the notes of his father which included the stillborn, misnomered opinion, *The King v. Wilkes.* In this opinion was the language which has been so controversially referred to ever since:

The power which the courts in Westminster Hall have of vindicating their own authority *is coeval with their first foundation and institution;* it is a *necessary* incident to every court of justice, whether of record or not, to fine and imprison for a contempt to the court, acted in the face of it, I Ventris I, and the issuing attachments by the supreme courts of justice in Westminster Hall for *contempts out of court stands upon the same immemorial usage* as supports the whole fabric of the common law; it is as much the *lex terrae* and within the exception of *Magna Charta* as the issuing [sic] any other legal process whatsoever. I have examined very carefully to see if I could find out any vestiges or traces of its introduction but can find none. It is as ancient as any other part of the common law; there is no priority or posteriority to be discovered about it and therefore (it) cannot be said to invade the common law, but to act in an alliance and friendly conjunction with every other provision which the wisdom of our ancestors has established for the general good of society. And though I do not mean to compare and contrast attachments with trial by jury, yet truth compels me to say that the mode of *proceeding by attachment stands upon the very same foundation and basis as trial by juries do—immemorial usage* and practice [emphasis added].[46]

Sir John Fox, in his classic treatise on the subject, has pointed out that though the early common law deemed disobedience to the king's writ a contempt, and the courts eventually used the king's seal to make their process effective, what started out as contempt of the Lord of the Court became contempt of the administration of justice instead, when the *Almon* case extended concepts of contempt as it did. He pointed out that the summary power to punish, which Justice Wilmot condoned, was beyond the embrace of previous contempt practice.[47] It had been suggested that the power to commit for contempt derived from a statute which empowered sheriffs to commit persons who resisted their process.[48] But this was after trial in the customary fashion. Justice Wilmot reasoned "that if resistance to a minister of the court is punishable" in this way, "*a fortiori* libelling a judge in his judicial capacity is so punishable." Rationalizing the power of judicial contempt as a product of the divine right of kings, Sir John Fox reports Wilmot's reasoning thusly:

[b]y our constitution the King is the fountain of justice and . . . he delegates the power to the Judges . . . arraignment of the justice of the Judges is arraigning the King's justice . . . it is an impeachment of his wisdom in the choice of his Judges . . . it excites dissatisfaction with judicial determinations and indisposes the minds of people to obey them . . . this is a most fatal obstruction of justice, and calls for a more immediate redress than any other. . . .[49]

His dream was to keep a blaze of glory around the court, that it would never be contemptible in the eyes of the public.

Justice Wilmot's proof of the supreme fairness of this contempt procedure lay in his reasoning that in the summary procedure before the court the party could acquit himself by his own oath, whereas a jury might improperly convict him upon false evidence. This logic, if not specious, lacks convincing certitude. In fact, later scholars have concluded that the idea that a sworn denial of a charged contempt cleared the contemnor, subject only to a charge of perjury, came into the law toward the end of the seventeenth century during the adoption of Star Chamber proceedings by the King's Bench courts. It was an anomaly which was discarded by the end of the eighteenth century.[50]

The analysis of the *Almon* case is as long and complicated as it is interesting. Suffice it to note the circumstances, that one may evaluate its influence upon the articulation of the law of contempt of court, as well as the propriety of its departure from the previous confines of the power.

For years, the situation remained static. Until the nineteenth century there were only two other cases of contempt of the court which arose out of the courts, and which were treated by summary procedures.[51] Interestingly, both involved libels of Lord Mansfield. However, in writing his famous legal treatise, Blackstone consulted his friend Justice Wilmot concerning the law of contempt. He reported then that the law was such as Wilmot had reasoned, but cited no authorities to support the conclusion. So, it has been accurately concluded:

The present law of contempt in this country has been founded . . . upon the statements of Blackstone in his Commentaries and Sir John Eardley-Wilmot in *King v. Almon* which concerned a contempt by publication. Oddly enough, neither of these authorities forms a legal precedent, for the opinion of Justice . . . Wilmot was never delivered, as the case was dismissed because of technical difficulties. It also appears that in all probability the statements made by Blackstone merely represented the views of Judge Wilmot, and that it may be said that the present scope of the summary power is due almost exclusively to the opinion of one man.[52]

By the twentieth century, the law of Wilmot had, like fine wine, aged to the point of unquestioning respect. English courts adopted the *Almon* decision, cited it, and extended it beyond even Wilmot's probable intent.

The sometimes blind inheritance of common law in American legal attitudes bore this Almon-phenomenon of England to the United States, where it was early inculcated as a rule of law. The sanctity given by Blackstone's approval of Justice Wilmot's opinion added to its prestige in the United States. Since the American colonists were by and large a product of the common law environment of England, it was very natural that their courts were endowed with procedures copied from mother England. Though these settlers consciously went about ameliorating many of the harsher aspects of English governmental practice, the general contempt of court power was not among the changes. This was probably because of the minor civil implications of the exercise of this power at that time, and the seemingly natural claim for the power by the courts themselves.

The first American federal legislation dealing with the contempt of court power was the Judiciary Act of 1789, which by its words gave federal courts "the power . . . to punish by fine or imprisonment, at the discretion of said courts, all contempts of authority in any case or hearing before same. . . ."[53] Impliedly, this included whatever the extent of the power of contempt of court was at common law. The first state legislation in America was passed in Pennsylvania, and it condemned as contempt official misconduct of court officers, disobedience to process, and misbehavior in the presence of the court.[54] (This excluded the vicarious kind of constructive contempt to the administration of justice which was approved by Justice Wilmot in the *Almon* case.) New York followed with similar legislation which was finally passed in 1829, also excluding the contempt, Almon-Wilmot species, but accepting without question the power of contempt of court in general.[55] The courts considered that the right to punish for contempt was one adopted from long precedent and essential to judicial efficiency. These statutes were followed in theme and extent by federal legislation in 1821, which aimed at alleviating both the uncertainties and the harshness of the original federal rule. This change was provoked by a heated controversy which arose out of the famous *Peck* impeachment case.

Until then, there were only a few federal cases in the lower federal courts arising under the 1789 statute, and they followed the common law rule with respect to constructive contempts.[56]

There was no question that the exercise by courts of the direct contempt power (disobedience to process or disrespect in the presence of the courts) was inherent and proper. Then, Lawless, an attorney from Missouri, provoked Congress into initiating impeachment proceedings against Judge James H. Peck for willful oppression. Peck was a federal judge who punished Lawless summarily under his assumed contempt power, for publishing a critical article about his conduct of a series of pending proceedings, which concerned the adjudication of land grants from the old Spanish-American authorities, and in which the judge had ruled unfavorably to the interests of Lawless.[57] Congressional hearings lasted almost a year, when the judge was finally acquitted by a vote of 22–21. One of the arguments made at these hearings was that the power of judicial contempt was not inherent but a product of the common law; therefore since *Almon's* case was not common law (it was never officially published and was unofficially published after the adoption of our Constitution), its effect was void. The judge claimed innocent and fair interpretation of the common-law power of contempt of court, basing his conclusions upon the English decisions that preceded his.[58] Yet the strong feelings about freedom of the press at the time of the Peck debates precipitated against this oppressive judicial power. One month after Judge Peck's acquittal, James Buchanan, later to become President but then Chairman of the Judiciary Committee and active in the impeachment debates, presented a bill to Congress which followed the New York–Pennsylvania treatment and omitted summary contempt power in cases where the act was not obstructive of the physical administration of justice. It was passed in 1831,[59] and covered misbehavior in the presence of the court or so near thereto as to obstruct the administration of justice, disobedience of process, and discipline of court officers. By 1860, twenty-three of the then thirty-three states had enacted legislation implementing the

federal policy concerning constructive contempts, and only a few states applied the rule of *Almon's* case. The current federal statute reads much the same as the 1831 statute,[60] though the Supreme Court cases have varied at different times in their interpretations of it, and are currently closely split as to allegiance to or departure from the English rule, the latter group currently prevailing. The rule has since pendulated both in the federal and state courts with respect to the interpretation of the statute's coverage of the constructive contempt power. This treatment will be thoroughly detailed in Chapter II.

When intrepid souls have dared to question the courts' right to the mighty contempt power, and at times in prefatory apologias to their decisions, judges have proffered several pat *raisons d'être*. One rationale has been necessity.[61] Without such a power, what would deter obstruction to the administration of justice? Would courts be merely impotent boards of arbitration without any control or effect?[62] This is not necessarily a matter of speculative conjecture. Our Supreme Court has only once exercised the contempt power, and it has been exemplary in effectiveness, power, and dignity. Though it is an appellate court, the point can be made that respect and efficacy may be predicated upon and may more likely result from qualities and powers more ideally suited to a democratic society than coercive contempt powers. And what of other countries which do not have similar powers, or which have them only in limited and circumscribed instances? Is the administration of justice chaotic elsewhere than in America? And is it so necessary for control and order to have such a power as contempt? Do courts not have other disciplinary and punitive sanctions equally effective, yet better procedurally dedicated to an ordered liberty? We shall see in later chapters that they do, and that the contempt power is not the only moat to separate the crass or mundane public from the majestic castle of the judiciary.

Another rationale, or the same one reduced one level, is expediency [63] and self-protection.[64] And expedient it unquestionably is. But is expedience a good reason if it is the cause of injustice, and is this not another way of saying it is necessary— more euphemistic, though intellectually no more satisfying?

And the same necessity argument, elevated one level, has been offered in the name of inherence.[65] Most cases, in fact, have considered it axiomatic that the power of contempt is inherent in courts and automatically exists by its very nature. This is easier to say than to disprove. However, the contempt power has been uniformly reserved to superior courts in both England and the United States.[66] If the power is inherent in courts, how can it be that some courts are without it? This anomaly of reason, especially if supplemented by the historical inconsistencies supporting the background for courts' contempt powers, weakens the claim that the power is innate in judicial bodies.

All these reasons seem no more than rationalizations which may not withstand the insights of critical evaluation, or historical consistency.

Of course, it may be argued that as a matter of common-law principle contempt is now valid despite errors committed ages ago. Who is to say whether Wilmot's error was overlooked or in fact acknowledged and accepted through the years because it was deemed desirable and worth legitimizing. Moreover, even if these historical flaws were overlooked, do not centuries of consideration and application evidence a sufficient enough adoption to exclude criticisms founded on such errors?

In any event, the general power of courts to punish for contempt was little questioned during these early days in the United States. In one reported case, Justice Field of the Supreme Court wrote that:

The power to punish for contempt is inherent in all courts; its existence is essential to the preservation of order in judicial proceedings, and to the . . . due administration of justice. The moment the courts of the United States were called into existence and invested with jurisdiction over any subject, they became possessed of this power.[67]

Whether it was deemed beyond dispute, or so natural and necessary as to be without question, or whether the arguments about the extension of the power (in constructive contempt cases) shifted the focus of legal opposition away from the attack upon the general power itself and concentrated against its specific extension is open to conjecture. Yet, it has been said, and repeated of late, that the power of contempt itself "is, perhaps, nearest akin to despotic power of any power existing under our form of government." [68] Justice Black, less impressed by 170 years of *Almon* precedent, has written about the contempt power that "the principle commonly referred to as *stare decisis* has never been thought to extend so far as to prevent courts from correcting their own errors." [69] Yet even the vigorous critics of the summary contempt power, who have recently sounded the call for change, impliedly go along with maintaining at least some contempt power for the courts.

Legal scholars have more recently, and after thorough historical study, raised serious doubts about Justice Wilmot's conclusions. Messrs. Frankfurter and Landis have written about the implications of the *Almon* case, that:

It has bedeviled the law of contempt both in England and this country ever since. Wilmot's opinion influenced the course of decisions during the nineteenth century, partly because he spoke with an air of great authority, and partly because the power which he claimed is not unappealing even to high-minded judges bent upon the quick dispatch of business.[70]

As late as 1958, Justice Black is recorded as having said that "the myth of immemorial usage has been exploded by recent scholarship as a mere fiction," but that the decision in the *Almon* case has "nevertheless exerted a balefull influence on the law of contempt both in this country and in England." [71] Nevertheless, Wilmot's "immemorial usage" became our law of the land, and the exercise of the contempt power in general now occupies so embedded a position of acceptance that, though modification in light of contemporary legal and governmental interests is possible, change will be difficult to bring about, and revocation of the practice nearly impossible. The law of contempt of court is very much with us today. Every state court has authorizedly acted against contempts; all federal courts have equally done so; and with the increasing business in the courts and the not occasional employment of the courtrooms as arenas for public as well as private legal disputes, the use of the judicial contempt power has caused far-reaching ripples in the pond of social consequence.

Contempt of Congress

As the American power of judicial contempt is the product of the transplantation of English common law (whether with good reason or not), so the use of the contempt power by our Congress harks back to Anglican beginnings. But, though the historical arena was the same, the participating power forces which provoked and the path of precedent which led to its acceptance were not. Nor was the unquestioning readiness with which the American legal climate accepted contempt of court concepts, the environment into which it was to be planted, though the future was to see the doctrine flourish.

As with contempt of court, the rationale for punishing contempt of legislative bodies was a carry-over from days of divine and kingly rule. The king could not only do no wrong; he would not tolerate being questioned or impeded, much less flouted or insulted.[72] The attitude of political subservience by individuals to government was inculcated into popular perspectives of state relationships. And as critics of the king were punished and pilloried, so were critics of the courts, original administrators of the king's will. But, the Parliament was not always in the powerful and prestigious position it occupies today. Nor was it so much a collaborative power of the royalty as were the courts. In fact, the Parliament rose as a popular governmental representative body only after years of power struggle in England with the king, and its position in government has, at least periodically, been one of antagonism toward the king and kingly powers.[73]

American courts and American legal historians have often referred to the history of the English Parliament in support of their theories about contemporary congressional contempt powers.[74] The frequency of their resort has been almost equaled by the variety of their conclusions. The fact that secondary sources are all that can be resorted to in resolving some of these academic arguments compounds both the variety and the intensity of these differences. However, proponents of our congressional contempt power agree in pointing to the parliamentary exercise of the power as the authoritative example of its use by legislative bodies. The arguments arise about the historical nature of the Parliament's power. Concededly, Parliament was once, long ago, a body which discharged both judicial and legislative functions. It was the high court of Parliament, a body of bishops, lords, knights, and burgesses who "exercised the highest functions of a court of judicature, representing in that respect the judicial authority of the king. . . ."[75] As such, they rendered judgments, as well as enacting laws. When this organization was changed and the Parliament more akin to what we recognize structurally today was created, the original body divided into the House of Commons and the House of Lords. The latter group continued to exercise appellate judicial functions, while the former was made a legislative branch, with only a very limited number of judicial powers. It has been considered that this original judicial capacity, which the House of Commons once had, supplied the true grounds for its exercise of the contempt power forevermore. At least, since disputes with the judicial contempt power were few, this was both an expedient argument, and one which followed with perfect logical, if not syllogistic, reasoning. Courts can punish for contempts, as kings could, and Parliament was once a court, so it too cannot be precluded from exercising the power, though now the House of Commons is a legislative body.

Other students of the legislative contempt power, while agreeing that the power exists, see it founded for far different reasons and criticize the conclusion that it all goes back to days of kings and courts.[76] One legal historian criticized the view that the English legislature's contempt power derived from its judicial days, and pointed out that "the first instance in which the House of Commons vindicated any power of privilege by imprisoning for contempt occurred in 1543, nearly three hundred years after the Commons had become a separate body." [77] Indeed, English historians themselves have reported different attitudes within the House of Commons as to its one-time judicial power.[78] The point which these men failed to consider in their search for mathematical, historic logic is that even though the cases which interpreted the power of the House of Commons to punish for contempt arose after the merger into the present Parliament and the abdication of its phantasmal judicial power, it is not clear whether the power was upheld on the basis of legislative necessity and custom or because of the analogy with the former judicial character of the House. There is as much reason to believe that the courts which upheld the power of legislative contempt did so on the theory that the House once had that former judicial capacity, than as not. In other words, though the cases arose after the House of Commons concededly lost its judicial character, the cases may well have been decided with that original capacity in mind. There is legal language which leads to this conclusion.

Thus, the use of contempt by the legislature would be a carry-over from days when it was a judicial body. This point is nowhere satisfactorily answered.

Another rationale claimed for the exercise of this power by the Congress as well as the courts has been necessity.[79] The cases often have reasoned that without such a power, the legislative body could not function. The power of the legislature was said to be governed by the same principles as was that of the judiciary. In other cases this necessity has been labeled self-defense.[80] Without the power to punish contempt, there would be no way to deter disrespect or encourage cooperation. Still another ground urged in defense of the exercise of the contempt power has been expedience.[81] This is, if more euphemistic, again less than satisfying intellectually; and essentially no more than another way of saying it is necessary.

This necessity argument has also circuitously been developed into one of inherency.[82] Certain cases have advanced the argument that the power of contempt is not only expedient and necessary but also so essential that it must be a natural, innate power of any legislature. I suggest that all these arguments—necessity, expediency, inherency—are but full circle around the same ground. The courts have, to one degree or another, recognized that the power is helpful to the completion of legislative tasks. And this it certainly is. To acknowledge the claims for the power by legislatures, courts have been wont to articulate some rationalization for its condonation. But other than this merry circle of need—usefulness—naturalness, there has been no one, agreed-upon-as-true explanation of the purpose and value of legislative contempt powers in the cases. The trouble here is compounded by the realization that many examples of what are now treated as contempts are usually covered by other legal sanctions, without the use of summary procedures. This will be discussed more thoroughly in later chapters.

In any event, the Parliament emerged as a powerful legislature during the end of the seventeenth century, and to insure its position, claimed and exercised the privileges and procedures thought befitting of its post, among which was the summary contempt power.[83] Here again, historical origins played only a convenient part in the adoption of the contempt power by Parliament. Undoubtedly, this institution, in its ascendency to power, realized the effectiveness of such a tool, and adopted it only coincidentally noting their atavistic judicial nature.

The original American colonies adopted many procedures akin to the motherland's common-law methods. Their assemblies exercised the contempt power in defense of privilege, to compel testimony, and to protect their dignity and position. The cases were many, and though their reasoning was not often questioned, they rationalized their power as one of inherent and necessary right—auxiliary to their legislative natures.[84] What was claimed to be inherent in the courts, also became inherent in the legislature.[85] Strangely, only a few states included this right in their constitutions. Defenders of the right of the legislature to punish for contempt attribute this silence to its supposed axiomatic or inferred implication within the grant of legislative powers in general.[86]

The federal constitution is also silent with respect to the power of Congress to punish nonmembers for contempt. It has been reported that "A proposal at the Constitutional Convention of 1787 to incorporate an explicit grant to the Congress for the exercise of these powers [to conduct investigations and punish for contempt] died in the meetings of the committee on style." [87] The reverse argument has been made by critics of the congressional contempt power in response to this silence; that is, since it was not granted, while other specific punitive powers were,[88] the intent, they claimed, was to deny the power.[89] For some time, the exercise of the power by the legislature went unquestioned, a situation which has been construed as popular, silent acquiescence and evidence, of a sort, of its propriety.[90] By congressional action, then, the problem was resolved, though after much debate within the Congress about whether it could cite for contempt. In 1795, a House committee investigating an alleged bribery of a member of the House cited one Randall, a nonmember, for contempt and imprisoned him for nine days.[91] This was the first recorded instance of congressional contempt by a nonmember for violating the dignity of the national legislature in America. During the next fifty years, both the House and the Senate cited individuals for contempt of their august selves. Though the procedures were summary, all who were cited were given the opportunity to present a defense and to be represented, to a limited extent, by counsel.

Finally, in 1821, the first American case to discuss the power of the legislature to punish for contempt was decided. An examination of this case, and another early decision of the United States Supreme Court, will illustrate the political misgivings toward application of the English contempt rule to Congress as well as the reasons advanced in support of adopting this legislative power, which prevailed at that time.

The case, *Anderson v. Dunn*,[92] arose out of an order by Henry Clay, then Speaker of the House, to the Clerk, and thence to the Sergeant-at-Arms of the House, Dunn, "to take into custody the body of the said John [Anderson], wherever to be found, and the same forthwith to have before the said House, at the bar thereof, then and there to answer the said charge. . . ."[93] This was done. Anderson was charged with abuse of the House and contempt of its dignity. The particular nature of his offense is not clear from the report of the decision, though a later opinion, based upon inference from the record, stated that the delinquency was an attempt to bribe a member of the House.[94] It has been reported that Anderson sent Lewis, a member of the

House, $500 for any "extra trouble" gone to in furtherance of a claim in which Anderson was interested.[95] The House, in debate, decided that it had the contempt power irrespective of any lack of specific constitutional authorization, in order to protect itself and to operate efficiently. After being taken into custody, Anderson was brought before the House and allowed to present a defense to the charges of misconduct against him. The House was adjourned each day, and Anderson was kept in custody during the adjournments, until the matter was finally closed, and he was judged guilty, reprimanded, and discharged from custody. Later, Anderson sued Dunn in trespass for assault and battery and false imprisonment. Dunn's defense was the warrant by and the authority of Congress. There was little American authority to guide the Supreme Court, and both parties argued in consideration of the English practice and the more settled theory of contempt of court. The Attorney General argued for the government that the power of Congress to punish contempts is a "principle of universal law growing out of the natural right of self-defence belonging to all persons," and that the "necessity of self-defence is as incidental to legislative, as to judicial authority." [96] Counsel for Anderson argued that whatever powers, akin to contempt, which Congress had, were inapplicable to Anderson, who was not an official of Congress. Their argument was that article I, section 5 of the Constitution gave Congress the power to determine its own rules of procedure within its walls and over its members. This implied the power to punish its delinquent members, if necessary. However, the power to punish "relates solely to the internal polity and economy of the House," and not to nonmembers like Anderson.

Supreme Court Justice Johnson affirmed the lower federal court's approval of Dunn's defense. His opinion included a philosophical discussion of the power of Congress, of facile erudition but less than satisfying reason.

First, the court reasoned that if Congress had no power to punish Anderson it had no power to compel his appearance, because the latter is an initiating process issued in the assertion of the former (punishing power). It followed by agreeing that there was no express congressional power to punish except over its own members. Consequently, if the power existed to punish nonmembers, it was one to be implied, though "the genius and spirit of our institutions are hostile to the exercise of implied powers." [97]

Leaving the genius and spirit of our institutions, Justice Johnson then verbally embarked upon a social compact theory and wrote that power, properly delegated and responsibly exercised, is for the good of all, as it is for the governmental body exercising that power. With this point made, he skipped to the power of contempt of court, about which he said:

Courts of justice are universally acknowledged to be vested, by their very creation, with power to impose silence, respect, and decorum, in their presence, and submission to their lawful mandates, and, as a corollary to this proposition to preserve themselves and their officers from the approach and insults of pollution.[98]

Enforced with this principle, he next switched to and displayed his supreme faith in the ideal of the legislature, thusly:

That a deliberate assembly, clothed with the majesty of the people, and charged with the care of all that is dear to them; composed of the most distinguished citizens, selected and drawn together from every quarter of a great nation; whose deliberations are required by public opinion to be conducted under the eye of the public, and whose decisions must be clothed with all that sanctity which unlimited confidence in their wisdom and purity can inspire; that such an assembly should not possess the power to suppress rudeness, or repel insult, is a supposition too wild to be suggested.[99]

The decision continued with a discussion of the fact that the offense by Anderson was committed in the House and was, therefore, within the express powers of Congress, and that the commitment was limited because "the existence of the power that imprisons is indispensable to its continuance; and although the legislative power continues perpetual, the legislative body ceases to exist on the moment of its adjournment or periodical dissolution." [100] Thus, the principle that imprisonment for contempt of Congress terminates upon adjournment of that body, as was the English rule.

With an admission that American legislative bodies do not have the omnipotence of the English legislative assembly (the only true precedent for the authority of Congress to punish for contempt, and, it could be argued, a fatal concession), a plea for moral self-restraint by the legislators in whose hands he had placed this power, and a paternal epilogue—"respectful deportment . . . will render all apprehension chimerical" [101]—the first American case was concluded. The power of congressional contempt was upheld, for reasons that the future would extend and upon ideals that would be ignored.

In 1874, the contempt power of Congress was again questioned,[102] under circumstances similar to those in *Anderson v. Dunn*. The Supreme Court of the District of Columbia followed the *Dunn* decision, and ruled that the power to commit for contempt existed in Congress, and so long as the Speaker of the House has jurisdiction over the premises, his ministerial function of committal was proper. The decision was brief, and relied upon stare decisis,[103] not questioning the reason or authority of Justice Johnson. In deference to the decision in *Dunn*, the court wrote that the issue had been decided after "stout contest and upon thorough deliberation," [104] and should have the respect of half a century of undisturbed age.

However, this situation was soon changed by the decision of Justice Miller in *Kilbourn v. Thompson*.[105] There, the United States Supreme Court was called upon to review a lower federal court ruling which dismissed an action by Kilbourn on the same grounds as those in *Anderson v. Dunn.*

The United States government had been a creditor of a company which was in the midst of bankruptcy proceedings. After a legislative investigating committee was appointed to inquire into the matter of the government's interest, the committee called Kilbourn and subpoenaed certain documents in his possession. He refused to answer certain questions or to produce the documents, for which he was imprisoned in the District of Columbia jail. On his release after bringing habeas corpus proceedings, Kilbourn sued Thompson for false imprisonment. A plea of justification was made by the Sergeant-at-Arms, on the basis of his congressional authority. The Supreme Court upheld Kilbourn, and he later recovered $20,000.

In curtailing the punishing power of Congress, the Court relied on the separation-of-powers doctrine and pointed out that except in limited instances, where Congress was expressly given the power to punish by the Constitution, its exercise of such a power was an improper assumption of judicial functions.

In support of this conclusion, the Court traced the history of contempt of the English Parliament, pointing out what it considered to be the misconceived impressions expressed in the *Dunn* case and the correct source of the legislative contempt power.

Noting in his opinion that analogy with the English legislature and its practice [106] failed because of its hybrid history of judicial as well as legislative powers, Justice Miller wrote:

[T]he powers and privileges of the House of Commons of England, on the subject of punishment for contempts, rests on principles which have no application to other legislative bodies, and certainly can have none to the House of Representatives of the United States, —a body which is in no sense a court, which exercises no functions derived from its once having been a part of the highest court of the realm, and whose functions, so far as they partake in any degree of that character, are limited to punishing its own members. . . .[107]

The *Kilbourn* case cited an earlier English case, which in discussing the contempt power of the House of Commons made an argument which Justice Miller undoubtedly looked to as authority for his decision. That case was *Kielley v. Carson*,[108] decided in Newfoundland in 1842, just thirty-eight years before. In that case, Kielley was held in contempt of the House Assembly of Newfoundland, a British colony. He claimed that the Assembly had no contempt power. In opposition to this claim it was said that the Assembly is analogous to the House of Commons and therefore did have the power. The court, in holding that there was no contempt power, distinguished the House of Commons as sui generis with respect to the contempt power of a legislature.

The House of Commons has this power . . . not because it is a representative body with legislative functions, but by virtue of ancient usage and prescription; the *lex et consuetudo Parliamenti*, which forms a part of the common law of the land, and according to which the High Court of Parliament, before its division, and the House of Lords and Commons since, are invested with many peculiar privileges, that of punishing for contempt being one. . . . [A]ll those bodies which possess the power of adjudication upon, and punishing in a summary manner, contempts of their authority, have *Judicial functions* . . . except only the House of Commons, whose authority, in this respect, rests upon ancient usage.[109]

The *Kilbourn* decision has been criticized for its historical conclusions. Yet, even amid the fuzzy haze of history, there is unanimity in the opinion that the American power of contempt of Congress is derived from English parliamentary powers of contempt. History also supports the finding in the Kilbourn case that this Parliament was once a holder of judicial as well as legislative powers. Whether the English decisions upholding Parliament's power of contempt are rationalized on the basis of that body's former judicial nature or upon the necessity or usage of Parliament qua legislature is the issue around which revolves the logical problem of precedent. However, no matter how one concludes in this debate, the fact nonetheless remains that Congress is not Parliament, that the power has been exercised for over a century, and that there are other rationales for its having the contempt power than the claimed parliamentary basis. The perfection of the precedential syllogism is important only in understanding the climate of the birth of the power, and its original *raison d'être*, and of course in weighing its position for the purpose of reappraisal.

The Court also discussed the *Dunn* decision, pointing out that its decision was consistent, at least historically logical, even with that decision. At the time of the *Dunn* case, said the Court, English decisions, interpreting the power of the House of Commons to punish for contempt, rationalized the exercise of the power upon the past use by that House of the power when it was also a judicial body. At the time of the *Kilbourn* case, however, the English decisions had changed, holding that the House of Commons was no longer a judicial body and could not consequently exercise any but legislative powers, which do not include the power of contempt of the legislature.

By dicta, if not strong implication, this case can be considered as holding that there is no congressional contempt power, other than as specifically granted to Congress by the Constitution. By actual decision, the case seems to hold that even if there is a congressional contempt power, the courts may still inquire into the jurisdictional basis of its exercise. Its more academic value lies in the historical discussion of the subject.

SEPARATION OF POWERS

The *Kilbourn* decision also raised serious issues about the departmental nature of the contempt power. American notions about the separation of governmental powers have played a less than academic role in later disputes about the contempt power.

In the *Kilbourn* case, the court set out its thoughts about the proper formula for the delineation of government powers:

It is believed to be one of the chief merits of the American system of written constitutional law, that all the powers intrusted to government, whether state or national, are divided into three grand departments, the executive, the legislative, and the judicial. That the functions appropriate to each of these branches of government shall be vested in a separate body of public servants, and that the perfection of the system requires that the lines which separate and divide these departments shall be broadly and clearly defined. It is also essential to the successful working of this system that the persons intrusted with power in any one of these branches shall not be permitted to encroach upon the powers confided to the others, but that each shall by the law of its creation be limited to the exercise of the powers appropriate to its own department, and to no other.[110]

This constitutional doctrine reflects an early American fear of the potential tyrannies of concentrated power, and a policy of caution about the unlimited absorption of powers by branches of government. However, it has been interpreted not as a rigid formula, but as a working political doctrine which must recognize the necessity for some interaction.[111]

The separation doctrine has raised puzzling questions about the inherency and necessity of certain applications of the contempt power. For example, the contempt power was originally a kingly executive power. Judicial and legislative bodies later assumed the power as administrators of the king's work. Our governmental executives are something less than kings and are denied contempt powers, while our courts and Congresses now claim inherent rights to its use. And, as it will be shown in Chapter III, administrative officers often exercise the power, though subject to complaints that their use of this autocratic weapon violates the separation of powers doctrine. If the power is innate in courts, how is it that legislatures have by statute so often limited the contempt of court power? Legislation, narrowing the scope and extent of the contempt power of courts, is not exceptional.[112] The typical response to complaints about this phenomenon is that the limiting legislation does not take away the court's power, but only regulates it. Another rationale for legislative qualification of court's contempt powers is that most courts are created by the legislature, and that body which creates may likewise qualify the power of its own creation. The Lord giveth, and the Lord taketh away. The constitution states that the judicial power of the United States shall be vested in the Supreme Court and "in such inferior courts as the Congress may from time to time ordain and establish." Some authorities have thought that even those courts which Congress has created can not later be denied their inherent contempt power, even by Congress.[113]

Similar questions could be asked about judicial invalidation of certain applications of the congressional contempt power and its rationalization with the separation of powers doctrine. The Constitution nowhere grants any contempt power to Congress and specifically limits the legislature to those powers "herein granted." Yet, Congress has claimed an inherent right to the contempt power and has itself described and limited its own power by legislation. Courts have also limited the Congress' contempt power in cases where it was abused. Typical grounds for judicial control have been the infringement of constitutional rights, and the misconduct of proceedings under the exercise of legislative contempt powers.

A third separation of powers question is raised by the executive pardon power. The Constitution states that ". . . he [the President] shall have power to grant Reprieves and Pardons for offenses against the United States, except in cases of Impeachment." It has been argued that if the executive pardon power was used to relieve a contempt conviction, it would cause a paralysis of judicial or legislative powers, and violate the separation of powers doctrine.[114] This argument was directly dealt with by the

Supreme Court in 1924. Chief Justice Taft disposed of the argument that an executive pardon of a contempt conviction, which arose out of a violation of a court order restraining conduct prohibited by the National Prohibition Act, would be an unconstitutional assumption of judicial power by the executive.[115] He ruled that contempt was an "offense" within the constitutional pardon power clause, and that use of this power by the President did not deprive the judiciary of its independence. The experience with the federal power allays fears of executive abuse or judicial dependence. Conversely, others have questioned whether the exercise of legislative contempt powers to compel executive officers might also violate the separation of powers doctrine.

A separation of powers problem concerning the executive and judicial branches of the federal government recently arose in the context of a civil contempt proceeding against a District Director of Internal Revenue and a section chief of the Justice Department's Tax Division. A Federal District Court in Wisconsin issued an order directing the release and return of certain levies which had been declared null and void. Certain government officials nonetheless held the assets in question illegally. The court fined them $800 for court contempt to compensate for losses sustained as a result of disobedience to the order of the court. In affirming this contempt action, the Circuit Court stated:

That the action of defendants was taken pursuant to instructions of superior authority is no defense. The executive branch of Government has no right to treat with impunity the valid orders of the judicial branch. An order issued by a court with jurisdiction over the subject and person must be obeyed by the parties. . . . And the greater the power that defies law the less tolerant can this court be of defiance.[116]

The separation of powers argument could well prevent attempts to change any aspect of the law of contempt, and may well be an important protagonist in the legal contempt dramas of tomorrow. So far, its consideration has been perfunctory, and the governmental branches seem to have reached an equilibrium of deference to one another.

In 1857, a federal statute was enacted authorizing punishment for contempt of Congress.[117] Prior to that time, the contempt power was exercised under a claimed, inherent right. The contumacious individual was brought before the Bar of the offended House by the Sergeant-at-Arms, at the behest of the officer of the House, and summarily dealt with. His imprisonment at the House, if any, concluded with the end of the congressional session. The procedure under the present statute requires the President of the Senate or the Speaker of the House, after a decision to punish an individual for contempt, to send the case to the United States Attorney for the district where the contempt was committed. He in turn, presents the case to a grand jury, which decides whether to indict the contemnor. If he is indicted, he stands trial in federal court as any other accused criminal.

The following procedure which is customarily followed when witnesses before congressional committees refuse to answer pertinent questions or to produce subpoenaed books or records was described to the Supreme Court by Solicitor General Rankin:

The chairman or other member of the committee before which the act or acts constituting the contempt occurred presents on the House or Senate floor a written report from the committee giving full details of the pertinent facts. This report, *inter alia*, recites the questions which the witness refused to answer and states that the questions were pertinent to the subject under inquiry by the committee and deprived it of necessary and pertinent testimony. Excerpts from the transcript of the proceedings before the committee, showing the exact context in which the questions were asked and the refusals made, are included in the report. In some instances the report is orally read by the Clerk; in other instances it is read in part, following which, by unanimous consent, on motion of the member presenting the report, further reading of the report is dispensed with and it is pointed out that copies of the report are available to all members. Sometimes the report is not read orally, but is summarized by the member presenting it, or a written summary of it is read.

The committee chairman or other member of the committee next offers a proposed resolution directing the Speaker of the House or President of the Senate, as the case may be, to certify the report of the committee as to the refusal of the witness in question to answer questions or produce books, "together with all of the facts in connection therewith," to the appropriate United States Attorney "to the end that the [witness] may be proceeded against in the manner and form provided by law." This resolution is then thrown open to debate, following which it is voted upon. Sometimes the debates are lengthy; sometimes they are brief; sometimes there is no debate. Where a number of related resolutions, each involving a different witness, come up for debate successively, it frequently happens that the first few resolutions are extensively debated and the later ones more briefly or not at all, but usually in such cases the range of the debates on the earlier resolutions is in fact broad enough to be applicable to all of the resolutions. When the vote is taken, the yeas and the nays may or may not be recorded, depending on whether or not a demand therefor is made by a member. If the resolution of citation is voted, a formal citation is transmitted together with the committee report directly to the United States Attorney for the district in which the contempt occurred.[118]

It has been pointed out that, while the custom is well established whereby the House or Senate, when Congress is in session, votes on a resolution of citation before the Speaker of the House or President of the Senate certifies the facts constituting the contempt to the appropriate United States Attorney for prosecution, this procedure may not be required by the literal terms of 2 U.S.C. 194. That no action by the full body of the particular House involved is necessary was suggested in *Chapman v. United States*.[119] It was also pointed out by one author, who is most experienced in the trial of congressional contempt cases, that "Although the statute leaves no discretion with respect to certifying the matter to the United States Attorney, it has been the practice, nevertheless, in recent years, to debate and vote on the requested certification." [120] The statute states that it shall be the duty of the President of the Senate or the Speaker of the House to certify the case forward to the United States Attorney, indicating that he would be required to do so no matter what the vote of the Congress was.

In any event, it is clear under the statute that, where the act or acts constituting the contempt are reported to the Speaker of the House or President of the Senate "when Congress is not in session," it becomes "the duty of" that officer to certify the facts constituting the contempt to the appropriate United States Attorney for prosecution without waiting for authorization for such action from the full body on the latter's reconvening. Such "recess" certifications were in fact made in several cases. [121]

Once in the hands of the United States Attorney, the statute directs that the case be presented for indictment by a grand jury. The words of the statute imply that the United States Attorney has no discretion in this matter. [122] The case is presented to him "whose duty it shall be to bring the matter before the grand jury for its action." What possible infringement this may be upon executive powers is mitigated by the practical control which the district attorney has over the grand jury. Thus, he may present the case in such a way as to control the true decision of which cases go to trial and which do not.

At least one writer has urged that the application of this statute and its later counterparts ideologically changed the purpose, if not the effect, of the contempt power to one of punishment instead of coercion. [123] He pointed out that in the majority of cases before the statute, the action of the particular house of Congress often changed the recalcitrant witness' attitude to one of cooperation. In many cases, the contemnor purged himself by cooperating with the Congress. Perhaps for this reason, if not from habit, the Congress at first was hesitant to act under the statute.

It has been reported that "until the twentieth century Congress was reluctant to use the statutory provisions of 1857 and continued to punish persons summarily." [124] More recently, all contempt citations have been pursuant to the statute. The statute was upheld formally by the Supreme Court in 1897.[125] Interestingly, punishment through the older practice is not precluded by reason of the fact that the same act is equally a statutory offense. Both powers are available. Since the 1857 statute, the focus of judicial review of congressional contempt cases has changed from one of inquiring whether the power existed, to what the extent of its application may properly be.

Yet, even in cases presupposing the propriety of Congress' use of the contempt power, historical debate about the source and nature of the power persisted. In 1917, the Supreme Court though recognizing the existence of the contempt power of Congress, if properly employed, harked back to the situation in England long ago, thusly:

Undoubtedly what went before the adoption of the Constitution may be resorted to for the purpose of throwing light on its provisions. Certain it is that authority was possessed by the House of Commons in England to punish for contempt directly, that is, without the intervention of courts, and that such power included a variety of acts and many forms of punishment including the right to fix a prolonged term of imprisonment. Indubitable also is it, however, that this power rested upon an assumed blending of legislative and judicial authority possessed by the Parliament when the Lords and Commons were one and continued to operate after the division of the Parliament into two houses either because the interblended power was thought to continue to reside in the Commons, or by the force of routine the mere reminiscence of the commingled powers led to a continued exercise of the wide authority as to contempt formerly existing long after the foundation of judicial-legislative power upon which it rested had ceased to exist.[126]

During the period of English history notorious for the emergence of an active and powerful Parliament, and typified by a broad use of the contempt power in asserting its authority, there were abuses and misuses at the expense of those not then in favor.[127] Yet, in more modern times there has been a shift toward restraint in the use of the contempt vehicle by Parliament. The Royal Commissions and Tribunals of Inquiry [128] more frequently have conducted the fact-finding investigations which legislative groups have been wont to handle in America, and they have generally done so without coercive powers.[129] Now, these Royal Commissions are the principal source of investigative work in England. They are composed of specialists; have no enforcing power except in specific and unusual cases where Parliament granted it in creating the Commission; and have been responsible for many of the recent great social reforms. Withal, their hallmark has been fairness, as much as efficiency. Of course, the Royal Commissions are instruments of the Prime Minister and the Cabinet, and as such are not truly legislative bodies. In England, the legislature does depend on these executives for legislative assistance, whereas in the United States a similar dependence might cause a separation of powers problem, but in any event would not have much support because of the political advantage and the minority party interest in investigatory powers.

On the other hand, the inverse is so of the situation in the United States. Originally, the power was used where it was necessary to urge compliance which, once given, dispelled the need for further action. The procedures, though summary, included some hearing with counsel. Nowadays, the statutory contempt vehicle is more freely used than ever, and often in an attitude of retributive punishment.[130] Crime, subversion, and security are investigated by the American legislature, whereas they are not in the English political arena.[131] The number of investigations here has greatly multiplied in recent years,[132] and the argument has been made that the use of the contempt power in many cases has become more a weapon against individuals, than a shield of the government.[133] Professor Gellhorn has pointed out that during the ninety-two years between 1857 (the date of the congressional contempt statute) and 1949, 113 witnesses were cited for contempt of Congress, while from 1950 to 1952, 117 witnesses were cited for contempt.[134] Do these figures indicate a sudden increase in contemptuous refusals to answer questions? Or do they rather suggest that many more questions are being asked, and that the areas of inquiry have been undergoing change? From 1789 until 1925 Congress had authorized 285 investigations, while during 1950–52, Congress authorized 225 separate investigations.

In the litigation of the past half century, the claims by individuals for broader judicial protection of constitutional rights have been, as often as not, subjugated to the claims of the legislature for greater investigatory power. In these disputes, the congressional contempt power has been the sword which the legislature has often sought and used.[135] Compare this phenomenon with the English system, from which our congressional contempt power was born, and it appears that although the coin has turned, it looks to history as authority for its new face.

It can be fairly concluded that the powers of contempt which are now exercised in the United States originally were adopted from English common law. The inconsistencies and inappropriatenesses came too as part of the inherited common-law package. Though times have changed, as have political climates, the power has remained, in fact increased. Paradoxically, the legislative contempt power has played a lesser role in modern English practice, while the American offspring has grown to proportions more extreme than its parent. This blind heritage, in the hands of irresponsible power holders, could create the anomalous result of kingliness in a government which was conceived to establish the sovereignty of men.

CHAPTER II

The Varieties of the
Contempt Power

Contempt of Court is the Proteus of the Legal World, assuming an
almost infinite diversity of forms.[1]

In a case entitled "The United States against Anonymous," a
federal court of 1884 noted that under older English equity procedures, the contempt power was classified into two types—
ordinary and extraordinary.[2] Later years were to witness such
developments in this area of the law that contempt practice could
certainly be called "extraordinary," in an artless sense of that
word, and in a sense which the equity chancellors probably never
had in mind. Actually, this distinction was no more than the one,
now made in America, between civil and criminal contempts.
But this penchant for dividing contempts into categories and
opposites has been typical and has grown to confuse and often
plague the common lawyer. It was as if our forebears were so
calculating that they not only endowed us with this debatable
legal tool, but so complicated matters as to make our use of it difficult, and at times incomprehensible. Interestingly, the court in
the *Anonymous* case also noted the distinction between direct
and constructive contempts, but refused to delve into the distinction because it was admittedly "unsatisfactory to all who
study this subject."

Later courts have offered different categorizations of the contempt power, but all have agreed that this power of courts is one of many varieties, each with significantly variant ramifications. At different times, various writers and decision-makers have applied their ingenuity to the task of classifying contempts. Lord Hardwicke's division of the contempt power in a 1742 decision is often quoted. He wrote:

There are three different sorts of contempt. One kind of contempt is scandalising the court itself. There may also be a contempt of this court in abusing parties who are concerned in cases here. There may also be a contempt of this court in prejudicing mankind against persons before the cause is heard.[3]

The Encyclopedia of the Laws of England mentions a distinction between contempt of the court's power (its ability to enforce obedience to its orders) and contempt of its authority (or its jurisdiction to declare law and the rights of private parties).[4] The ordinary-extraordinary distinction disappeared from legal literature after the federal case already mentioned.

All these variations apply only to the contempt of court power. Contempt of Congress is of one basic kind, and these shadings are not applied. Congressional contempt is criminal, deriving from a federal criminal statute, and is prosecuted procedurally as such. By contempt of court standards, which thankfully are not applied, these contempts could be called criminal (to punish a wrong) or civil (to coerce cooperation), direct (as it usually is) or indirect.

These isolated hybrids, while academically perplexing, have not persisted beyond their own times and cases. Only two dichotomies have been uniformly accepted and are still applied today. They are the civil-criminal division, and the direct-indirect distinction. These two classifications are always made, and though cases usually turn upon a decision as to one of the two dichotomies, they both are not mutually exclusive. That is to say, though each contempt can be criminal or civil, direct or indirect, criminal or civil contempts are at the same time direct or indirect as well. The opposite is also true.

One must note that these classifications are signally important. With each labeling of a given contempt, a different door is opened to a different legal arena and a new association of participating procedures and characteristics. These classifications go to the heart of an accused contemnor's liberty and property rights. The decision-maker's every treatment of a contempt case involves a kaleidoscope of legal procedures. One turn, one move of position causes a swirl of new and special legal relationships between government and the individual. This aspect of the law of contempt is as reasonable as Russian roulette. Often also the results are tragic.

To shrug this off as an unimportant procedural matter is to overlook the crucial point. Because each determination of the classification of a contempt a fortiori defines the treatment of the contemnor which will follow.[5] And every contempt has, as we shall see, specific procedures, limitations, and treatments of its own. These procedural differences will be described in Chapter IV, but their import can be sensed from a few only cursory and inconclusive comparisons. For example, direct contempts are dealt with summarily, indirect contempts demand some hearing; direct contempts are insignificantly protected by the First Amendment, constructive contempts usually are protected; criminal contempts are pardonable, civil contempts are not; civil contempts allow for punishment which could conceivably continue without end, while criminal contempts have vaguely limited punishments; the privilege against self-incrimination and the criminal Statute of Limitations apply to criminal but not civil contempts; the burden of proving the offense is greater for criminal than for civil contempts; the civil contempt sentence can be purged while an adjudication of criminal contempt is fixed and final. The variations on this theme go on and on. These are but a few of the more glaring examples, which underscore the perceptive Holmesian comment that the substance of the law is secreted in the interstices of procedure.

Of course the classification problem is not peculiar to the law of contempt. In many situations, courts are called upon to classify acts of legal import as intentional, willful, reckless, in good faith, testamentary, voluntary, or their opposites. The list is a long one. But contempt is peculiar to the classification problem. Nowhere else is there such recurring confusion and mistake as here. This intellectual debacle results from a variety of contributing forces, prime among which are anomalous historical precedent, senseless judicial tenacity, and continuous disagreement. An analysis of the development of these classifications of the varieties of the contempt power should prove the need for thorough reevaluation of the whole subject, which results from the presently confused state of the law in this area.

Civil and Criminal Contempt

The English common law early recognized the unsuitability of the procedures of typically civil actions in law or equity with those developed to enforce the criminal law. This procedural difference brought about the development of a distinction between the treatment of civil and criminal contempts, which though insignificant then has grown, become more complex, and today plagues the American courts. Halsbury reported that older English law distinguished criminal contempts by their procedural implementation as much as by any innate substantive differences which might have existed between them and other offenses.[6] So it was that a contemnor could be attached on Sunday for the benefit of a private party for a civil contempt, but not for the good of the state in a criminal contempt case.[7] And the parliamentary privilege was disallowed as a defense to a criminal contempt, though it would bar attachment for a civil contempt.[8] There was no appeal from an order of committal or attachment in criminal contempt cases; nor was there a power in the Crown to remit a criminal contempt sentence.[9]

Seemingly trivial special treatments like these have unwittingly matured into a body of law with some rhyme, but less reason, and have provided later lawyers with the hapless lot of developing sensible theories and methods for treating the consequent problems of classifying contempts. No resulting conclusions are very satisfactory; all contain some truth, but none go beyond the extent of general observation; and all apply no more than an *ad hoc*, after-the-fact categorization which is not sufficiently helpful to the decision-maker of today nor fair to the actor (the unknowing contemnor) of tomorrow.

This unfortunate and troublesome result is, at least in part, because the original law of contempt embraced only what is now known of as criminal contempt. The contempt power was directed at offensive conduct which derived its criminality from the active interference with the crown or its acting official agents. What is now called civil contempt was originally called contempt in procedure and was considered a quasi-contempt; contempt in theory and name alone. It was not what was classically understood to be contempt. It was akin to the novel and peculiar crime of contempt, but was quite apart in purpose and procedure. Primarily, it was an equitable civil procedural device which was used to secure obedience to court orders. Yet, confusion probably grew from the double-edged nature of the power, in ways so similar to criminal contempt. Halsbury described this aspect in the following words:

In circumstances involving misconduct, contempt in procedure partakes to some extent of a criminal nature, and then bears a twofold character, implying as between the parties to the proceedings merely a right to exercise and a liability to submit to a form of civil execution, but as between the party in default and the state, a penal or disciplinary jurisdiction to be exercised by the court in the public interest. Misconduct of this kind consists in disobedience to . . . orders for the payment of money . . . or in wilful disobedience to any order or process or in the breach of an undertaking given to the court.[10]

Lord Chancellor Brougham tried to express this in the Wellesley case in 1831. Criminal contempts, he wrote, are acts not unlike civil disobedience, though usually more aggravated in nature. However, the former is a wrong savoring of criminality and dealt with penally. The latter is a civil matter (unless it is accompanied by criminal incidents) which is not punished in a penal sense and is only subject to civil process.[11] The power of equity courts to imprison in aid of civil process compounded the similarity of civil and criminal contempts, which arose from their usually similar natures and names.

So, it seems that there was not, as is now the case, a body of law dubbed contempt, but divided into two separate parts—civil and criminal. Rather, there was a body of contempt law, and a distinct procedural device, like contempt, called contempt, but not really contempt.

This chameleonic characteristic is one which has been a continuous cause of the misapplication and enigma which has followed in later treatment of the civil-criminal distinctions. The unfortunate nomenclature of civil contempts, and certain of its similar summary procedures have occasioned its being grouped together with what were at least historically "true" contempts, and eventually being intermixed and confusingly misapplied, sometimes in an unwarranted punitive sense. Today, the law of contempt embodies both civil and criminal contempt, and though both were born from different history and reason, they are considered but nuances of each other and are often applied interchangeably. Civil contempts are now often treated in ways which are extraordinary and would not be tolerated were they not garbed in that title "contempt," which we shall see is the cloak for a peculiar and sometimes severe area of the law. Whether the law of contempt is good or bad, the argument is even stronger against contempt procedures in essentially civil matters, which are rarely treated with criminal sanctions or followed by criminal stigmas.

Perhaps this confusion can be sensed from a review of some of the treatises and legal decisions concerning this issue. A review of the leading authorities of the past and a passing evaluation of their treatments will indicate both the nature and the extent of the problem of classifying civil and criminal contempts.

In 1884, Stewart Rapalje whose *Treatise on Contempt* [12] is one of the few books on the subject, put his hand to the task of making sense of the existing civil-criminal distinction. He reported that it was impracticable to distinguish every act of contempt in terms of its civil or criminal nature. His conclusion was that the main distinction between the two consisted of the passive non-compliance between private parties typical of civil contempts as contrasted with the positive obstruction or active disrespect to the court which characterized criminal contempts.

Civil Contempts are those quasi contempts which consist of failing to do something which the contemnor is ordered by the court to do for the benefit or advantage of another party of the proceeding before the court; while criminal contempts are all those acts in disrespect of the courts or of its process, or which obstruct the administration of justice or tend to bring the court into disrepute, such as disorderly conduct, insulting behavior in presence or immediate vicinity of the court, or acts of violence which interrupt its proceedings; interference with property in the custody of the law, misconduct of officers of court, etc.[13]

He added that to try to formulate a rule that would always apply was "impracticable." Time has proved this evaluation to be an understatement. It is impossible.

About twenty years later, James Oswald compiled an encyclopediac book [14] dealing with the contempt power and also directed his acumen toward resolving a sensible dichotomy between civil and criminal contempts. His conclusion was that criminal contempts were positive acts of deliberate interference with the law, and as such were public offenses, while civil contempts involved merely passive inaction in regard to civil obligations, and could result only in private injury. Both these scholars seemed to agree that the object of the contemptuous act determined the gravamen of its social effect, and thereby its characterization as civil or criminal. Since these men are relatively unchallenged as expositors of the law of contempt, their unsatisfactory conclusions are the more serious. Though common-law countries are not as seriously bound by the law in legal treatises as other countries, we are nonetheless led and taught by such authority, and in the instant situation have little else to help us in this confusing area.

These formulas for distinction afford no clear guide for the actor, who cannot know whether his conduct goes so far as to interfere with the law in general, or whether it is merely an interference with a private party who is an adjunct to the administration of law. The greatest percentage of cases of contempt could fall into either category, depending not upon the application of the Rapalje or Oswald formulas, but upon the discretion of the particular decision-maker. Not only does this do havoc to the law of contempt, but it also violates a strong principle of criminal law which directs that a law be clear enough to forewarn all potential violators of the consequences of their future acts. These formulas also overlook the fact that all true contempt derives from some offense to the law, whether the "law" in such case be a judge, king, congress, or a pending litigation. Any further distinction between law as an official body or proceeding and law as manifested through some private participant to a legal proceeding becomes hazy and is bedded in insubstantial reasoning.

In retrospect it is easy to criticize, but difficult to clarify complex issues and their past treatment. But guides like those just described miss one essential element of legal rules, the capacity to forewarn or to create justified expectations of later legal consequences. This characteristic in the context of classifying contempts compounds the otherwise existing confusion and, while often wise in the instant situation, propagates the difficulty and often the injustices attached to the problem.

Finally, in 1904, the Supreme Court directly addressed itself to the problem of classifying contempt of court as civil or criminal.[15] The source of the controversy was a procedural one. A district court had issued an injunction against certain parties to a pending suit. Bessette, a man who was not a party to this suit, was subsequently convicted of contempt by the court for acts violating its injunctive order. He attempted to appeal this conviction. The Supreme Court was called upon to decide the proper form for appeals of this kind. Until that time, contempt was not reviewable except upon writs of certiorari or prohibition, questioning the jurisdiction of the lower court. There was no jurisdiction to review criminal cases on appeal. The Supreme Court interpreted intervening federal statutes as extending the jurisdiction of appellate courts, to cover criminal cases through means of direct appeal of the whole record of the lower court, or by writ of error raising only questions of law. The court then classified contempt as criminal and therefore within this extension of appellate jurisdiction. Since Bessette was not a party to the original suit, out of which the injunction and the contempt arose, he could not bring a direct appeal on the record of the original case. He could, however, raise questions of law through a writ of error—the record of the lower court as to the facts in the original case remaining conclusive. In order to arrive at its ruling, the Supreme Court had to and did classify the contempt as a criminal matter, thus within the new statute's coverage. Referring then to distinctions made by lower federal courts in earlier cases, the Court confessed that "it may not always be easy to classify a particular act as belonging to either one of these two classes. It may partake of the characteristics of both." The Court rightly admitted that it is often impossible to decide whether a court order is to secure the private remedy of a person or to carry out its own work. About contempts in general, the Court went on to say, "that they are criminal in their nature has been constantly affirmed," and "the mode of the trial does not change the nature of the proceeding or take away from the finality of the decision." The Court, by implication, adopted the test of the lower federal courts which classified contempts according to whether the aim was to punish a wrong to the court, or to preserve or enforce the rights of private parties.

Here again, serious fault can be found with the formula. Most official legal sanctions are as much calculated to give efficacy to the legal process in a given case, as to insure the private redress of any of the parties. The test applied does not seek to classify contempt by any of the criteria ordinarily applied in distinguishing crimes from civil wrongs. The language of criminal law nowhere appears in discussions of contempt.

For example, it is axiomatic, capital letter criminal law that two requisite legal ingredients are necessary to prove any crime. Generally, the first is an intent by the wrongdoer to commit the act in question. This is called *mens rea*, or criminal intent. Second, there must be an act manifesting that intent and completing the prescribed conduct. This is called *actus reus*, or criminal act. In contempt cases, though there are references to legal requirements of willfulness, the strict *mens rea* standards which are applied in ordinary criminal cases are overlooked and irregularly required. Moreover, the *actus reus* in contempt situations is confusedly mixed with civil wrongs and is ill-defined and so sweepingly inclusive as to scoop up almost any act without forewarning. Furthermore, there is no distinction between other ordinary crimes and contempts—one act could be both. This latter confusion and intermingling is important since once an act is classified as a contempt all the peculiar contempt procedures follow on the rationalization that the wrong is special or sui generis—even though the exact same act is a crime of the ordinary kind as well.

The issue was brought before the Supreme Court again in 1914.[16] The case typified many to come in the era which saw the development and rise of the labor power in this country. Injunctions during these years were liberally issued against interference by labor leaders with court orders concerning action by organized labor. Disobedience to these court orders was treated as contempt. In the *Gompers* case, the court had to determine whether a contempt was civil, and could consequently be reconsidered on the merits of the record as a whole. The court echoed the theme of the former *Conkey* case. "Contempts are neither wholly civil nor altogether criminal." But, it went on to hold, "It is not the fact of punishment but rather its character and purpose that often serve to distinguish between the two classes. . . ." Then the court went on to set out its formula for classification:

If it is for civil contempt the punishment is remedial, and for the benefit of the complainant. But if it is for criminal contempt the sentence is punitive, to vindicate the authority of the court. It is true that punishment by imprisonment may be remedial, as well as punitive, and many civil contempt proceedings have resulted not only in the imposition of a fine, payable to the complainant, but also in committing the defendant to prison. But imprisonment for civil contempt is ordered where the defendant has refused to do an affirmative act required by the provision of an order which, either in form or substance, was mandatory in its character. Imprisonment in such cases is not inflicted as a punishment, but is intended to be remedial by coercing the defendant to do what he had refused to do. . . . On the other hand, if the defendant does that which he has been commanded not to do, the disobedience is a thing accomplished.

Imprisonment cannot undo or remedy what has been done nor afford any compensation for the pecuniary injury caused by the disobedience. If the sentence is limited to imprisonment for a definite period, the defendant . . . cannot shorten the term by promising not to repeat the offense. Such imprisonment operates, not as a remedy coercive in its nature, but solely as punishment for the completed act of disobedience.[17]

This unfortunately rhetorical dialectic again falls short, by its own standards, of satisfying the classification problem. If the character and purpose of punishment is determinative of the nature of the act of contempt, there can be no justifiable expectation before the decision of punishment of what that determination will be. This is a matter of the subjective intent of the decision-maker. The court admitted that "either form of imprisonment has also an incidental effect," that in cases of civil remedial punishment "there is also a vindication of the court's authority," and that in criminal punitive punishments "the complainant may also derive some incidental benefit from the fact that such punishment tends to prevent a repetition of the disobedience." Argument can be made with this reasoning if one can accept the conclusion that in most contempt cases there are no prime and incidental aspects of the exercise of the contempt power. In almost all such cases, the prime purpose of the use of the power is to assert power by government over interfering individuals. All such cases derive from a recognition of such a governmental supremacy, and all cases involve some power gain to government and any participant to the particular governmental proceeding.

In civil contempt cases, though the rationale may be assistance to a private party litigant in the execution of his civil remedies, there is an exaltation of government and a strengthening of its control and power through the judicial process. Likewise, in criminal contempt cases, rationalized on theories of protection of sovereign efficacy and punishment and deterrence of wrongs to

the state, there usually inheres a coercive, private, typically civil
element, such as the extraction of cooperation from a recalcitrant
witness under threat of punishment or the protection of the fairness of a trial for one criminally accused.

Reference again to the historical nature of the contempt power
indicates that in any event, contempt of any kind or classification
could historically only be a governmental power to be used essentially for governmental purposes, any private aspects notwithstanding. This is incontrovertible fact and history. If the purpose
of civil contempt departs from this quality, it is a contempt in
name alone. Its ancestry supports this fact, though its contemporary application clouds the clear import of history. I suggest
then that the nature and purpose of punishment under the contempt power is all too often the same in civil and criminal cases,
from standpoints of pragmatic effects and political realities. The
suggested differences are for the most part unjustified and, as
further development will indicate, exist only in the tangle of
procedure and practice that has resulted from years of confusion
and irrational allegiance to an unsatisfactory fiction.

The court in the Gompers case was guided in its decision about
the nature of the contempt proceeding by such ephemeral aspects
as the intent of the parties, the title of the action, the characteristics of the past proceedings, the relation of the contempt proceedings to the original action, and the prayer for relief. Marshal-
ing these incidents, the court decided that the aggregate of facts
showed that the contempt was civil. Indeed, later courts have in
fact done little more in their treatments of the civil-criminal contempt dichotomy, while avowing allegiance to various equa-
tions.

Another aspect of this last case points up still another rule to
which courts have often referred in their decisions about the civil
or criminal character of contempts. The Gompers court, and
many to follow, resorted to the unfortunate expression made in

an earlier case that civil contemnors carry the keys to their own prison door.[18] This is the rationale by which the punishment of civil contempts is considered unlike other criminal punishments and not a true sanction, since the man imprisoned can control his incarceration by doing a required act. By such specious reasoning it follows that if he does not cooperate to attain his release he is not truly being punished, but is doing some masochistic act which the state cannot control and for which it is not responsible.

This phrase has been almost uniformly accepted. It seeped into American law under the following rationale. Governments are founded to administer justice and courts are established to control this process. Though the power to imprison in essentially private matters is drastic, the court has no alternative until some better device is discovered. The idea is traceable to the language in an old English decision:

The law will not bargain with anybody to let its courts be defied for a specific term of imprisonment. There are many persons who would gladly purchase the honors of martyrdom in a popular cause at almost any price, while others are deterred by a mere show of punishment. Each is detained until he finds himself willing to conform. This is merciful to the submissive, and not too severe upon the refractory. The petitioner, therefore, carries the key of his own prison in his own pocket. He can come out when he will, by making terms with the court that sent him there. But if he chooses to struggle for a triumph —if nothing will content him but a clean victory or a clean defeat, he cannot expect us to aid him. Our duties are of a widely different kind. They consist in discouraging, as much as in us lies, all such contests with the legal authorities of the country.[19]

This "carry-the-keys-to-his-prison" expression has caught the fancy of later judges and students of the contempt power as to have become a legal cliché. It is an unfortunate one because of its seemingly obvious good sense, as well as the semantic cleverness which has made it such a favorite phrase, notwithstanding what I think is a clear absence of realism.

First, incarcerating a man until he does a certain act is as much a punishment of his original refusal to do that same act as it is a coercion of his doing it in the future. The interest of the state and the interest of personal parties are inextricably entwined. In all criminal punishments, the aim of incarceration is assumedly to deter others and reform the individual from future misconduct, and to penalize the commission of a completed act. This does not mean, in any other case, that the criminal punishment is anything less than a sanction of completed conduct. Second, the contemnor's conduct is often a product of strong principles which he holds and which conflict with governmental functions at a given point or of a disputed point of law about which he is often not unfairly or unreasonably adamant. Sometimes, the required act is impossible to perform. Imprisonment in such cases is not only an extraordinary deviation from general practice, but is often not truly calculated to change affairs by inducing a change of heart or mind. In cases arising out of legal disputes, the contemnor generally complies with the court after final litigation of his legal arguments. The *United States Mine Workers* case is such an example.[20] There a union leader and his union were punished for a contempt which arose out of a dispute over the meaning of a certain labor law about which even the Supreme Court could not agree. Once the courts decided the legal issues, the union conformed, and it might well have conformed then without threats of punishment.

In adamantine cases based on moral principle, the chances of coercing a change are unrealistic and often lead to embarrassing hardship. As an example of this point, the *Uphaus* case immediately comes to mind.[21] In contempt cases like this, where the issues are grounded in deep personal ideals, there is little hope of inducing a moral change. While it is not necessarily bad for man to suffer for his convictions in order to do homage to society, it is cruel and onerous to continue his punishment indefinitely, as might be the case in a civil contempt situation. This trait of individualism can withstand punishment, but it should not be killed. Moreover, the unalterable and crucial fact remains that a man is imprisoned in civil contempt cases as a legal consequence of his past and current conduct, no matter what logical legerdemain is employed about prison keys and doors or future conduct. And this occurs despite the fact that the imprisonment results from a civil action which characteristically does not employ such powers.[22] The duration of this imprisonment is unlimited, it could conceivably last and on occasion, has lasted much longer than punishments in more grievous criminal contempt cases. One article reported a case where a man was incarcerated for a civil contempt for nine years for refusing to be coerced into answering certain questions.

Any facile cliché then overlooks the fact, the law, and hardly assuages the indignity and harm to the individual involved. Nonetheless, the cliché and the reason upon which it was founded have hardily withstood years of use, and now support the civil side of the contempt-conviction coin.

This particular issue underscores the basic question concerning civil contempt. Is it best for government to imprison an individual to coerce him to act in a special way in the future? One may initially recoil at the idea of imprisoning men who have not committed crimes. Yet, it is perplexing to imagine the situation where governmental operations were at the complete caprice of the citizenry. It is my feeling that some compromise can be discovered. This problem will be one of the subjects of the final chapter of this book.

For some considerable time, courts continued to reiterate the purpose-of-the-punishment test as an index to classifying contempts as civil or criminal.[23] That the test was subjective and that results could often not be anticipated was accepted with no reported concern. Courts continued to ask: Is the punishment exacted in order to vindicate the authority of the law in general, or is it to benefit a private party to a legal proceeding? Thus posed, the classification question was automatically answered on the basis of the punitive or remedial effect of the punishment. The former meant the contempt was criminal; the latter that it was civil. And often the "keys to the prison" aphorism was used to rationalize or intellectualize the justness of civil contempts. In a great many cases it was impossible to know how an act of contempt would be treated until the court acted. The test was a reflection upon completed acts, not a key to direct action in the future or to apprise the actor of the consequences of his conduct.

Courts often voiced the conclusion that contempts are sui generis, neither civil or criminal in the ordinary sense of those words.[24] They would therefore marshal the characteristics of the whole proceeding, and label the contempt according to the predominant nature of the case. Finally, after years of fluctuating between these general tests, Judge Learned Hand wrote a decision in a case in the Second Circuit Court of Appeals, which eventually had some elucidating effect upon the classification enigma.[25] That case arose out of another suit in which defendant had sued the New York Stock Exchange and over six hundred different parties, alleging a damaging conspiracy under the antitrust laws. While that action was pending, the defendant "kept up a sporadic fusillade of broadsides sent to all . . . defendants" abusing and annoying them. The District Court ordered him to stop. He continued. The District Court found his conduct contemptuous, and he appealed to the circuit court. Judge Hand commented upon the confused and inadequate status of contempt classification which followed the *Gompers* decision. He pointed out in his decision that determining the civil or criminal nature of a contempt upon such incidents as the title of the proceeding, the conduct of the case, and the like, was to unduly elevate the import of purely formal elements of a case. Previous cases had determined the character of contempts as civil or criminal upon such formalities as the title of the proceedings,[26] the nature of the relief sought,[27] whether the contemnor testified,[28] who conducted the contempt proceedings (the government or a private party),[29] or to whom the fine was ordered to be paid.[30] Disagreement about which aspects were conclusive to the classification existed both between and within various jurisdictions.[31]

The awkwardness of this approach was pointed out by one author,[32] who noted that any given distinction between civil and criminal contempt may in one sense be the basis of a classification and in another the consequence of that same classification. For example, since the method of reviewing contempt cases is determined by the classification of the contempt (civil contempt was reviewed by a direct appeal, and criminal contempt by a writ of error), it is circuitous to use this aspect of the proceeding at a later stage to reflect upon the proper classification of that same contempt.

Judge Hand, with more success, also noted that this practice was unsatisfactory. He pointed out in his opinion, that this classification technique has defeated its own purpose, namely advising the respondent at the outset of the nature of the case against him. "Surely," he implored, "it should be possible to find some simple and certain test by which the character of the prosecution can be determined." Bound by judicial precedent and his tacit duty not to judicially legislate, Hand outlined those aspects of contempt cases which he felt might better control the classification problem.

Criminal prosecutions, that is, those which result in a punishment, vindictive as opposed to remedial, are prosecuted either by the United States or by the court to assert its authority. The first are easily ascertainable; they will be openly prosecuted by the district attorney; it would not seem to be of consequence how they are entitled when that is true. In the second the court may proceed sua sponte without the assistance of any attorney, as in the case of disorder in the courtroom; there can be little doubt about the kind of proceeding when that is done. But the judge may prefer to use the attorney of a party, who will indeed ordinarily be his only means of information when the contempt is not in his presence. There is no reason why he should; but obviously the situation may in that event be equivocal, for the respondent will often find it hard to tell whether the prosecution is not a remedial move in the suit, undertaken on behalf of the client. This can be made plain if the judge enters an order in limine, directing the attorney to prosecute the respondent criminally on behalf of the court, and if the papers supporting the process contain a copy of this order or allege its contents correctly. We think that unless this is done the prosecution must be deemed to be civil and will support no other than a remedial punishment.[33]

In response to this appeal, the Federal Rules of Criminal Procedure were soon amended to include the requirement of notice to the contemnor of the nature of the contempt charged in all criminal contempt prosecutions. "The notice shall state the time and place of hearing, allowing a reasonable time for the preparation of the defense, and shall state the essential facts constituting the criminal contempt charged and describe it as such." [34]

The clarity which this statute seemed to ensure was somewhat blurred by the subsequent decision in the *United Mine Workers* case.[35] There, the court held that the same act may constitute both a civil and criminal contempt, and that disposition of both in one proceeding is proper, even though the contemnor's procedural protections are likely to become obscured. In a dissent to that decision, Justice Rutledge noted that no other proceeding in the common-law system but contempt could be compounded into a civil and criminal hodgepodge. With typical directness and insight, he said, "our system does not comprehend a power so unconfined anywhere within its borders, and it is time the large confusion about this were swept away."

A case soon to follow indicated that this admonition was to continue unheeded.[36] That case involved a contempt arising out of a failure to provide documents to the Securities Exchange

Commission (SEC) in the course of an investigation of an illegal sale of securities. A district court, assisting the SEC, ordered the defendant to produce the documents. He refused and was adjudged in contempt. The court imposed an unconditional fine, indicating that by prior standards, the contempt was criminal. The commission appealed and asked for a remedial penalty calculated to coerce compliance with the order to produce. The Court of Appeals held that "the nature of the relief asked . . . is determinative of the proceeding." [37] Here, the purpose of the court's power was to bring about certain conduct, more than to avenge an injury to some public interest. The contempt proceeding was brought as part and in aid of the original proceeding, solely to compel production of the documents in question. The circuit court concluded that the case was not one of criminal contempt, or of an admixture of civil and criminal contempt, but solely one of civil contempt. Therefore, it substituted imprisonment for the fine ordered by the district court. The Supreme Court affirmed,[38] but added some gratuitous and confusing language. Admitting the "dual function of contempt" to vindicate the public interest, and to coerce or compel conduct, the court suggested that "imprisonment as a coercive sanction" would not preclude imposition of a "fine as a punitive exaction." This confusing rule is nothing more than a lingering on of the difficulty pointed out by Halsbury, long ago. Following older precedent criticized by Justice Rutledge, the majority of the court allowed room for a combination of civil and criminal contempt in one proceeding. A confused Justice Rutledge concurred in this case, and trying to understand the import of previous decisions of his brethren, urged that if the *Mine Workers* case overruled the *Gompers* decision that civil and criminal contempts could not be combined, Rule 42B notwithstanding, then this case should be sent back to the district court which could apply both contempt sanctions. The answer ought to have been that the court then would not be applying both kinds of contempt but one—embracing the aspects of both. Indeed, this is all that can be safely said for civil and criminal contempt differences, in general.

I suggest, in summation, that all that can be gleaned from the past is that the legal rules supporting both civil and criminal contempts have been liquefied to the point where one often washes into the other. Today, civil and criminal contempts combine to form the law of contempt, though historically one was a contempt power, and the other was a procedure for civil execution, unfortunately and confusingly labeled, and having certain similar characteristics as "true" contempts. The fact that so many typically civil remedies seem so much like a form of criminal contempts and appear to aid the judicial governmental process as much as the private individual party, also lends to the confusion.

As a result, one is left with but few and vague guides. A wrongdoer may never know, at the time of his wrongful act, whether he has committed a civil or criminal contempt or what the form of his sanction will be. Courts appear to survey all concomitants of a case and decide on the basis of the special characteristics of the act, the remedy sought, the nature of the action, and the aim of the remedy, whether the act looks like what has been vaguely considered civil or criminal contempt in the past. To this end the key issues considered by courts have been: who will primarily gain from exercise of the contempt power; is exercise of the power to punish a completed act or to coerce a future one; will the contempt proceeding constitute a separate action or will it be part of the execution of the original one; and what standard indicia of civil or criminal proceedings appear to attach to the processing of the power in the instant case. Characteristically, certain kinds of offenses have been treated as criminal contempt, such as obstruction of court proceedings or court officers, attacks on court personnel, publications obstructing trials, and interference with parties, and jurors. Personal characteristics like deliberateness, bad faith, and fraud have also inclined the decision-makers to classify contempts as criminal.[39]

Such acts as disobedience to judgments, orders, or court process, and the like, have been considered civil contempts. Though this is the usual case, certain acts of disobedience to court orders have been deemed to have reached such a point of contumacy as to warrant classification as criminal.[40] Civil contempts usually arise out of equity actions because of the peculiar in personam character of these decrees,[41] and criminal contempts often are of a gravity which would suggest some public interest. Yet, a governmental body may seek civil, remedial contempt relief,[42] and individuals may institute criminal contempt actions, though both practices are unusual out of the contempt arena. The peculiarities of certain civil contempt cases have resulted in certain extended imprisonments which would seem to indicate a gravity lacking in the typical civil situation. A thorough consideration of the cases leaves a distinct impression that courts apply an *ad hoc* kind of accounting to contempt situations and arrive at conclusions which, no matter how just in the immediate case, compose only the most casual and intellectually unsatisfying link with any body of law or legal principle.

Direct and Indirect Contempt

Besides the isolated hybrids of contempt classifications like those mentioned earlier and the civil-criminal distinction, one other classification has regularly been applied to contempts. That is the distinction between direct and indirect contempt. This distinction is traceable only to the procedural differences by which the common law punished certain contempts summarily and others only after some proceeding on the substance of the charge. This was discussed in Chapter I, and thoroughly treated by Sir John Fox in his book *Contempt of Court*. The essential reason for summarily dealing with certain acts of contempt and trying others in the usual procedural manner was that the former class involved either court officers or conduct by strangers to the court, but in the court's presence. In these cases, close judicial administration and the judge's personal knowledge of the offense reasonably disposed of the usual objections to summary treatment. The *Almon* case disturbed this distinction and brought certain contempts committed by strangers and not in the court's presence within the summary contempt power of the courts. This tale has been told, and we now know that for better or for worse American law is wedded to the principles of the common law in this respect.

The distinction between direct and indirect contempt is now always made. Upon the classification hinges such important privileges as the right to a jury trial and the right to be heard before a court which is not involved in the contempt itself, as well as the protection of the First Amendment. But even here, the courts have had problems of classification which are confusing and at times procedurally expensive to the contemnor. Very generally, this distinction was based upon the immediacy and location of the contemptuous act. Direct contempts were spontaneous, aggressive offenses expressly aimed at the court, itself, or at parties to the judicial process, which were committed in the presence of the court, and which tended to physically obstruct the administration of justice.[43] The prime example would be misconduct in the view of the court. No list could boast conclusiveness. Examples are myriad and run the gamut from striking a judge, juror, attorney, or witness to failing to produce a witness or to testify in a matter properly before the court. The conduct itself was offensive without proof of what was precisely the actual obstruction or interference with justice.

Indirect contempts were acts of misconduct, apart from the immediate proceeding in time or location, which by implication tended to interfere with the administration of justice.[44] Bribing a juror or a witness at a distant place or publishing prejudicial statements about a pending case are obvious examples of this offense. The title indirect contempt was originally used synonymously with the terms consequential or constructive contempt, but in substance meant the same thing. Nowadays, the term indirect contempt is used to include all nondirect contempts with one usual exception. Contempts by publications in the press have as a matter of custom been called constructive contempts, until now the term constructive contempt is almost one of special connotation, reserved usually for press contempt cases. There is no special reason for this except commonly accepted practice and habit.

There is little essential difference between direct and indirect contempts. Both are contempts in the historical sense of the word. Both are implied offenses to the workings of judicial government. There are no special causes or reasons for the distinction other than the historical confusion already mentioned in Chapter I, and which will be discussed further in the section of this chapter dealing with constructive contempt. But the treatment of the difference by the courts and the serious consequences of each classification in terms of procedural rights makes the subject one worth examination. Unfortunately, there has been some confusion in these cases, and the writings on the subject are less than appreciably helpful. A thorough reading of the appropriate cases, texts, and articles affords the reader with a special sense for guessing how a given contempt might be classified in the future. But, it is difficult to advance beyond this inarticulate "feel" approach —a result which some may find less than satisfying. Most writings merely present a "buckshot" approach of dozens of examples of each specie, and conclude with only vague, incomplete, or inadequate syntheses.

DIRECT CONTEMPT

Of direct contempt, Rapalje listed performing military maneu-
vers near the court while it is in session, insulting protests against
judgments of a court, assault and battery near the courtroom,
threatening witnesses near the courtroom, and blaspheming the
judge, to name just a few illustrative examples.[45] Edward M.
Dangel, another of the few scholars who have even attempted to
make some scheme from the broad- and ill-defined state of contempt law also attempted to explain by example.[46] He also added
that direct contempts were open insults to judges while they
were presiding, resistance to court powers in its presence, and
only such acts as the court personally knows about or which take
place in such a way as to impede proceedings. Disorderly conduct,
insulting demeanor, disobedience of court orders are the typical
vague descriptions given to direct contempts. H. S. G. Halsbury,
James F. Oswald, and the few other writers in this area have
offered little more.

INDIRECT CONTEMPT

Probably the only all-embracing and accurate definition of
indirect contempt is that it is composed of all contempts that are
not direct. Here again, the instances are often too unrelated and
vaporous to be summarized in a helpful descriptive sentence.

Typical examples which are clumped together as illustrative
of indirect contempts are only slightly helpful. All the contempts
by publications are indirect. Most contempts which occur distant
to the court geographically are too, unless they so causally effect
"the administration of justice" as to have a clear and obvious impact upon the court. Acts occurring when the court is not in session or disobedience to court processes away from the court itself
but which tend to impede justice are definitions. Preventing service of process, improper communications to or by jurors, with-

holding evidence from the jurisdiction of the court, bribing a witness or juror are examples. Those contempts about which the court has no firsthand knowledge is a favorite definition. Failing to obey orders of court in a place distant from the court is a typical example.[47] The temptation to follow this precedent of explanation by mass example should be resisted. Though a better explanation is evasive, a continuation of the list of examples and hypotheticals can only compound the existing confusion. Yet there are some golden threads of reason running through the rationales for the direct-indirect contempt distinction, and their examination may be of some help.

Direct contempts are said to be more readily recognizable. They are obstructive acts or inaction or words in the presence of the court which interfere with the administration of justice in obvious, usually physical ways.[48] The issue which typically arises is whether the act was "in the presence of the court." For this purpose, the act may be in the actual presence of the court or in sufficient proximity to have an actual as opposed to a remotely causal effect on the court's work (such as during trial intermission, on the court steps or in the corridors, lounges, or jury room). In these direct contempt cases, the court acts summarily against the contemnor, because any formal proof would be superfluous and merely ceremonial. The personal knowledge of the court is said to supply the necessary proof for conviction. The court need not prove what it already knows.

The interference with the administration of justice in indirect contempt cases is more speculative than in the direct contempt situation. Consequential contempts are said to *tend* to defeat the administration of justice. On strictly theoretical grounds it might be questioned how a court could be obstructed without personally knowing of the obstruction (for example, an unsuccessfully attempted bribe may be an indirect contempt, though there was no actual interference with the administration of justice), or indeed whether many acts which are considered indirect contempts actually do obstruct justice. A clear and convincing example of the latter objection is the contempt-by-the-press case, where it is only conjectural whether an actual obstruction results from the so-called contemptuous act. In cases of contempt by the press this presumption of interference with justice is harder to imagine than in the case of an attack upon a juror. Yet even those contempts which include some physical disruption of the judicial process often involve a more tenuous obstruction to the ways of justice in general than some apparently indirect contempts. Thus, the question whether a remedy as drastic as the contempt power is necessary to right the wrong in indirect contempt cases is not easily answered categorically.

The general "presence of the court" test is muddied by inclusion of "impact on the court" rationales. Here, courts have circumvented the requirement of actual presence in direct contempt cases by construing some constructive or fictitious legal presence of the court out of a direct contempt whose directness is physical *only* in actual effect or impact on the court. One judge applied this latter test in arriving at what seemed like a very reasonable opinion, but which really destroyed the foundation for distinguishing direct and indirect contempts. "It is a mistake," he wrote, "to say that all contempts not committed in the presence of the court are constructive only. The mere place of the occurrence may not be an absolute test of that question, and it may depend on the character of the particular conduct in other respects. . . ." He went on to explain: "to ride one's horse into the tavern where the judge sleeps . . . may be only constructively a contempt, as it very indirectly obstructs the course of justice, if at all; but when it takes the form of an assault upon an officer, as when he was beaten and made to eat the process and its seal . . . the impediment to the efficient administration of justice may be quite as direct . . . as if the party had ridden his horse to the bar of the court and dragged the judge from the bench to beat him." [49] A true lawyer, the judge cited cases to indicate that his allusions were not facetious. However, this kind of logic destroys the only valid reason, if any there be, for summarily trying direct contempts. There is no need for proof where the contempt occurs in the court's actual presence. But, there is a necessity for proving the offense where the court does not of itself know about the contempt. This is so no matter how direct, in a literal sense of the word, the contemptuous act is.

Another rationale for the use of summary procedures in direct contempt cases is the defensive need, asserted by courts in this type of case, to protect the trial from obstructive interference.[50] Less kindly observers have stated that the summary treatment of direct contempts is an example of the judiciary assuming the administration of criminal law by legislating unto itself the power to punish without a jury trial, in clear violation of the Constitution.[51]

Still, courts have continued to classify some contempts as direct and to proceed summarily against them, where the act arose out of incidents about which the court could only have had second-hand knowledge. An example would be the case involving tampering with the jury in the jury room. The rationale for considering this conduct a direct contempt is that the court is figuratively present in all parts of the place set apart for its use. Thus, though the court does not witness the contemptuous act, the threat to the administration of justice is immediate and severe enough to present a direct demoralization of the court's authority. Drawing an analogy to the doctrine of constructive presence in the criminal law, the same author has suggested the possibility that this tendency to create direct contempts out of what are really indirect contempts "presage the eventual extinction of the generally accepted differentiation between direct and indirect contempts." The cases since this comment was made have not borne out that prediction, though the theory has not infrequently held true.

On these occasions, there have been absurd and confusing results, like that in a recent decision of the Ohio Supreme Court.[52] A steel workers' union and two of its officials were found guilty of direct contempt when pickets prevented a sheriff from executing an order to take possession of trailers located on the picketed property. The court decided that the contempt was direct because the conduct obstructed the court's process, and was consequently "in the constructive presence of the court." This was despite a pertinent state statute which specifically classified resistance to process as indirect contempt. The court concluded by intoning the following reason: "If power, distinguished from jurisdiction, exists independently of legislation, it will continue to exist, notwithstanding legislation."

Thus rationalized, the case was one proper for summary treatment. However, the judge allowed a hearing because he didn't have any knowledge of the contemptuous act. The defendants were found guilty of criminal contempt even though a grand jury had refused to indict on a proposed charge of interfering with a court officer.

I submit that though inclusion of these acts within the direct contempt category may make good sense in certain situations these decisions cloud the consistent theoretical rationale for that power, and leave the potential offender with few justifiable expectations of the potential consequences of his conduct. It is further suggested that if summary procedures are continually applied to direct contempt cases, these situations should be limited strictly to acts which are direct in a physical, geographical sense, so that courts can act upon information which comes to them through their own sensual perception. Summary treatment should be withheld, at least in cases where commission of the contempt is only inferrible, no matter how directly related it is to the court.

This is a significant distinction, sometimes overlooked by courts in their decisions. Since the applicability of summary procedures and the dispensation of certain constitutional rights follow the classification of contempt as direct, there is a serious importance in paying strict service to this distinction.

These two criteria are all that can be found to distinguish direct and indirect contempts. Yet the two tests—actual personal knowledge of the court and significant causal impact upon the proceedings—are inconsistent. The former makes sense from the standpoint of avoiding proof of the offense and condoning summary procedures. The latter does not; it is only direct in a theoretical sense, no matter how the conduct effects the trial. It may be that this latter group was included within the category of direct contempts in order to insure summary judicial control of proceedings where it was badly needed. This would include instances where the misconduct occurred before the court itself or where conduct was so extreme as to demand swift and forceful treatment. If this is so, all that can be said to identify direct contempts is that they are offenses which the court in its discretion considers severe and important enough to treat summarily.

Today, by federal statute,[53] the indirect contemnor has certain specific procedural protections. One accused of indirect contempt must be granted a hearing after due notice of institution of proceedings against him by a complaint or a show cause order, service, and pleading. He must be given the right to be represented by counsel, to cross-examine witnesses, and to offer testimony in his own behalf. He can demand a jury trial in situations where it is allowed by sister statutes; and if the contempt involves criticism or disrespect of a judge, that judge is disqualified from deciding the contempt matter. Bail must also be allowed.[54] By contrast, the direct contemnor has only the guaranteed right to an order of contempt reciting the facts, signed by the judge, and entered in the record, and the right to appeal his conviction to a higher court. For a variety of pragmatic reasons, which will be described later, this right to appeal is of questionable value.

Another infrequent problem, arising out of the classification of contempts as indirect, is the possibility of violating the double jeopardy clause. The constitutional problems with which the contempt power in general is fraught will be covered in a later chapter. Suffice it for now to point out that most examples of indirect contempts are wrongs which are specially covered by other noncontempt criminal laws. So, the contemnor could be punished for a single act, not only for contempt, but also for subornation of witnesses, bribery of jurors, criminal libel, stealing documents, fleeing from a jurisdiction, fighting with a court officer, perjury, and a whole gamut of possible wrongs which could equally be considered indirect contempts.

An extreme example of this strange result was reported in an opinion of Justice Holmes in 1906.[55] In that case, while an appellate review of a criminal conviction of a Negro for raping a white woman in Tennessee was pending, a mob lynched the Negro. The federal courts had ordered his safe detention pending appeal. The Court evidencing the ultimate sensitivity of its honor decided that the lynching was done "with intent to show contempt for the order of this court." There is no saying what contempt it showed of the lynched man. There is no question that the court's order was disobeyed. However, the prime offense was murder, and any conclusion that disrespect of the court was the essence of the misconduct is farfetched. This is an example of the expedience and versatility of the contempt power, by which it can be applied to almost any governmental problem as a catch-all for offenses and a means of circumscribing normal procedural protections. I question what kind of respect judicial reasoning like this fosters in the public attitude toward government. Stretching legal powers for even the most noble ends often compromises the image of government. The breadth and vagueness of contempt law could often lend itself to frustrated or aggressive prosecution.

Again, I am left with more a confession than a conclusion about whatever legal principles attach to the law of direct and indirect contempts. Whether one uniform procedure governing all contempts would have the virtues of expedience as well as fairness and good reason and which substantive offenses ought to be covered by that procedure will be discussed in the final chapter. Special treatment in the contempt-by-the-press cases will also be discussed in later chapters, but some background of the constructive contempt doctrine should be included at this point.

Constructive Contempt

The indirect contempt cases arising out of press publications have a history and significance which warrant singular mention. These cases depart from situations involving actual physical disobedience or disturbance to the governmental body, and deal with acts which by implication affect the administration of justice through criticism, pressure, and interference with participants to the judicial process. Actually, it could be argued that any alleged contempt is by implication only. What indignity the sovereign suffers from obstruction toward its governmental representatives is speculative in many cases, especially press cases, and many consider that freedom to criticize or dispute government has an ultimate value of endearment and respect—that the maverick proves the solidarity of the flock. Nonetheless, such conduct has been deemed to impliedly, if not actually, dim the blaze of glory which the law sees as the aureola of sovereign government. Constructive contempt sees this implication reduced one level and is based (according to Blackstone) upon a want of regard for the courts which deprives them of authority, and thereby imperils the good order of the kingdom.[56] The actual harm to government in these cases is often speculative, and the speculation is based on the main inference that any contempt actually does harm. Yet, through the exercise of the constructive contempt power, courts have been able to go beyond the judicial world and exercise their controls over areas otherwise tangential to the judicial process. The litigated cases in this area have often involved situations with political overtones. This subject is dealt with in Chapters I and IV, but a more thorough examination here should be helpful.

The constructive contempt doctrine is directly traceable to eighteenth-century England and the famous case of *King v. Almon*, the background of which was described in Chapter I.[57] Though the rule was imported into American law, the treatment of this power by the English and American courts has been polaristic. This is as much owing to differences in concepts about the propriety of the contempt power as to the extreme difference in attitude toward the press, the usual subject of the constructive contempt power. For it is the press which is the object of the exercise of constructive contempt powers by courts, almost to the exclusion of all other potential offenders. For this reason, the particular backgrounds of the status and freedoms of the press both in England and America should be kept in mind during any perusal or study of these comparative case treatments, lest the full appreciation of the function and interrelation of this law upon society be only superficially understood. Constructive contempt cases have been generally considered as the protagonists to the free press versus fair trial legal dramas.[58]

One view of the history of the English press concludes that freedom of the press there is dormant, if not dead.[59] The English press originally operated under Royal grant or prerogative. The press was the tool of the crown and operated only so long as it remained in favor.[60] With the rise of libertarian principles during the time of Locke and Milton, there began an easing away from absolute royal control of the press. However, even in mid-seventeenth-century England, licensing ordinances controlled the press to some degree. The last such act expired in 1679, was revived, and was finally allowed to lapse by Parliament. In 1694 it expired. Nowhere in the English Bill of Rights is there any enunciation of the policy concerning freedom of the press. Likewise, the Magna Carta is silent on this subject. So it has been argued that this freedom of the press is a negative one, unlike that in our own country. Of course, such a policy as freedom of the press need not be expressed in formal writings to exist with the blessings of government. However, the situation of the press, viewed merely through the constructive contempt perspective, could lead one to conclude that whatever sanctity the English press does know can easily be, and has often been, dissipated by government.

Freedom of the press in England has been equated by other writers as an equivalent only of freedom from prior restraint. One book described press freedom in England as the right to publish anything so long as it does not injure third parties or the public.[61] That through the disciplined practice of constructive contempt by the courts in England, publishers are in effect buying their freedom, fine by fine, is so, if only in the contempt context. Less harsh observers have argued that the press is by appropriate standards quite free. Without digressing from the prime focus of this subject, it should be at least understood that there is a definite relation between legal doctrines of contempt, and the status of the press's liberty—a relationship which the cases will show severely subjects English journalistic freedom to the majesty of the court's control of the administration of justice.

The concurrent analogy which runs through any comparison of the English with the American cases is the status or social position of the judiciary in these respective countries. Whether this status is the chicken or the egg to the law of contempt is conjectural—certainly the two are consistent and understandable when seen in juxtaposition. The American lawyer is usually awed by the manners of the English courts and barristers and the active control and dignity of the English bench. This condition is reflective, if not the cause, of the English law of constructive contempt, as is the more freewheeling, critical press and bar in America consistent with our contempt law.

In the *Almon* case, for the first time (recorded) a court decided to summarily punish an individual for critical words written about a member of the judiciary and concerning a court proceeding. Citing no authority as precedent for summarily punishing this conduct, the court asserted an innate right to so act, claiming the sanction of immemorial custom and usage for authority and precedent. About this decision, Sir John Fox, the most thorough scholar of this subject, wrote that "the judgment seems to have been based rather upon what the court considered the practice ought logically to be than what it actually was. . . ." [62] Nonetheless, this case was the beginning of the law of constructive contempt. That case was followed by only two more constructive contempt situations in the eighteenth century.[63] Both arose out of alleged libels of Lord Mansfield, as did the *Almon* case. Sentencing was rigid, and convictions were predicated upon bringing courts or court officers to obloquy or unduly affecting pending proceedings. Sir John Fox, in his book, cited abundantly from the cases decided in England during the nineteenth century which followed or applied the rule of the *Almon* case, and which indicated its acceptance as authority by the English courts. In an appendix to his decision in a recent case, Justice Frankfurter, possibly indicating his personal propensity toward adoption of the English rule, included a memorandum of English cases decided between 1902 and 1945, which carried the application of the *Almon* rule by English courts almost to date.[64] The thrust of the *Almon* case has been broad, as it has been persistent. The rule has undergone doctrinal changes and extensions, until now it is probably beyond the scope that even Justice Wilmot intended or even envisioned when long ago he set down the rule.

Publications about evidence which might later have been ruled inadmissible at trial have been held contemptuous by English courts,[65] as have been articles criticizing a prosecuting attorney,[66] articles describing a newspaper's private detective work on a case,[67] posters concerning a related but different trial,[68] articles concerning matters not brought out in open court,[69] and even news films of an arrest.[70]

The applicability of the constructive contempt doctrine has been broadened to embrace innocent distributors of contemptuous matters,[71] matter written without knowledge of the judicial process toward which it was held to be contemptuous,[72] matters written both before a case came to court and after a trial ended,[73] and personal criticism of judges.[74] A review of some of the cases will indicate to the subject of the American press, a frightening picture of the state of press affairs in a jurisdiction which strictly applies the constructive contempt power.

Sir John Fox reported that there were no instances of summary punishments for constructive contempts in English history until early in the eighteenth century. Though contempt could recognizably be committed out of the presence of the court, the unusual summary procedures of direct contempt cases were withheld, and proceedings against strangers to judicial proceedings for contempts out of the court were by indictment, information, or action at law.[75] Then, in 1742, Lord Hardwicke wrote the decision in *Roach v. Garvin*.[76] In it, discussing the rationale for constructive contempt convictions, he coined a phrase which was later to be adopted and unduly extended by subsequent judges writing about this subject. He wrote, "There cannot be anything of greater consequence than *to keep the streams of justice clear and pure,* that parties may proceed with safety both to themselves and their characters." That gratuitous remark, in a case which dealt with a publication concerning a matter then before the court, was later to be seized upon as a favorite judicial cliché to support the right of courts to punish all constructive contempts.

Later, in the *King v. Davies,*[77] another court dealt with an article about a woman who had been arrested for abandoning a child. She had not yet been committed for trial. The *Southwest Daily Post* printed an article about "traffic in babies" which reflected upon the character of this woman. About a month later, she was charged with attempted murder arising out of the abandonment of a child. Because of the article, the editor of the *Post* was convicted for contempt. The court ruled that the High Court had contempt jurisdiction to protect the administration of justice in inferior courts, even in cases which might never come before it, so long as the possibility existed that it could possibly come before it at some time. Blending this with the "streams of justice" phrase of Lord Hardwicke, the court, citing its opinion in a prior case, wrote:

We adhere to the view we expressed in that case that the publication of such articles is a contempt of the court which ultimately tries the case after a committal, although at the time when they are published it cannot be known whether there will be a committal or not. *Their tendency is to poison the stream of justice in that court, though at the time of their publication the stream had not reached it;* and as such articles are calculated to interfere with the power of the court that tries the case to do effective justice, it is a contempt of any court which very well may try the case, but in fact does not do so, as well as the court which actually tries it [emphasis added].[78]

Thus David Davies paid £100 for his journalistic mischief, which was considered likely to pollute justice, and thereby contaminate the public welfare. The tendency of such conduct, reasoned the court, was to deprive the judiciary of the power to do what was its end, namely to administer justice duly and impartially. The phantom of Justice Wilmot and Almon pervaded the opinion.

In 1956 this polluted stream doctrine was further extended.[79] The Sunday edition of *The People* ran an article on vice and prostitution, in which it attacked one Micallef. Unbeknown to the editors, publishers or printers, Micallef had recently been charged with keeping a brothel, and shortly after the publication of their article, he was committed for trial. The Attorney General successfully moved for an attachment, and the court agreed that a contempt had been committed. Lord Goddard wrote that *mens rea* (criminal intent) was not essential to constitute the crime of criminal contempt. He cited older cases which held that intention or knowledge was no prerequisite for a contempt conviction. Newspaper publishing, he wrote, is "a perilous adventure," to be undertaken with the assumption of the risk of possibly publishing matter about subjects which the law would forbid, should it later be presented at a trial. Recognizing other cases which held that intent to interfere with the administration of justice was essential to convict for contempt, the court said that it withheld imprisonment, but fined the respondents £500.

This decision raises a serious problem with respect to the doctrine of *mens rea*, and carries the *Almon* and *Roach* decisions to a point of print-at-your-own-risk. It then appeared that the stream could be poisoned before it began to flow or even where it was not known to exist. No intention to prejudice the administration of justice was necessary to hold a publisher in contempt, since the courts would infer an attempt to obstruct justice.

It might have been argued that contrivance or carelessness by the offender would incline the court to impute *mens rea*, as is the case with homicide arising out of carelessness or corporate crimes.[80] But this was not indicated in the opinion. Rather, the court applied an absolute liability, considering the contemnor's state of mind as relative only to the sentence. This situation has provoked the comment, perhaps contemptuous:

It would clearly be inconvenient if the law made it necessary to prove knowledge in every case, as this would encourage ignorance on the part of editors and reporters, it may be doubted with all respect whether it is necessary for the law to be as Draconian as it now is in order to guard against any possible pollution of justice.[81]

The *New Statesman* case [82] was one which, besides being a *cause célèbre* about which most people had some comment, extended still another tributary of the polluted stream concept. One would guess that after a criminal proceeding terminated, press comment would be proper. Two problems then arise: When, for this purpose, is the trial over? Are post trial comments within the court's contempt power, and if so, by what rationale?

In the *New Statesman* case, the court dealt with comments published about a Catholic judge's verdict in a birth control case. Dr. Marie Stopes, a famous advocate for birth control, was sued for libel by the *Morning Post*. She had suggested that the paper refused to publish her advertisements because of Roman Catholic influences. The libel action was successful. *The New Statesman* then ran an article which said:

The serious point in this case, however, is that an individual owning to such views as those of Dr. Stopes cannot apparently hope for a fair hearing in a court presided over by Mr. Justice Avory—and there are so many Avorys.

Supposedly recognizing the authority that judges as individuals are subject to criticism, the court held in this case that the statement was contemptuous because it scandalized "the court itself." The court drew a distinction between criticism of a judge personally and imputation of his partiality, finding the latter contemptuous. Its rationale was that the public confidence in the fair administration of justice was affected in the latter classification, and that constituted more than mere criticism. The court again harked back to Justice Wilmot and the *Almon* decision, in finding the defendants in contempt "not for the sake of the judges as private individuals, but because they are channels by which the King's justice is conveyed to the people." This decision was despite or, according to the author of the opinion, in line with established English authority that the contempt power is not to be used to vindicate the judge as an individual.

The reader is left with alternatives by this decision, each bothersome. If the case, despite the language in the opinion, was based upon some interference with the dignity of particular trials, we are left with an unwarranted extension of the polluted stream doctrine, since the trial was over and any imputation of justice was by this time quite remote, if it existed at all. If, on the other hand, the case was decided on some rationale of heretic criticism of public officials, the contempt doctrine is extended to comments about judges personally, notwithstanding long precedent and strong language disallowing convictions for such conduct.

A later case reached a similar result.[83] In *R. v. Colsey*, the editor of *Truth* was ordered to pay a fine of £100 and costs for having commented on Lord Justice Slesser's judgment in the case of *R. v. Minister of Labour* in the following terms: "Lord Justice Slesser, who can hardly be altogether unbiased about legislation of this type, maintained that really it was a very nice provisional order or as good a one as can be expected in this vale of tears." Lord Justice Slesser had been Attorney General in a former Labour government which supported this legislation. Professor Goodhart has commented on the case as follows: "This case seems to carry the doctrine of constructive contempt to its extreme limits, for the administration of justice can hardly have been seriously endangered by the editor's mild but expansive humour." [84]

Better reasoned cases have left the judges to private actions for libel for such comments, not governed by the summary procedures applicable in contempt actions. One writer has called for a distinction between contempts by publication which are merely defamatory, and those which actually are obstructive of judicial proceedings.[85] Precedent against allowing criticism of particular judges and judicial decisions after the proceedings have terminated is another dangerous extension of the constructive contempt doctrine. This leaves little area for the exercise of criticism of the judiciary, so valuable, as admirers of Dickens or Daumier will attest, to a free society.

A recent case extended the constructive contempt practice beyond even the *New Statesman* case, by including in the harsh embrace of the contempt-minded courts the innocent distributor of matter which is subsequently found to be contemptuous.[86]

The trial of Dr. Adams for the murder of an old lady, who was his patient, and under whose will he was named as a beneficiary, was one of world-wide interest and notoriety. *Newsweek* magazine printed a European edition of their weekly in which there were some comments prejudicial to Dr. Adams. That issue was written in the United States, printed in Amsterdam, and distributed in England. There was no editor or manager for *Newsweek* in England, and the distributor claimed ignorance of the prejudicial article. The court, scooping deep into the barrel of responsibility, held the distributor in contempt, seemingly because someone had to be responsible, and since he was in charge of circulation within the country, he was the only one the court could punish in a case of this kind. Otherwise, foreign publishers could take commercial advantage of their immunity and reap profits irresponsibly where local publishers could not because of their susceptibility to sanction by the English courts. Thus the news vendor was added to the list of occupations made hazardous by extension of the contempt doctrine. This is economically harassing since the small news vendor is less able to insure himself from this judicial jeopardy than the publisher, and certainly less financially able to withstand the sanctions of the court. The most local, informal traffic in writings could bring the same result, and Britishers might well alter an adage and warn "beware of men bearing gifts, if they are writings."

Justice Goddard, the author of this opinion added the apologia: "This jurisdiction is discretionary and the court can be trusted not to exercise it except against those who can fairly be said to bear some responsibility for the publication." Yet, in this case, the defendant did not know or have reason to know that the publication that they distributed contained improper remarks. Moreover, as a practical matter, it may well be impossible for a distributor to ascertain improprieties in articles which he distributes. His brief contact timewise with the voluminous amount of materials with which he deals compounded by the imprecision in defining what is contemptuous (especially in the eyes of the layman) make his position quite precarious.

The court disposed of two cases which the defendant relied upon in his defense by holding that conduct which prejudices the fairness of a trial is in a class by itself and is not to be treated by any loose analogies. One case which the defendant raised in his defense held that, in cases of defamation by publication, a distributor is not liable if he can prove that he was unaware of the defamatory material, and that he was not negligent.[87] Both conditions were conceded in the *Newsweek* case. The court held nonetheless that the law of defamation is not analogous to the law of contempt. Defendants also pointed to an older decision involving a case where an individual loaned his friend a copy of a newspaper.[88] The newspaper contained contemptuous matter. In excusing the defendant from contempt liability, the court recognized that it would be going too far to hold one responsible for not guessing the implications of the contents. To this, the court replied that dissemination was defendant's business in the *News-week* case, and circulation was greater, more pervasive, and had a socially significant effect. There is language in the opinion indicating that this case was a limited policy decision by the court, based upon the practical consequences of that article, and the lack of proprietary responsibility of the magazine to the control of the English courts.

The Administration of Justice Act of 1960 [89] has made some considerable procedural changes in English contempt law. Section 11 makes lack of knowledge "having taken all reasonable care" a defense to a contempt charge. This was obviously aimed at the decisions in the *Odham's Press* and *Griffiths* cases.

The status of press control by English courts through the exercise of the constructive contempt power is still frightening to one who is reared in the climate of a freewheeling press. Yet Englishmen will be quick to state that the press is free in their country, albeit less free than in America. That freedom is not an absolute license is a favorite defensive retort. In practice, the English press knows a freedom from prior restraint, but a very sensitive and rigidly construed responsibility for that which is published. A practical aspect of the English contempt attitude of favorable value is the deterrent effect it ought to have on press misconduct. Certainly, it must have its effect on manners, decorum, and the taste of the press. Still, one wonders about the caliber of some of the existing English tabloids.

The greatest failure of English contempt law is its disrelation with its most valuable object—protection of fair trials. It is of little service to an accused person who is written into jail by a prejudiced press that the publisher or editor is fined or imprisoned. His victory is a hollow one unless the conviction is reversed. The contempt vehicle is only indirectly curative of unfair trials, if at all, though this is its most valuable purpose. However, many of these cases conform to the original purpose of the contempt power which was to punish disobedience and disrespect toward the sovereign and his officials.

I suggest that there is sound reason for discouraging, by use of the contempt power, the dissemination by mass media of information which might later be used as evidence at trial.[90] This would be a rationally connected means to a legitimate end—protecting the evidentiary rules of judicial proceedings. There is serious question, on the other hand, about the value of carrying this rule any farther. Editorial opinion-venturing, criticism, description, these aspects of the journalism of law are invaluable and certainly outweigh any claims for abstract judicial purity which may be offered in defense of the broad application of the constructive contempt rule.

THE AMERICAN RULE

Our First Amendment has been the wall to stop the flood of constructive contempt convictions in this country. It is more than a policy declaration. Rather, it has served as the establishment of a sanctity upon the role and the power of the press and a deterrent to its dissipation by legislative ruling or judicial review. The latitude of American courts in dealing with the press is a cause both of the gauche, sensationalistic press—all too frequent in this country—and for, on the other hand, some of the social reforms, the great informational interchanges, and the general enlightenment of the population in matters of public interest. For this latter reason primarily, the use of constructive contempt against the press by American courts has been sporadic and unsuccessful. The original acceptance of the contempt doctrine as part of our adoption of the common law was typified by debate and confusion. Recent decisions by the Supreme Court have quite emasculated its effect as a control upon the press. This situation stands alone as a denial by the American courts of the fullest application of the English contempt doctrine. Though constructive contempt cases are not the only ones where the First Amendment has been raised to restrain contempt powers, it has been the area where the most success has been achieved. There is nonetheless one minority of our Supreme Court which has even recently called for adoption of the broader English constructive contempt rule. A perusal of some of the leading cases will indicate its status as a power of American courts.

The first American cases involving use of this contempt power arose in the states at the end of the eighteenth century, and most often involved provoking political comments by the press.[91] These cases followed the English rule of *Almon's* case, and adopted Lord Hardwicke's famous phrase from *Roach v. Garvin.* The court considered its power to use the contempt process as adopted from long precedent and essential to judicial efficiency. Justice Wilmot's immemorially used power became our law of the land. However, public opinion demanded a greater respect for the young American press than that shown in England, and in 1809 this interest was recognized. After several states enacted statutes confining the summary power of contempt to official misconduct of court officers, disobedience of process, and misbehavior in the presence of the court which obstructs the administration of justice, the federal rule was enunciated.[92] By its general wording, it impliedly adopted the English common-law rule. It covered "all contempts of authority in any case" at the discretion of the court. Until the famous case concerning Judge Peck, there were only a few inferior federal court cases dealing with the contempt power, and they followed the English common-law rule. After the *Peck* case, and the new federal statute which followed, the trend was away from the broad common-law rule and more in conformity with a liberal press. The story of this legal episode has been urbanely treated in early articles on the subject of constructive contempt.[93] The bill passed in 1831 still, in effect, defines the offenses punishable as contempt of court.[94] The present statute includes misbehavior of any person in the presence of the court or so near thereto as to obstruct the administration of justice, as well as misbehavior of court officials, and disobedience of resistance to official writs. It has been argued that the federal statute's wording was based upon the early Pennsylvania and New York statutes which preceded it, and was meant to cover direct contempts of the court in a physical sense. This would indicate a policy of protecting the court members and the court itself, but not the sanctity of a fair trial in general. The statute, it has been argued, excluded from summary treatment publications out of court, even if they tended to interfere with the administration of justice. By 1860, twenty-three of the then thirty-three states had enacted legislation implementing the federal policy, and only a few state cases applied the rule of *Almon's* case.

After the Civil War, a revival of the common-law rule could be noted. States recognized contempt powers both to protect the dignity of the courts and to prevent obstruction of the administration of justice. Many states held that legislative inhibitions to the contrary were unconstitutional and need not be heeded.[95] The federal rule swung back to the English approach in 1915 when the Supreme Court upheld a district court judge who found a critical newspaper publisher in contempt of court for commenting upon a pending proceeding.[96] Since that case, lower federal courts have gone both ways on the issue of constructive contempt,[97] though the current Supreme Court, with a minority usually dissenting, has favored the more liberal American adaptation of the English rule.

At first the federal statute's wording "so near thereto as to obstruct the administration of justice" was interpreted to mean having a reasonable tendency to obstruct. Justices Holmes and Brandeis dissented to this construction in the *Toledo* case, arguing that the statute plainly and directly dealt with accomplished

facts of interference and should not be construed to cover speculative obstructions like those involved in these situations.

The "causal" rule of the *Toledo Newspaper Co.* case was directly altered in 1941 by the holding of the Supreme Court in
Nye v. United States.[98] There defendants sought to influence an
administrator in his suit for wrongful death brought in a federal
district court. The act in question took place 100 miles from the
court, but was direct misbehavior and involved a pending action.
They were found in contempt of court by the district court and
fined. Then they appealed to the Supreme Court. Justice Douglas,
for the majority, held that the words "so near thereto" in Section
268 of the Judicial Code should be construed as having a geographical rather than a causal connotation. Since the conduct did
not occur physically within the vicinity of the court, it was no
interference with the administration of justice in the better interpretation of that section. "It is not sufficient that the misbehavior charged has some direct relation to the work of the
Court." Denying that the acts had a reasonable tendency to sub-
vert the administration of justice (or closing their eyes to it) the
court indicated their fear of criminal conviction without jury
trial, as is the case with contempt. Perhaps these verbal gym-
nastics in interpreting Section 268 were more provoked by the
court's dislike of the procedures of contempt convictions, than
the reprehensible nature of defendant's conduct or any scholarly
distinctions about the proper extent of the contempt power.
After all, the words "so near thereto as to obstruct the administration of justice" in their most literal, common sensible interpretation mean near enough to a trial to obstruct it. Moreover,
the fact that the "so near thereto" clause follows the words "in
the presence of the court or . . ." indicates quite clearly that the
statute meant to cover those acts actually in the court's presence
as well as others near and affecting the trial, but not in fact in the
court's presence. Otherwise, why add the clause?

Whatever the court's motivation, the effect was to change again, through statutory construction, the power of the courts to punish what was classically defined as constructive contempts. Justice Stone dissented in the *Nye* case on the rationale that if the acts affected the tranquillity of the court, they should be within the contempt statute's "near" clause in a causal proximity sense. This attitude is traceable to Bacon's noted Essay on the Judicature, where he wrote: "The place of justice is an hallowed place; and therefore not only the bench, but the footplace and precincts and purpose thereof ought to be preserved against scandal and corruption." [99]

Indeed, one commentator has argued that the jurisdiction of the court to punish for contempt should be based on the harm done and not on any arbitrary measure of "presence of the court." [100] Does the publication affect the judge in the agony of his decision?

Several mid-twentieth-century cases were decided by the Supreme Court, which evidence a settled policy or direction away from the English rule. However, those cases were more concerned with preserving the power of the press than with scholarly distinctions about the extent or propriety of the contempt power itself. No polluted stream theories were adopted from English cases decided around this time. Since they arose out of state decisions, these opinions extended the federal rule to the states through the implications of the Fourteenth Amendment.

The first of these came to the Supreme Court in 1940 and involved a Los Angeles newspaper and a California labor leader.[101] A newspaper editorial attacked two union members accused of assault and urged the judge to deal strictly with them. The trial was over and the two defendants had already been found guilty. Only the issue of sentence remained. Two other editorials commented upon accused persons already found guilty before Los Angeles courts, but awaiting sentence. A companion case in-

volved a telegram from labor leader Harry Bridges to the Secretary of Labor which was printed in a local newspaper. The
telegram threatened union action if a pending trial resulted in a
certain way. In separate cases, California courts found both the
newspaper and Bridges in contempt of court,[102] and they joined
in an appeal to the United States Supreme Court. Justice Black,
writing the majority decision overruling the California courts,
said that the First Amendment, guaranteeing free speech and
press, disapproved English practices restricting this enlarged
American liberty, and that one of the objects of the American
Revolution was to rid us of the English style of freedom of the
press. Recognizing the perplexity of this conflict, he wrote "For
free speech and fair trials are two of the most cherished policies
of our civilization, and it would be a trying task to choose between them." The choice of the majority was free speech. This is
in line with the thinking of one segment of the post New Deal
Supreme Court that First Amendment liberties are absolute directives which must predominate in almost all cases of conflict.

Justice Black's theory was that, historically, the intent of the
Constitution writers was to give the press a liberty of the broadest
scope consistent with orderly society. Dismissing the issue of the
state-federal conflict, which the majority resolved by holding that
the First Amendment is incorporated by the Fourteenth and
binds the states, the Court applied the clear and present danger
test enunciated by Justice Holmes in the *Schenck* case.[103] Applying what they called the working principle of the clear and present danger test, the Court found that the publications were not
substantive evils serious or imminent enough to be punishable.
Disrespect of the judiciary and interference with the administration of justice was negligible and not worthy of censoring utterances of public interest.

Justice Frankfurter and a concurring minority dissented, arguing that the majority's interpretation of freedom of speech tore

at the historical powers of state courts to protect the states' administration of justice. In his view, free speech was "not so absolute or irrational a conception as to imply paralysis of the means for effective protection of all freedoms secured by the Bill of Rights," such as fair trial. Drawing a distinction between comment and the free flow of doctrine, with intimidation which subverts a pending judicial proceeding, Justice Frankfurter saw the latter in the instant case. His rationale for use of the contempt power was that courts are not organs of popular will, as are the executive and legislature, and therefore they more seriously need this power to facilitate their function.

The next case of import in this trend arose in 1946.[104] There, the publishers and editor of a Florida newspaper were cited for contempt based on two editorials and a cartoon criticizing the leniency of a Florida court. There was no jury involved, and two of the three cases commented upon were not pending. The Florida courts held that the article impugned the court's integrity and thereby impeded the administration of justice in pending cases. The United States Supreme Court, reversing the conviction, stated that in close cases the need for freedom of public comment outweighs its undesirable influence upon pending proceedings. Under the circumstances, Justice Reed wrote, the evil held contemptuous was not serious enough to warrant interfering with free comment. Justice Frankfurter, dissenting again, urged that freedom of the press is not an end in itself but only a means to that same end. Freedom gives power, but power in our democratic society implies responsibility. Freedom of the press does not mean freedom from responsibility for its exercise. His approach shows less interest in protecting the judiciary as individuals than in protecting the function which judges exercise, especially as it effects the balance of state and federal powers. The states must have discretion in fashioning their own criminal remedies.

Following this decision, came *Craig v. Harney.*[105] There, newspapermen were convicted for contempt for publishing several articles critical of a lay Texas trial judge and his decisions. As if answering Justice Frankfurter, the court, through Justice Douglas, found the conviction violative of the First Amendment and announced that there is no aspect of the judiciary which gives them any peculiar right to censor the press. Justice Frankfurter dissented, pointing out this time that the court was dealing with the state law of contempt, and not the federal statute as was the case in *Nye.* Once declaring that First Amendment cases are issues of federal law, so the court can independently consider the facts of the case, the majority of the court held that the insulated dichotomatic power of the states was gone.

The *Baltimore Radio Show* case followed.[106] There, the Supreme Court denied certiorari from a decision of the Maryland Court of Appeals which reversed a contempt conviction issued by the Criminal Court of the City of Baltimore. Two tragic murders of little girls in the Baltimore-Washington area occurred within ten days of one another. Public alarm and concern was tremendous. Then one night a radio announcer began his program with the words "Stand by for a sensation." He went on to report that the killer was apprehended, identified, had confessed, and had a criminal record; and, further, that the subject had reenacted the crime and dug up the death weapon. These facts were true. The reported facts became vital evidence at the subsequent trial. Because of the great public interest in the case, the broadcast had a pervasive impact in the community. In fact, the defense attorney waived jury trial because he felt he could not risk it in such an aroused community.

The trial court found this broadcast contemptuous, likely to prejudice indelibly any potential jury, and fined three broadcasting companies for contempt. The state court of appeals reversed, and the United States Supreme Court affirmed that reversal in a per curiam opinion. Justice Frankfurter filed an opinion, nonetheless, indicating some empathy for the trial court's ruling, and citing a number of twentieth-century English cases of constructive contempt. Indeed, there are other commentators who agree that American courts would do well to emulate the English treatment.

Of interest is the 1951 case of *Shepard v. Florida*.[107] This case involved a Florida trial of four Negroes for the rape of a white girl. The press took great interest in the trial. It reported about a confession which was never offered in evidence at trial; it called for the supreme penalty; and it generally reflected the fever-pitch of a rampant community which burned Negroes' homes and tried to run some people out of town.

Justice Jackson, joined by Justice Frankfurter, in a concurrence to a per curiam opinion which held that the defendant was deprived of due process of law, wrote:

But prejudicial influences outside the courtroom, becoming all too typical of a highly publicized trial, were brought to bear on this jury with such force that the conclusion is inescapable that these defendants were prejudged as guilty, and the trial was but a legal gesture to register a verdict already dictated by the press and the public opinion which it generated.

Motions for continuance and change of venue were denied. Trial was by jury, unlike the *Craig, Pennekamp,* or *Bridges* cases. Unopposed, deliberate, and pointedly, Justice Jackson wrote that trial courts, by reason of recent decisions, have become disabled from dealing with press interference with the trial process, unless the interference takes place in the court's immediate presence, "the last place where a well-calculated obstruction of justice would be attempted. These convictions, accompanied by such events, do not meet any civilized conception of due process of law. The case presents one of the worst menaces to American justice."

The Supreme Court in utter frustration recently reversed a state murder conviction because press notoriety had been so great as to prevent a fair trial. In a concurring opinion to this unanimous decision, Justice Frankfurter again voiced his contempt for the press which misuses its freedom in such a way as to deprive individuals of their constitutional right to a fair trial. "The court has not yet decided that, while convictions must be reversed and miscarriages of justice result because the minds of jurors or potential jurors were poisoned, the poisoner is constitutionally protected in plying his trade." [108]

The result of these cases raises some questions about the status of the press in relation to criminal trials. Will the Supreme Court deal differently with the press in jury cases? In *Pennekamp*, *Craig*, and *Bridges* the court spoke of the fortitude of judges before press criticism, while in *Shepard*, they recognized the due process problem where there is a jury trial in an environment of great publicity. And what of the social responsibility of the press? When the press becomes an instrument of injustice, as in the *Shepard* case, may the courts not inhibit their freedom before they prejudice the trial? Should the press in the exercise of its valuable liberty be totally unfettered? Is the Supreme Court as concerned with articulating the proper modern power of the historical contempt vehicle, or is their concern more directed at controlling the summary process of this criminal sanction? Indeed can there ever be a right decision, when the Court must balance values like the safety of society and the security of individuals on the one hand, with the enlightenment of society and the liberty of the press on the other? Either choice involves an irreparable loss. Erosion, through majority or minority decision, of basic liberties, as are involved in such a conflict as this, must lead to a crumbling of one or the other value. Should decisions involving important and traditional institutions of our society be made by policy-oriented factions of the Supreme Court, changing according to membership and partisanship rather than through action by other organizations of government more reflective of the popular will in these matters? Are the procedural techniques, like *voir dire*, instructions, continuance, and change of venue, which American courts use as a substitute for the English constructive contempt power in these cases, a better solution? Is it possible to restore some narrowly confined contempt power in press cases, which would avoid constitutional restrictions and still be effective? Some statutory scheme like that which Professor Donnelly and I suggested in a recent article or like that which will be described in the final chapter of this book may be a suitable alternative.[109]

These are the issues with which the status of American law is left. Certainly, the consistency of recent constructive contempt decisions indicates that the American view is doctrinally as established in favor of the press as the English view is, unquestionably, against it. Both the English and American counter-views allow for some justification of expectations of decisions. Perhaps, this is all that judges can do. If this is so, we might better look to the legislature to find a solution which is not a compromise, and which is not an esoteric preference of values, but which brings an approach to the problem which will preserve the essence of both values—the freedom of the press and the fairness of trials.

These cases and these situations are not meant to be exhaustive of the problems provoked by the constructive contempt doctrine. Instead, they are intended merely as an exemplary thermometer of the degree and direction of its acceptance. More doctrinaire reviews of this subject have preferred an approach that traced the elements of the offense chronologically. I have preferred a doctrinal comparison.

In constructive contempt cases, as contrasted with all other contempt cases, American courts seem to be less impressed or guided by historical precedent and practices than with deciding some realistic, workable rule by which vital, competing interests can best be harnessed. This kind of sensitive jurisprudence is all the more appreciated in an area of law least famous for just that, and too often inhibited by the deeds, good or bad, of the past.

CHAPTER III

Extensions of the Contempt Power

Contempt powers have not been confined wholly to the worlds of judicial and legislative officialdom. The twentieth century has seen the rise to prominence of administrative agencies as a fourth branch of government, as well as the increase in governmental activity through officials, who defying precise or singular classification into standard categories, have been casually labeled "quasi" judicial, legislative, or executive officers. Even conservative advocates of the standard American tripartite form of government have recognized this vast constellation of governmental bodies and officials which are not purely legislative, judicial, or executive. It cannot be denied that the vastness and complexity of contemporary governmental business has occasioned an era wherein important official business has been conducted by administrative officers, and these other hybrid officials, who often have assumed many of the important functions of the traditional three other branches of government.

Do any of these agents and agencies have contempt powers; or indeed ought they have such powers? These governmental representatives should not be overlooked in assaying any problem of present governmental power, and the contempt power is no exception.

Executive Officials

The development of the Anglo-American contempt power from its derivation as an aid to the king and those governmental representatives who carried out his executive mandates in his name was described in Chapter I. Might it follow that the contempt power, being executive in origin, could rightfully be bestowed upon our own executive branch of government? This rhetorical logic would overlook the great difference between the English monarchy of the fifteenth century and the American presidency of the twentieth if not the eighteenth century. The President of the United States is not divine, as the king was supposed to have been. Moreover, his lack of monarchial divinity was a result of calculated constitutional design and not the sheer misfortune of a heavenly miscalculation. As a matter of fact, our government was deliberately planned with checks, balances, and separations of power to deprive our President of the autocratic powers of the king. This change in the nature of executive power would be inconsistent with the use of the contempt power by our modern executive officials. Fortunately, few people have seriously suggested it; thus we have been saved from what might have been a dangerous and for the most part an unnecessary extension of power which elsewhere has been misused, if not abused.

Though few writers have ever suggested that our executives should exercise a contempt power, and though few executives have ever themselves asserted any claims to the power, Wigmore has written that "the Executive of the State has a limited inherent power, comparable to that of the legislature, to employ testimonial compulsion for aiding the executive purposes."[1] However, he added, "the exercise of the power has rarely been attempted, and the legitimate scope of its inquiries would be difficult to define." Wigmore has listed some limited instances where executive officials have been granted specific powers of compulsion by statutes. Some of these isolated examples of state statutory grants have given limited contempt powers to such minor executive officials as a fire marshal, district auditor, state professional board members, police commissioners, municipal commissioners, and in some cases an attorney general.[2]

Advocates of an executive contempt power could argue that all rationales for judicial or legislative contempt powers could apply as rationalizations for an executive power as well. Certainly, executive officers would find such a power expedient, necessary for self-defense and for competence and efficiency. In fact, since all contempt powers historically derive from the power of the English kings to punish interference with their governmental processes, it could be argued that the power, if inherent at all, inheres in the executive as much if not more than other government branches.

Those cases which have dealt with disputed claims for executive contempt powers have usually been disposed of on the ground that contempt is a judicial power, so that its use by executive officers would violate the separation of powers doctrine.

One Kansas case, as long ago as 1897, dealt with this issue.[3] The case arose out of the use of the contempt power by a notary public. The contemnor in that case argued that the contempt power is judicial, notaries are executive officers, and therefore executive use of the power would be prohibited by the separation of powers doctrine. The court held "there is no such thing as contempt of executive authority which is punishable. While an executive officer might be constituted a court, judicial power cannot be conferred on him as merely ancillary to the exercise of purely executive power."[4] The court cited other state decisions, which struck down similar legislation granting contempt powers to executive officials, as authority for the fact that the power to imprison for contempt is essentially judicial. No legislation can "give it residence elsewhere." A dissent noted that other states have with impunity conferred judicial contempt powers upon mayors, coroners, court clerks, commissioners, and other similar executives, and that limited grants of these judicial powers to executives should be proper. The distinguishing basis of these two rationales lies in the courts' considerations of whether the mere exercise of a judicial function by a nonjudicial officer carries with it other implicit judicial powers like contempt. Those courts which have denied such grants of the contempt power have usually based their denial on the ground that one who administers a judicial function acts only in a ministerial capacity and lacks the judicial contempt power. Those courts which have upheld this use of the contempt power have done so on the ground that the official, acting in a quasi-judicial capacity, could use the contempt power to perfect his judicial work. The generally accepted rule seems to be that the contempt power should not belong to all who exercise any judicial function,[5] even though in the case of executive officers it could be argued that the power could be implied from general constitutional grants of executive powers.

It is paradoxical that the ground for denying executive contempt powers has been that the power is inherently judicial. History indicates, as I have shown in Chapter I, that the courts were originally given the contempt power only because they were acting for the king. The use of the power by the courts was to punish an offense to the king, for whom the courts acted. With the gradual changes in English governmental power structures and the rise in individual judicial powers, the courts claimed inherent rights, as courts, to the use of the contempt power. American courts, needing no derivative powers from executive government, claimed the power as one innately judicial. Now, the executive officers of government are most often denied the power because it is confined to the use of courts only. The reason for the contempt power seems to have shifted in this sense a full 180 degrees.

Though theoretical arguments and all pragmatic grounds for use of the contempt power (expediency, necessity, self-defense) apply to executive officers as much as they do to judicial and legislative officers, the use of the power has consistently been denied to the former. The probable reason for this phenomenon could be attributed to deep-seated psychological resistance in American political thought to the possession of any autocratic powers in the hands of executive officials. The result of, if not the reason for, this situation is correct and is satisfactory, sensible, and politically workable.

Grand Juries

Grand juries are juries of inquiry which assist the criminal courts by receiving complaints and accusations, hearing state's evidence, and finding indictments in cases where they decide that a trial should be had.[6] Their significance in America is apparent. The Fifth Amendment to the federal constitution provides that "No person shall be held to answer for a capital, or otherwise infamous crime, unless on a presentment or indictment of a Grand Jury." Most state constitutions have similar provisions.[7]

The investigative process of the grand jury requires some means of enforcing the appearances and testimony of witnesses. This necessity provokes contempt problems analogous to the problems of legislative committee investigations and administrative agencies. The manner of dealing with contempts of grand juries is basically similar to the way they are disposed of by these analogous bodies.

Neither federal nor state grand juries have ever themselves

had direct contempt powers.[8] It has always been assumed that this power was absent.[9] The reason for this is undoubtedly the close relationship between grand juries and the courts, through which contempts of the former are considered and punished as contempts of the latter. Grand juries have traditionally been labeled "arms" or "appendages" of the courts.[10] Therefore, a contempt of the arm is considered a contempt of the corpus itself.[11] Contempt of a grand jury is contempt of the court, much in the way that contempt of a congressional committee is deemed to be a contempt of the Congress it represents. It has always been a simple matter for a grand jury to seek the aid and assistance of the court in contempt matters. In fact, the lay makeup of the common grand jury makes such a procedure a sensible necessity.

The actual mechanics of the practice followed in the case of a contemptuous refusal to testify before a grand jury is outlined in the *Federal Grand Jury Handbook:* "Refusal to testify must be carefully recorded. Then, accompanied by a United States Attorney, the Grand Jury may bring the matter before the court with a copy of the record, in order to obtain the ruling of the court as to whether the answer can be compelled or not. This is because of the technical questions involved."[12] There have been comparatively few difficulties, from the government's standpoint, in employing this procedure, and fewer demands for a more direct method of punishing such contempts. Probably, a more direct procedure would be unconstitutional. The Supreme Court has held that a secret contempt proceeding denied that due process of law which is guaranteed by the Fourteenth Amendment.[13] Since grand juries investigate *in camera,* an adjudication of contempt in the secret atmosphere of the grand jury room would be unconstitutional. However, there has been a decision which upheld such a secret trial because the defendant failed to object at the time.[14]

This practice is well established whereby the grand jury invokes the aid of the judiciary in punishing contempts of the jury. Since the basis of the wrong derives from an implied injury to the court, this procedure satisfactorily follows in theory and practice. This was the firmly established practice at common law, and today it has been continued under those statutes which have enumerated judicial contempt powers. The underlying reason for this dependence was articulated in a recent case:

A grand jury is clothed with great independence in many areas, but it remains an appendage of the court, powerless to perform its investigative function without the court's aid, because powerless itself to compel the testimony of witnesses. It is the court's process which summons the witness, and it is the court which must compel a witness to testify if, after appearing, he refuses to do so.[15]

A lower federal court recently outlined the specific physical steps which must be taken before disobedience to a grand jury becomes a contempt of court.[16]

I. The witness must be called before a legally constituted Grand Jury and placed under oath.

II. A pertinent question must be propounded to the witness by the prosecuting official or a member of the Grand Jury.

III. The witness must refuse to answer the question on the ground that an answer would tend to incriminate the witness under some Federal law [or upon some other legal ground].

IV. The Grand Jury, the prosecuting official and the witness (with his attorney, if he has one) shall come before the Court in open session.

V. The Foreman of the Grand Jury (or the prosecuting official) must inform the Court of the matters set forth in paragraphs I through III above, and ask the advice and assistance of the Court in connection with the privilege claimed.

VI. The Court hears the question which the witness has refused to answer. (This is done by having the Official Court Reporter take the witness stand and read the question to the Court and to those present.)

VII. The Court makes certain that the witness understands the question that has been put to him. (If the witness does not understand the question, it must be re-framed so that there is no doubt that he does understand it.)

VIII. The Court then proceeds to consider the bare question, which the witness has refused to answer, and determines whether or not, from the face of the question, an answer could, in fact, tend to incriminate the witness under any Federal law [or if his reason for refusal is proper and recognizable].

IX. If the question does not, on its face, disclose that the answer would tend to incriminate, the witness is then given an opportunity to be heard and, if it is desired, to introduce any relevant evidence which substantiates the claim that from the implications of the question, in the setting in which it is asked, there is a real and appreciable danger that the answer would be dangerous because an injurious disclosure might result from it [it can be assumed that an opportunity would similarly be given to argue any other defenses which were offered to warrant the witness' refusal].

X. If, after a consideration of the question in the light of the evidence adduced, any other relevant facts, and the applicable law, the Court is satisfied that an answer would not tend to incriminate the witness under any Federal law, the Court then rules that the privilege may not be validly claimed and directs the witness to return to the Grand Jury room and answer the question.

XI. Should the witness continue to refuse to answer the question, this fact is reported to the Court in open session with the Grand Jury, the prosecuting official and the witness (with his attorney, if he has one) present.

XII. The Court again hears the question as in step VI.

XIII. The Court then, in the presence of, and on behalf of the Grand Jury, puts the question to the witness and inquires:

A. If the witness understands the question;

B. If the witness understands that the Court has ruled that the privilege against self-incrimination may not be validly claimed for that question, and the Court has ordered him to answer it;

C. If the witness has given all the reasons that he has for his refusal to answer the question; and

D. If the witness still refuses to answer the question as directed by the Court.

XIV. If the witness affirmatively answers each of the four questions set forth in step XIII, the witness has committed a contempt in the presence of the Court. The Court may then certify that it saw and heard the conduct constituting such contempt, and may proceed to punish the witness summarily under the provisions of Rule 42 (a) of the Federal Rules of Criminal Procedure.

The mechanics of this procedure cause certain problems with the practice under the federal statutes. Courts of the United States are granted the power to punish contempts of their authority arising out of misbehavior in their presence and disobedience to their orders.[17] Under the Federal Rules of Criminal Procedure, the contempt proceeding may be summary, if the contemptuous act is committed in the judge's presence, though notice and hearing are required in all other contempt situations.[18]

Employing the generally accepted common-law notion that a grand jury is a part of the court, it is reasoned that, under these provisions, a contempt in the presence of the grand jury is a contempt in the presence of the court. This fiction may be satisfactory for the limited purpose of predicating some basis for a contempt of court situation, but it is unsatisfactory and arguably unconstitutional, for the purpose of dispensing with normal procedural safeguards in the processing of the contempt action. In other words, the "presence of the court" requirement of the statute empowering the courts with contempt powers is satisfied in the contempt of grand jury situation, but it should not apply to the sections of the Federal Rules of Criminal Procedure which determine the procedural implementation of the power. While a mere "metaphysical" presence would suffice for the purposes of invoking the judicial contempt power to punish contempts before grand juries, an actual physical presence should be required before the requirements of notice and hearing on the charge are avoided. In the one case, the concept of presence is reasonably extended in order to give the court power; but in the other there is no reason to circumvent procedural safeguards, since the court may actually have no knowledge of the act it is seeking to punish, and some hearing would be necessary. For this reason, in the federal courts summary proceedings to punish contempts "in the presence of the court" are limited to those acts of contempt which the judge himself personally hears or sees.

Another interpretational difficulty is encountered with the statutory requirement that contempt must be a "misbehavior." When a witness refuses to testify before a grand jury, he has not misbehaved in the presence of the court. Only after the court itself has ruled on the witnesses duty to testify, and ordered him to testify, and he still refuses, can there be a contempt of the court. But, then the contempt would be a disobedience to a lawful order of the court, and not misbehavior in its presence, as the general contempt statute contemplates. This distinction would depend on where the subsequent refusal took place. If it was before the court, it could be deemed a misbehavior in the court's presence, and therefore it would be summarily punishable. If, however, the later refusal took place before the grand jury, the contempt would be based not on a misbehavior before the court, but upon a disobedience to a lawful court order. If this was the case, notice and hearing would be required before the court could punish the contemptuous refusal, because under the Federal Rules of Criminal Procedure only contempts in the presence of the court can be summarily punished. Thus, a court can defeat a contemnor's right to argue about the use of the contempt power by the simple expedient of requestioning the witness in its own presence. The avoidance of notice and hearing provisions of the Federal Rules by thus acquiring summary jurisdiction seems arbitrary, and has been criticized. In that case, where notice and hearing requirements of the Federal Rules were circumvented by just such a proceeding, Chief Justice Warren wrote: "Given the purpose of rule 42a with its admittedly precipitous character and extremely harsh consequences, this court should not countenance a procedure whereby a contempt already completed out of the court's presence may be reproduced in a command performance before the court to justify summary disposition." [19] This particular case also happened to involve the longest sentence in history for contempt of a grand jury—fifteen months.

Still another problem was recently raised about contempt of grand jury procedures.[20] In this case, the federal court cleared the courtroom and held a secret hearing on the contempt of the grand jury charge. The contemnor argued that though grand jury hearings are closed to the public and grand juries act as representatives of the court, in this situation the proceeding was judicial and, therefore, he was entitled to a public hearing. The closed proceeding was upheld, though Justice Black wrote a dissent in which he criticized the practice of labeling criminal prosecutions contempts in order to avoid the safeguards of the Bill of Rights which apply to ordinary criminal trials. The secrecy of the grand jury, he wrote, should not extend to the courtroom. When the grand jury comes to the court for enforcement, the secret grand jury ends, and a public trial begins.

This current procedure is cumbersome, and its very awkwardness can cause legal problems like the one raised in the last case. Since the grand jury has no individual contempt power, and since any contempt before the grand jury is ultimately one of the court, much of the superfluous running around under the present practice could be eliminated. The procedure for dealing with a contempt of an order of a grand jury which was detailed earlier calls to one's imagination a picture of harried people traipsing from grand jury to courtroom and back, while different people keep asking the same witness the same question and ascertaining if he really understands what he is doing.

From my experience with federal contempt of grand jury practice, I am aware of the practical difficulty with and the lack of dexterity of the present procedures. First, in most cases the witness knows from the beginning just how far he will challenge the grand jury. Sometimes, his disobedience is based on an ethical reluctance to testify until he is ordered to by the court. Such is the case, for example, of an attorney who is asked to disclose confidential communications of a client. He might properly refuse and require a court order before such a disclosure, and such an insistence would reflect professional conscientiousness, not contumacy. Moreover, a witness before a grand jury might legitimately question the relevancy or constitutionality of his being forced to answer a particular question. After adjudication of the issue, which he would have every right to, such a witness may cooperate without further dispute. Since respectable legal minds have differed on issues such as these, a witness might well raise such questions without being considered contemptuous.

However, the truly obstinate and contumacious witness usually knows all along that he will not cooperate, no matter who orders him to do so. In such a case, the present practice is frustrating, and often plays into his hand. Often, he will delay by occasioning numerous trips from the courtroom to the grand jury room, raising frivolous and purely dilatory legal arguments, and when ultimately faced with answering the grand jury he will often perjure himself. None of these tactics aids either the witness or the government, but sends both down a delaying and wasteful sidetrack.

I suggest that a better procedure, one calculated to allow the witness a fair opportunity to resolve sincere legal questions before cooperating with the grand jury as well as afford the government an expeditious and reasonable way to go about its business, could be devised. Such a procedure should attempt to avoid some of the constitutional objections recently raised and treated by the Supreme Court. The following alternatives are suggested. First, the witness should be thoroughly questioned by the grand jury. Then, if the jurors feel that any refusals to produce documents or to testify are contemptuous, the grand jury with its recorder and legal representative should go to court. This proceeding should include two phases. The first phase should be in closed court. It would be nothing more than an extension of the grand jury proceeding, but would include the aid of the court and judge. The grand jury should place the matter in the hands of the judge, who would hear the questions and answers. The public should be excluded to insure the privacy and sanctity of the grand jury. Since the body is acting for the court, there is nothing irregular with its seeking its assistance, adjudication, and power. The court would then rule on the witness' claim. If this satisfies the witness, the grand jury should retire to its room and continue its work. If the witness indicates to the court that he will not obey its order concerning the matters raised, the proceeding should move directly into its second phase. This would be a judicial proceeding for contempt of court deriving from the grand jury. Here, the public should be allowed to be present. The witness should be allowed counsel and a hearing at least as full as Rule 42B allows. The court should advise the witness of its consideration of his defense and hear argument by counsel before issuing its order. Intellectual distinctions between contempt in or out of the court's presence or contempt based on misbehavior or disobedience to orders should be discarded. The fullest fairest judicial proceeding should follow, and the contempt of the witness should be adjudicated then and there. Trips to the grand jury room should be avoided, as should repeat performances of the questions, answers, and arguments. The witness, now with advice of counsel, should make his choice: to return and cooperate with the grand jury or be adjudicated in contempt of court.

The alternative to this procedure, and one which has been used in cases where the contempt arose out of misconduct before a grand jury[21] (as opposed to disobedience to its orders) would be for the grand jury to return a presentment to the court outlining the contemptuous conduct alleged to have been committed before it.

Such a practice could be used to initiate any contempt proceeding based on contemptuous conduct before a grand jury. The court could then hold a Rule 42B hearing or a trial on the presentment, and resolve the issue in one step. This alternative could be used in cases of contempt based on disobedience to orders of a grand jury to produce or testify, as well. After presentment, the recalcitrant witness would have a trial on the issue he raised in defense of his conduct. The advantage of full and fair hearing would prevail, though the nature of the grand jury inquiry would become public. This result, heretofore avoided with good reason, should be balanced against the value of a full and open fair hearing which would inhere in such a practice. My former proposal appears to include the better features of both alternatives—celerity, fairness, and protection of the secrecy of the grand jury.

The issues discussed here along with the broader constitutional issues which are related and will be discussed in the next chapter, and compounded by the fact that there are a great number of contempt cases arising out of grand jury proceedings, lead to the conclusion that procedural change is warranted in this area. Some method of enforcement is necessary to the effectiveness of grand juries. Present procedures under the current contempt practice are unsatisfactory. Either the suggestions offered here or a more basic change in contempt practice in general (which will be the subject of Chapter V) would provide satisfactory reform.

Referees

A referee is one to whom a cause pending in a court is referred by the court to take testimony, hear the parties, and report to the court.[22] As special agents who carry out limited judicial functions for the courts, their relation to the judiciary is direct and their claims for contempt powers are natural and, theoretically, derive from the established power of the courts themselves. The problems referees encounter, and for which they might use a contempt power, are exactly the same as those the courts themselves experience—insubordination and noncooperation. However, referees are not considered to have any inherent contempt powers.[23] Their use of the power is usually conceded, but the source of their power is agreed upon as purely statutory. Bankruptcy referees are the most common examples of this type of official, and an examination of their contempt powers is generally informative.

Courts of bankruptcy have jurisdiction to "enforce obedience by persons to all lawful orders by fine or imprisonment." [24] Referees in bankruptcy are officers appointed by the bankruptcy courts to conduct administrative and quasi-judicial functions under the bankruptcy law, and to assist the courts and relieve the judges of details, "by taking charge of all administrative matters and the preparation or preliminary consideration of questions requiring judicial decision, subject at all times to the supervision and review of the court." [25] Their contempt powers are purely statutory, and any contempt is considered a contempt of the court they represent, as opposed to contempt of the referee himself.[26] Section 41A of the Bankruptcy Act defines the statutory contempt power of referees as the power to punish: disobedience or resistance to lawful orders, process, or writs in proceedings before referees; misbehavior during a hearing or so near as to obstruct the hearing; neglect to produce pertinent documents when ordered to do so; and refusal to appear when subpoenaed, or to take the oath, or to testify.

The bankruptcy courts have inherent contempt powers because they are courts. The court's powers under the bankruptcy statute are not the source of the court's contempt power, for the creation of the court itself invested it with that power. The bankruptcy court judge has the contempt power, and it has been made clear that the bankruptcy statute conferred no powers in this respect enlarging the general judicial contempt power. "Any act, matter, or thing which any United States court may punish as a contempt may be punished as such by a court of bankruptcy; and any act, matter, or thing which can not be punished as a contempt by other United States courts can not be punished as such by a court of bankruptcy." [27] This general power combined with the power under Section 11 of the bankruptcy law gives the courts power "to enforce obedience by bankrupts, officers, and other persons to all lawful orders by fine and imprisonment. . . ." Examples of bankruptcy situations which might give rise to the use of the contempt power are false testimony, interference with property under the court's control, interference with court officers, or misbehavior in the presence of the court.

Where the contemptuous conduct occurs in the presence of the referee, he must certify the facts to the judge.[28] Failure to so certify would allow the aggrieved party to petition for review.[29] The referee then serves an order on the contemnor to show cause before the court why he should not be punished for his contempt.

The referee's certification to the court is akin to a pleading. The judge then hears the evidence and acts, much in the same manner of procedure as it does with other contempt of court matters. The certification of facts by the referee usually holds great weight in the court's decision.[30] And, this may approach absoluteness in cases of direct contempts (in the referee's presence), since in these cases there is usually no notice or hearing by the court itself. The general rules of defenses and purgation as well as the usual distinctions between kinds of contempt are made in these cases.[31] In civil contempt cases, the party who obtained the order which was violated usually moves for punishment of the contempt, though a third party may do so with the special permission of the court. In criminal contempt cases anyone may move for the contempt sanction, and the court itself may do so on its own motion. Clear and convincing proof of the contempt is usually called for, and the courts may act summarily as they do in nonbankruptcy contempt cases.[32]

Referees, masters, and receivers are officials who perform specific functions in aid of the judicial process. They are appointed to carry out some function in aid of the appointing court. The reason for the use of the contempt power by these officials is the same as that of grand juries. Contempt of the authority vested in them by the court is contempt of the court itself.

Notaries Public

The right of a notary public to exercise the contempt power depends on two preliminary requisites. Either the power must be granted in the statute which generally empowers the notary or the notary must be considered a "quasi-judicial" official. In most cases, neither requisite exists, and the problems concerning notaries' use of the contempt power have been minimal.

Notaries are not modern innovations upon the ordinary three branches of government. Historically, they derive from the tabularius and notarius of ancient continental legal systems.[33] Their functions now are quite the same as they were originally— to draw legal documents, certify them, and to perform limited official acts with respect to the affirmation and certification of legal papers.[34] Notaries have been recognized in common-law and civil-law countries. Though in the United States they are now sometimes executive appointees, their powers are delimited by the legislature.[35] However, their acts are considered to be in aid of the judicial as well as the executive process.[36] But they are not extensions of the court as are grand juries or referees, so their use of the contempt power cannot be based on derivations of judicial powers.

Nonetheless, in exercising their official functions, notaries can be faced with exactly the same problems which are treated with the contempt power when they are encountered by the courts or congresses.[37] However, their lack of any direct relationship with the courts has necessitated the creation of a different manner for dealing with these problems.[38]

Unlike other officials or agencies treated in this chapter, notaries have at times exercised direct contempt powers (without application for the assistance of courts). Yet, unlike the analogous practice of courts and legislatures, the exercise of this direct contempt power by notaries is purely a result of statutory authority.[39] There is no common-law contempt power based on need, inherency, or the other grounds usually offered by more traditional bodies. In fact, arguments that notaries had an inherent or implied contempt power were specifically rejected on most of those occasions when they were raised.[40] The usual grounds for these rejections have been that the contempt power is too autocratic to be allowed, by mere implication, to petty officials, or that the power is strictly a judicial one, never inhering in nonjudicial officers.

Some courts have indicated that a clear statutory grant of the power would be upheld.[41] Other states have declared such statutory grants unconstitutional; [42] and still others have upheld such statutes.[43] Those courts which have denied the constitutionality of these statutes have done so on due process [44] or separation of powers theories.[45] These decisions emphasized that notaries are executive or ministerial officers, while the contempt power is strictly reserved for the judiciary.[46] But the courts are in disagreement about the nature of notary power, and in many of those cases which upheld contempt statutes for notaries, the courts rationalized the constitutional question by classifying the notary as a judicial officer.[47] For example, courts have said that the taking of a deposition is a judicial function, therefore the use of the contempt power by one who is taking the deposition would be appropriate.[48] In another case, a notary's contempt power was upheld against due process objections when the court held that, under the particular statute involved, the power itself was nonjudicial, and could thus be exercised by a nonjudicial officer.[49] In some situations, state statutes still exist though the constitutional objections to their applicability have not been raised.[50]

This disagreement is not troublesome since those statutes which do exist are rarely used, and those cases where the use of this statutory power was questioned have been few. In these few cases the particular statutes were strictly construed.[51]

As a matter of policy it might be better if the direct contempt power was denied to these minor governmental officials. As one author noted:

> The universal character of the notary public, their almost unlimited number, their practical value and wide importance as executive officers in the commercial world, and the ease with which appointment to office without special qualifications or merit, may be secured, renders the question of clothing them with high and arbitrary powers so closely touching the rights of citizenship a very serious one.[52]

In cases where there is no statutory grant of the power, some other method of dealing with contempts at depositions has been sought. Normally, an application to the court is required.[53] Sometimes, courts will act upon a mere certification of the facts by the notary to the court.[54] Usually some intermediate court enforcement order is required before the court will punish misconduct as a contempt.[55] Since notaries are not truly court officers, this latter procedure is the least objectionable.

Similar rules apply to coroners and commissioners.[56] The contempt power is not often recognized with respect to these officials, and then only if it is specifically and limitedly granted by statute.

Miscellaneous Officers

Beyond these specifically discussed officials, there are numerous other minor officers of semiexecutive, legislative, or judicial natures, who also have infrequently used contempt powers of some limited extent. Except for the general policy issue of whether these petty officials should have any contempt power, there have been few discussions, arising out of actual cases or otherwise, about their use of the power. One New Jersey court voiced the generally accepted reluctance about broad extensions of contempt powers to all minor officials: "The power is great, and its exercise without review, where there is jurisdiction, and hence our duty to be careful not to extend it beyond the recognized bounds of the common law." [57]

Nonetheless, there have been statutory grants of contempt powers to a number of minor officials whose situations are too typical and relatively unimportant to consider at great length. These miscellaneous grants of the contempt power have not usually fared well when questioned in court, as their constitutionality is dubious, and the policies which might support them are minor.[58]

Administrative Agencies

Generally speaking, administrative agencies are governmental units empowered to administer or enforce existing legislation. The so-called regulatory agencies, like the Interstate Commerce Commission, the Federal Communication Commission, and others, are created by the federal legislature, but are considered independent bodies.[59] Of the numerous other agencies, some have been created by the legislature, and others are created by and are under the control of the executive branch of government. This latter group includes the various cabinet offices of the federal government, such as the Departments of State, Agriculture, and Interior. In all instances, the agencies are "administrative" rather than solely "judicial," "legislative," or "executive," though they may possess some characteristics of each.

Does or should an administrative agency have contempt powers? These agencies are faced with the same problems, which when encountered by the courts or the legislatures, have been considered to warrant the use of such a power. Witnesses who are called to attend hearings may refuse to appear, testify, or produce papers and records. Parties to disputes often refuse to comply with final orders which are issued by the agency. Attorneys, witnesses, parties, even spectators may be disorderly or disrespectful at investigations or hearings. The power to meet these problems through use of the contempt device has, as we have seen, been considered to be inherent in both purely legislative and purely judicial bodies. Moreover, in many cases, administrative agencies carry out "quasi-judicial" or "quasi-legislative" functions. For present purposes, an administrative body will be considered as such solely because it is so labeled by common understanding. However, it will become clear that the label itself is less significant in determining the consequences relative to administrative use of the contempt power than are the particular functions of the agency. These functions have been considered to be the pertinent issue in decisions about administrative contempt powers.[60]

Problems with respect to the maintainance of order or the compulsion of compliance to administrative subpoenas and orders are mitigated by the observation that most people are cooperative. It is only in unusual cases that noncompliance becomes a problem. In 1941 the National Labor Relations Board (NLRB) reported that not more than 6 out of 5,000 orders issued actually required enforcement proceedings.[61] In the same year, the Office of Indian Affairs disclosed an amusing, though perhaps atypical, picture of how minimal the contempt problem is, with regard to the attendance of witnesses:

[P]arties are generally able to induce their witnesses to attend the hearings. Furthermore, the Indians on many of the reservations have come to regard the examiner's annual visits as a festival period during which friends and relatives may convene for social purposes. It is not unusual, therefore . . . for the examiner to be concerned by the presence of too many, rather than too few witnesses.[62]

Though the problems may have been few, comparison with the disciplinary problems of courts and Congress, as well as recognition of the tremendous increases in the bureaucratic administration of government, may well indicate some increase in the future problems in this area, as a result of more claims by the agencies for broader administrative powers like contempt. As this chapter should indicate, existing agency mechanisms for dealing with contempt are generally inadequate from the agency standpoint (securance of compliance with their mandates), and from the point of view of the individual (whose private rights may be interfered with by agency activity). The purpose of this part of the chapter is to thoroughly examine the current contempt practices of administrative agencies and to analyze the problems which they provoke.

At present, there are four general procedures which are typically used by agencies to compel compliance or punish recalcitrance or misconduct. The choice of one method as opposed to another depends upon the constitution or statutes under which the agency operates, the type of conduct considered contemptuous (whether it is actual misbehavior or disobedience), and the end sought by the agency (coercion of future conduct or retribution for past acts). The four available procedures are:

1. Direct punishment by the administrative agency for contempt of its authority.[63]

2. Prosecution of the contemnor under a statute making noncompliance with subpoenas, or other contumacy before administrative agencies an ordinary criminal offense.[64]

3. Application to a court for an enforcement order, which if disobeyed will subject the individual to punishment for contempt of court.[65]

4. Application to a court for an immediate punishment of the contempt of the agency, as if it had been committed before the court.[66]

Procedures 1, 3, and 4 are mutually exclusive, while procedure 2 could be used concurrently with any one of the others. Procedure 1 could be statutory or inherent, while the other three (2, 3, and 4) are always statutory. Each of these methods of agency power will be considered in relation to their use, nonuse, or misuse by Federal and State Administrative Agencies.

DIRECT POWER: FEDERAL ADMINISTRATIVE AGENCIES

Federal administrative agencies have never directly fined or imprisoned an individual for contempt. Unlike the national Congress and judiciary, federal administrative agencies cannot claim any implied contempt power from some other constitutional grant of specific powers. The United States Constitution does not even mention administrative agencies. The authority for the very existence of administrative agencies is therefore implied, and any inference of powers from this inference of existence is so speculative that even the more active advocates for an effective administrative contempt power have sought other rationales.

Furthermore, no federal agencies have ever explicitly or impliedly been granted the direct contempt power by statute. As a general rule, agencies must resort to the judicial process by one of the indirect statutory procedures already mentioned. These indirect procedures are currently the only means of punishing federal administrative contempts. However, though agencies have never been granted a contempt power of their own, it should be noted that there are no express constitutional prohibitions on their use of such a power. But, for various constitutional, historical, and practical reasons, which will be discussed, agencies have rarely claimed any inherent right [67] to the power, and on those occasions when they have, they were never upheld.

Control of Misconduct in Their Presence. On occasion, when faced with physical disorders, the federal agencies have assumed that since they are given the statutory power to enact their own procedural rules and regulations, they could provide for certain self-protective measures against contumacious witnesses, spectators, parties, or attorneys. Agency regulations usually empower individual hearing officers to exclude a contumacious person from participating in the immediate proceeding.[68] The assumption that they have this implied power has been judicially approved.[69] Of course, this power is appreciably less severe and more reasonable than the traditional contempt power. A typical provision (in the National Labor Relations Board rules) provides that "misconduct at any hearing before a hearing officer or before the Board shall be ground for summary exclusion from the hearing." [70] While this limited power may be validly implied from the statutory authorization to make procedural rules, it has been thought of by the agencies as inherent.[71] Such a narrow power is not truly punitive or coercive, but is merely a true method of self-defense, employed as a substitute for the traditional contempt power. In fact, the agencies have assumed that they could not exercise such a power of punishment by fine or imprisonment. The NLRB has said of this exclusion rule:

Its purpose is not to punish offenses against the Board's dignity, but to assume and defend the control of the Board's hearing by its agents when challenged by contemptuous conduct during hearings, *the Board, lacking power to punish for contempt,* must have and does have the elementary power to exclude the guilty individual or individuals [emphasis added].[72]

This power in the hands of any lawful governmental body ought to be unobjectionable, and is even consistent with the denial of a true contempt power. Contempt, as it is known in Anglo-American jurisprudence, allows summary imprisonment or fine. Mere exclusion from a hearing room, if it does not unjustly deprive a person of counsel or of a full hearing, is proper and considerably less severe than ordinary contempt punishments. Some right to prevent obstruction of the performance of lawful functions, not in the least way constituting an imprisonment or fine, is both sensible and fair. Any abuse of the power by unjustified exclusion, which might result in a denial of adequate representation or hearing, could presumably be raised as a violation of due process of law on an appeal from an adverse judgment in the particular proceeding.[73] Furthermore, any individual who feels that he has been abused by such an exclusion is usually afforded an appeal within the agency itself.[74]

In the case of an attorney whose livelihood depends upon his right to appear and practice before administrative boards, such an exclusion would be more serious, and might border on punishment, as opposed to mere self-defense by the board. Some agencies require a special license of attorneys who regularly practice before them. Denial of the right to appear in these cases would be equal to a severe fine. In some cases, the agencies have exercised more stringent measures like this. For instance, at one time the NLRB claimed the "inherent" right to suspend or disbar exceedingly contumacious attorneys from practicing before the Board.[75] In a proceeding involving the suspension of an attorney who physically assaulted an NLRB officer without provocation, the defendant claimed that without an authorizing statute or regulation the Board had no power to suspend or disbar him for contempt. The Board ordered the defendant suspended for two years and said:

> The Board believes and finds that, as a quasi judicial agency entrusted with enforcement of a declared public policy, the Board possesses, as it must, an inherent power reasonably to control practice before it in the interest of preventing disruption of its proceedings and to protect its processes and agents from being held up to disrepute. The Board also believes and finds that it is empowered to conduct such proceedings as may be necessary to that end.
>
> Such power is as indispensable to the regular conduct of this agency's business and to the proper administration of justice by it as the corresponding power of a court [Power to suspend or disbar] is necessary to the court. Such power is a natural and necessary concomitant of the Board's basic statutory functions; no express statutory provision is required to create it.[76]

On appeal to the district court this decision was reversed.[77] The court agreed that the power to control attorneys by admission and disciplinary action was a "highly important one" but said: "It is not, as is the case in judicial courts of general jurisdiction, an inherent power, but is one which, if it exists, is given by the legislative authority creating such agency."

Since this decision the NLRB has adopted a regulation permitting suspension, after due notice and hearing, of an attorney

for "misconduct of an aggravated character."[78] While this suspension procedure is direct, it is not, nor was it considered to be
an exercise of the traditional contempt power as it is known and
practiced in the courts. Suspension or disbarment is not considered a penalty or fine,[79] although it may often be a severe
punishment.[80] Suspension and disbarment proceedings are rationalized on the peculiar status of attorneys as officers of the courts
or agencies before which they practice, and consequently on
their proper susceptibility to summary disciplinary proceedings
short of fine or imprisonment. This is less objectionable where
full notice and hearing are required, as is the general practice.[81]
Moreover, the suspended lawyer can, presumably, obtain judicial
review of disbarment as with any final agency order.[82]

Notwithstanding the apparent limited and infrequent exercises
of suspension, disbarment, and exclusion, the federal agencies
have never successfully attempted to exercise summary contempt
powers in the traditional sense and these limited practices have
been employed only in cases of direct physical disorder.

DIRECT POWER: STATE ADMINISTRATIVE AGENCIES

Administrative contempt practice at the state level differs
somewhat from federal procedure. While there is absolutely no
direct contempt power in federal agencies, some states have bestowed the power, either by statute [83] or constitutional provision,[84] upon particular state agencies. In three states (Missouri,[85]
North Carolina,[86] and New York [87]), the power has been recognized as inherent or implied. Other states have denied the existence of any inherent or implied contempt powers in administrative agencies.[88] But one writer has observed that even where it is
denied "it is presently done in terms that imply that the power
might be exercised by such bodies if it were conferred by statute." [89] In eleven cases where statutory grants were made, five
were invalidated [90] for one of several characteristic grounds,

which will be discussed later. The other six statutes found continue to stand as valid, though several of them have never been questioned.[91] Constitutional provisions allowing administrative contempt powers are found in four states; [92] but in each the reference is to only one specific agency.

For the most part, the state administrative agencies are as devoid of direct contempt powers as are the federal agencies. The result has been a concoction of varied statutory procedures, generally conforming to those four already outlined. Sometimes all four procedural methods for handling contempts of administrative agencies can be found among the several agencies of one state.[93] Exclusion, suspension, and disbarment proceedings are also available to state agencies.[94]

REASONS FOR DENIAL OF DIRECT POWER

The general denial to state administrative agencies of a direct contempt power and the consistent absence of the power in federal agencies are consequences attributable to various historical, legal, and practical forces.

The nonexistence of a direct contempt power in the federal administrative process is usually attributed to the adventitious potency of certain dicta pronounced by the first Justice Harlan in the famous *Brimson* case in 1894.[95] That case dealt with a statute which permitted the Interstate Commerce Commission to apply to a United States Circuit Court for enforcement of subpoenas issued by the agency. It was argued that the statute was invalid because it violated the separation of powers doctrine, and because it failed to present the court with an actual case or controversy as required by the Constitution.[96] While proceeding to hold the statute constitutional, the court wrote:

Of course, the question of punishing the defendants for contempt could not arise before the commission; for, in a judicial sense, there is no such thing as contempt of a subordinate administrative body. No question of contempt could arise until the issue of law . . . is determined adversely to the defendants and they refuse to obey, not the order of the commission, but the final order of the court.[97]

Then Justice Harlan added the dictum that has since had such a far-reaching effect:

Such a body [as the ICC] could not, *under our system of government, and consistently with due process of law,* be invested with authority to compel obedience to its orders by a judgment of fine or imprisonment. . . . [*T*]*he power* to impose fine or imprisonment in order to compel the performance of a legal duty imposed by the U.S. *can only be exerted* under the law of the land *by a competent judicial tribunal* having jurisdiction in the premises [emphasis added].[98]

This assumption, that due process is per se violated by permitting anyone but the courts to deprive an individual of his liberty or property, had been previously expressed in a number of state cases in relation to local due process provisions.[99] A concurring opinion in one of those cases presented the argument lucidly.

A citizen can only be imprisoned by due process of law. . . . If the (Agency) had jurisdiction to adjudge that the appellee should be imprisoned there was due process of law; if it had no jurisdiction to imprison, there was not due process of law and the appellee was unlawfully deprived of his liberty.

In free countries courts always have assumed jurisdiction of questions involving personal liberty, and so they must, or else free government, securing personal liberty, ceases to exist. When that great right comes in issue, the courts hear and decide, and the authority of executive or administrative officers is at end. Whatever else such officers may be empowered to do, they can not be empowered to sit in judgment upon the right of a citizen to his personal liberty. Only the courts can give the command which takes from the citizen his liberty and places him within prison walls, and they can only give it in accordance with the law of the land. However extensive the authority of the board may be, it is always ministerial or administrative, and hence does not go far enough to adjudge imprisonment, for it is beyond the power of the legislature to invest it or any administrative board with that high judicial function.[100]

Remnants of this attitude continue to lurk in the minds of modern authorities. One leading author in this field has suggested that: "It is the absence of administrative powers of imprisonment that sharply distinguishes a legal system like the Anglo-American from those which prevail in those countries we disparagingly describe as totalitarian." [101]

ARGUMENTS AWAY FROM THE GENERAL RULE

But, other contemporary writers have disputed the *Brimson* dictum, and claimed that more recent developments have enfeebled, if not destroyed, its constitutional potency. These men have pointed to parallel situations which may indicate that modern federal courts would find the rule and reason of the *Brimson* dictum archaic, and would uphold a statute which granted an agency a direct contempt power. The trends which have moved these men to advance this theory are threefold. One is the generally accepted recognition of the expansion of administrative powers to include the power to impose civil remedial fines. Another is the power, also recognized only in limited situations, of administrative powers of detention. And third, some writers have suggested analogy with those state decisions which have upheld the right of state governments to blend traditionally legislative, judicial, and executive branches of their government consistent with the due process clause of the Fourteenth Amendment. These three trends warrant further explanation and comment.

The Power to Impose Civil Fines. The argument that analogy with the right of administrative boards to impose fines would support legislation permitting fines for civil contempts of agencies, is best taken. Penalties for violations of agency regulations and fines for contempt are without essential distinction. And the Supreme Court has upheld the constitutionality of legislation which sanctioned administrative imposition of civil penalties for violations of agency regulations on several occasions.[102] This rule is defended on the ground that formal adjudication in many petty cases would be both needless and meaningless, and that measures of culpability are often better measured by administrators having some expertise in the local matter.[103] But this reasoning has not gone uncriticized. Professor Bernard Schwartz, in commenting on a New York statute which granted an insurance commissioner the power to impose penalties of up to $1,000 upon violators of the New York Insurance Law, said: "It is difficult to imagine a statute more repugnant to the basic principles upon which our administrative law is grounded. It violates the fundamental rule that the imposition of a money penalty is with us a judicial not an administrative function." [104] Administrative expertise could be offered to support many departures from proper traditional practices; but it is a more questionable ground for extending fact-finding functions which determine culpability, and which in turn lead to penal consequences. Nonetheless, in the context of the present issue, the comparison is compelling.

Powers to Detain. The second parallel drawn by advocates of a direct administrative contempt power, or at least by critics of the comments of Justice Harlan in the *Brimson* case, is to the practice of administrative detention. This is a much less palatable analogy.

Temporary detention by administrative officials has been condoned in some circumstances, but they are unusual. "The power to detain the person as an incident of administering health laws is of course widely exercised," [105] and resort to judicial proceedings in such cases is often unnecessary. Similarly, aliens may be arrested by immigration officials and detained indefinitely for ultimate deportation; [106] and mentally ill persons may be administratively institutionalized for indefinite periods.[107] Imprisonment for contempt is to some degree similar to these practices.

Certainly, the power to imprison one for contempt, at least where it is exercised to coerce compliance rather than to punish recalcitrance, is in furtherance of an agency function. It is also, theoretically, a more temporary confinement than that permitted for deportation or public health protection purposes. In the latter situation, release is at the discretion of the administrative officer, while in a civil contempt case the individual may be emancipated at his own will; he need only offer to comply.

However, in another, more vital sense, comparison fails. Detention in the health and deportation cases is preventive, not punitive; this is not so with contempt confinement. Although the primary purpose in contempt cases may be to coerce obedience, the contemnor is in fact being punished for each day he continues to disobey. The indefinite imprisonment is a social sanction meted out until the primary object of compliance can be realized. The uncertain length of the sanction does not diminish its punitive nature.

Courts should be hesitant to circumvent the general rule that penal sanctions are matters of criminal law and its administration and, as such, warrant a trial by jury, before a court of competent jurisdiction, after indictment by a grand jury.

In *Wong Wing v. United States*,[108] the Supreme Court considered a federal statute which provided that Chinese aliens who were found to be unlawfully in this country, in the summary consideration of a judge or court commissioner, could be imprisoned for a year and then deported. A commissioner of the federal district court in Michigan ordered Wong Wing imprisoned, pursuant to this statute, for 60 days. On appeal, the Supreme Court held the law unconstitutional, in violation of the Fifth and Sixth Amendments. The court reasoned that imprisonment at hard labor was an infamous punishment and, as such, was a proper sanction only for an infamous crime. The punishment was said to establish the nature of the offense. Thus, faced with punishment of an "infamous crime," the court declared the mandates of the Fifth and Sixth Amendments applicable. Since there was no proper judicial trial, the detention was deemed unconstitutional.

Advocates for an administrative contempt power might argue that contempt, and particularly civil contempt, is not a crime—infamous, petty, or otherwise. To be sure, the courts have continuously referred to contempt in the mystical phraseology, "sui generis." Such reasoning by fiction should not be extended beyond its existing applications.

The admonition advanced by Professors Clark Byse and Walter Gellhorn in a recent discussion of the problem of administrative imprisonment should be heeded: "So long as imprisonment is the sanction should the law not insist that, however the statute may denominate the proceeding, it is in fact and in custom a criminal proceeding?" [109]

In a footnote, these authors referred to an "historical exception" to this general rule; namely, imprisonment for civil contempt. The reference should be clearly restricted to the established practice of courts and legislatures. To be sure, there can be no such exception for an administrative contempt power. It would be strange indeed to label that an "historical exception" which itself has so confused a history.

State "Due Process" Decisions and the Separation of Powers Doctrine. Finally, some analogy has been made to certain cases which have upheld the right of state governments to mix executive, legislative, and judicial functions into one department, consistent with Fourteenth Amendment due process requirements. The argument has been made that, since Fifth Amendment "due process" is substantively the same as Fourteenth Amendment "due process," these cases may hint of a disposition to allow some mixing of governmental functions at the federal level, as well.[110]

For example, the Supreme Court has upheld the constitutionality of an Illinois statute which granted certain judicial functions to administrative quasi-executive officials. The argument that this delegation of power violated the due process clause of the Fourteenth Amendment was dismissed because it was held that: "The true meaning [of the due process clause] is, that the whole power of one of these departments should not be exercised by the same hands which possess the whole power of either of the other departments." [111] In another case, a lower federal court upheld a statute, which gave an Optometric Board quasi-judicial and quasi-legislative powers, where similar due process arguments were raised. [112] And the Supreme Court more recently upheld a state statute which invested a local fire marshal with judicial powers, among which was the civil contempt power. [113] Might it then be assumed that, by analogy, the Supreme Court would uphold a federal statute which granted judicial contempt powers to an administrative agency in the face of the argument that this violated the due process clause of the Fifth Amendment? Certainly such a stand by the Court would conflict with the significantly prevailing attitude in American administrative law that the power to imprison or fine are so peculiarly judicial that they must be confined to courts, no matter what the case may be with respect to the delegability of other traditionally judicial powers.

Beyond the due process issue there is a further question concerning the separation of powers problem with respect to direct administrative contempt powers. Could it be argued that, though the power to imprison is essentially a judicial function, it would be an exaltation of form over substance to permit courts to impose that sanction while denying it to administrative agencies. In certain instances, all that really distinguish a court from an agency are legislative semantics and the black robe of justice. Thus, it has been suggested that the constitutional objections presented by the *Brimson* dictum might "be easily dispensed with . . . by simply terming an administrative agency a 'court' or an arm of the legislature."[114] This approach has been taken by several states which have upheld grants of the direct contempt power to administrative agencies.[115] While these cases did not consider the due process problem, their holdings are significant because they meet the argument that contempt is a purely judicial power by holding that the agency is functioning like a court. Such cases are best restricted to their peculiar facts; for while some agencies exercise substantially judicial functions (like workmen's compensation boards), the great majority of them differ from courts in great extremes of functions, procedures, personnel, competence, and prestige.

The greater significance of this line of cases lies in their disposition of a basic objection generally raised in cases denying the contempt power to agencies. It is often urged that the contempt power, regardless of the nature of its sanction, is exclusively judicial and, in accordance with strict separation of powers theory, must be restricted to judicial usage. This argument is prima facie defeated by the established existence of a legislative contempt power. It might be said that this seeming inconsistency is merely an exclusive "exception" to the general rule. The Supreme Court may have implied as much in the landmark *Anderson* case,[116] which initially upheld the legislative contempt power. The Court there said that "neither analogy nor precedent would support the assertion of such powers [contempt] in any other than a legislative or judicial body." But, while this declaration is a positive admonition against further extension of the contempt power, close examination of the Court's holding indicates that the extension of the power to the legislature was not meant as a mere "exception" to an otherwise rigid rule. On the contrary, the Court avoided conceptual arguments revolving around the alleged nature of the power and implied that necessity was the true basis of the power in the legislature and the courts. This conclusion is consistent with the historical and legal analyses of the usage of contempt powers.

Where state courts have declared the contempt power to be inherent in a particular agency, it has been on the ground of necessity. It is equally as necessary to administrative efficiency, as it is to judicial or legislative efficiency that some method of obtaining swift compliance be available to the agencies. "To the extent . . . that the agency requires the contempt power for the proper performance of its duties, the theoretical argument seems as strong as that which justifies the existence of the contempt power of the other branches of government." [117] As one writer noted, "If the function of the contempt power is administration of justice, it is a narrow view which would distinguish between administrative and judicial departments." [118] Though legislative and judicial contempt powers are implied from (and perhaps dignified by) constitutional grants of other powers,[119] whereas administrative agencies are creatures of statute, the enormous and significant growth and vitality of the administrative process in recent times might call for equal powers. Indeed, agencies have nowadays achieved the stature of a fourth official department in our historically and constitutionally triune government. To ignore this reality in the assessment of governmental powers would be shortsighted.

While the arguments based on necessity avoid conceptual difficulties revolving around the separation of powers debate, courts do often choose to involve themselves in such conceptualism. This is so, although strong arguments are offered to show the invalidity of the idea that contempt is exclusively judicial. It has already been shown that, historically, contempt was actually neither judicial nor legislative, but was in fact executive in origin. It is indeed questionable whether contempt bears the innate characteristics of any peculiar governmental department. As a matter of fact, the argument is compelling that if the power is distinctive of any branch of government it is probably more administrative than anything else. This proposition was clearly expounded in a lengthy Connecticut opinion in the late nineteenth century. There, the Court said:

[T]he power itself [contempt], while essential to judicial proceedings, is not distinctively a judicial power; it may be exercised by administrative as well as by judicial officers, and in its essence, so far as it can be called distinctive of any department, it is distinctively an administrative power. The principle on which the power rests is, that when immediate enforcement of law is essential to its execution, the State cannot permit a citizen to obstruct, by his disobedience, such immediate execution of law, and has the power to invest the officer charged with the administration of law, whether he be a judicial or administrative officer, with authority to compel, in such case of emergency, immediate obedience in the manner prescribed by law.

The real nature of the power is to compel a citizen to answer a proper question; when a refusal to answer obstructs the necessary, immediate execution of law, has been obscured by the habit of calling every such refusal a contempt. *It is a contempt, in the sense that every open defiance of law is a contempt of the authority of the State; it is a contempt of court when done in the course of a judicial trial; but the summary enforcement of an answer is not an exercise by the court of its judicial power to punish contempt of court as a criminal offense, but of its administrative power to enforce a law, which if enforced at all must be enforced at once* [emphasis added].[120]

Although this reasoning has logical merit, it has never been adopted by a subsequent case although it has been subscribed to by some writers.[121] One writer has expressed much the same argument by suggesting that there is an "essential unity of all administration of justice," and to claim that the contempt power is judicial merely "recalls the rather deep rooted belief in the separation of functions of administrative justice from judicial justice, inculcated by ancestral conceptions of Constitutional doctrines of triune government."[122]

The argument that the contempt power could be administrative as well as judicial or legislative is at least logically sound in theory. Though contempt may not be used by courts, except in the furtherance of their judicial functions, it need not necessarily follow that the exercise of the power is therefore judicial. It is still primarily a power used to *administer* a judicial function. When the legislature uses the contempt power it is in furtherance of its legislative functions, but the power is not, therefore, legislative. So it could be accurately concluded that the power is neither judicial nor legislative but truly administrative, because it is a "power used to enforce a law by whomsoever it is exercised." [123]

Though these arguments may have validity, the same result might nevertheless be reached even if it were assumed, *arguendo*, that the contempt power is purely judicial. After all, an administrative agency is normally "quasi-judicial" in nature anyway, and will usually exercise numerous powers traditionally thought of as judicial. Why should the addition of this particular "judicial" power suddenly violate the doctrine of Separation of Powers? Thus, it has been said:

[T]he exercise of the contempt power by an agency is no more judicial in nature than the exercise of its power to conduct hearings, to arrive at findings of fact, and to issue orders, all of which are constitutional. Furthermore, the independent administrative agencies, as presently constituted, combine legislative, executive and judicial functions; it seems illogical to argue, therefore, that the addition of one more "judicial" power—if contempt be so characterized—will violate the doctrine of Separation of Powers.[124]

That the contempt power is more drastic than those other judicial powers often bestowed upon administrative agencies could be the practical reason for its special treatment. But this is not a sound theoretical reason for a denial of the power, nor is it based on any separation of powers rationale.

As a matter of fact, the two constitutional arguments offered as reasons for denying direct administrative contempt powers are bedded in identical fundamental reasons. The "due process" argument in effect says that the contempt power is judicial, administrative boards are not courts, therefore their use of the power would be a denial of due process of law. The "separation of powers" argument holds that the contempt power is judicial, administrative agencies are not judicial bodies, therefore their use of the power violates the separation of governmental powers doctrine. Both arguments would falter in the face of an admission that the contempt power may be administrative as well as judicial or legislative.

The Practical Arguments. The preceding discussion of the established rationales for denying the direct contempt power to administrative agencies was designed to show that in logic there is little basis for denying the power to agencies while it continues to be upheld in courts and legislatures. There is no doubt that courts will continue to justify their use of the power upon debatable historical and legal conceptions. However, it remains to be answered whether these past standard rationales are necessary any longer in light of more persuasive arguments developed from experience. Thus, might it be well to follow the famous Holmesian aphorism, and search for the true experience rather than the purest logic from which administrative contempt powers may be sustained.

In this respect several factors become important. First, though historical or logical reasoning with respect to the policies concerning administrative use of the direct contempt power may be basically erroneous, the duration of its acceptance may signify that the error was considered and deemed worth perpetuating. The aura of validity may ripen from long acquiescence and application. If the dictum in *Brimson* is no longer valid, it nevertheless has been compounded so long and well that it would be unlikely that a court would question it. Justice Frankfurter has said:

Congress has never attempted . . . to confer upon an administrative agency itself the power to compel obedience to . . . a subpoena. It is beside the point to consider whether Congress was deterred by Constitutional difficulties. *That Congress should so consistently have withheld powers of testimonial compulsion from administrative agencies discloses a policy that speaks with impressive significance* [emphasis added].[125]

But mere acquiescence in an error, though it may be a fortunate one, may at best be a weak legal basis for any judicial position. There are, however, strong strains of policy which continue to insist on a denial of the contempt power to agencies. The "real problem" is not one of due process or Separation of Powers but is "a counterpoise of the administrative advantages of the contempt power against the dangers incident to its use." [126] It is here that serious objections to the use of the contempt power by any governmental body would reverberate even more strongly against any attempted extension of the power to a body which has heretofore not generally used it and apparently has not suffered much from its absence.

A recurrent objection to administrative agencies in general has been the broad discretion they have in the exercise of their functions.[127] They apply no fixed rule of law in the more constricted judicial sense, but rather act according to considerations of policy, reason, public convenience, or national interest. Administrative actions may be brought for numerous political and ulterior reasons, which might vary with the men who control the particular agency. The criticism has been made that: "The fate of individuals subject to its jurisdictions depends on the discretion of the men who run the agency; the individual is faced with a government of men not of laws. . . ." [128] Such qualities are particularly dangerous when augmented by an autocratic power like contempt. These negative features and their potential dangers are very real. Unlike many judicial appointees, administrative personnel are appointed for short periods of time and are pragmatically subject to the vicissitudes of party politics. Economic survival for these men often depends on whether they make the "right" political choice as to decisions and defendants. The chairmen of the federal agencies are usually presidential appointees subject to removal at the chief executive's pleasure. In turn the chairmen control the personnel and policies of their agencies. Hiring, firing, and promotions are within their domain.[129] The political dependencies are evident and probably inevitable.

Though this political receptivity is assuredly the case in the legislature, it is clear that the federal judiciary is not subject to such pressures. The strongest reason for this phenomenon is that appointments to the federal bench continue as long as the life and good behavior of the appointee continue. Examples are easily called to mind where judges after appointment to the bench exercised the strongest independence of mind and action, often to the surprise or disadvantage of their appointors. Whereas the political independence of the federal judiciary is renowned, other governmental officials are sometimes driven to abuses of power to curry favor or to maintain their office. But with the administrative process there is not even the indirect restraining force of an electorate, as there is in the legislative arena. Perhaps this circumscribed, independent nature of judicial power rather than any theoretical arguments about the nature of different governmental bodies is the actual reason for concluding that the contempt power ought to be limited to courts.

Recent presidential task force reports have pointed up this problem.[130] They illustrated that the quality of administrative personnel is all too often critically low. The comparisons of pay, education, and prestige to those in other governmental positions reflect deficiencies in the agencies' composition which speak forcefully against any increase of their powers. Of prime concern is the frequent lack of legal training of administrative officials. It is bad enough that judges, assumedly experienced in

American theories of criminal justice, can avoid the employment of common judicial safeguards in contempt proceedings. But it is even more dangerous to permit hearing officers or trial examiners, who may be inexperienced in law, to exercise such an autocratic power like contempt.

While the competency of administrative officials in their particular fields may be high, their judicial capacities may not. As one writer put it:

we must not lose sight of the fact that the expertness of an administrator is substantive rather than procedural in nature. In most instances he has been picked because of his specialized knowledge of a particular business or industry. In the great majority of cases he must be loyal to the political forces. Although administrative officials are usually men of high integrity, they tend to exalt administrative convenience and the national advantage at the expense of the individual and his freedom. The official in his zeal to achieve a desirable result may impose an unreasonable burden upon the subject.[131]

Finally, the many objections to the use of the contempt power by the courts and the legislatures apply with equal if not greater force to any proposed extension to administrative bodies. A power already wielded by too many, and often too harshly, is better limited to its present bounds.

Thus, for various practical and politically sound reasons, the denial of direct administrative contempt powers seems justified. However, for the sake of governmental efficiency, some methods of compulsion or punishment might nonetheless be warranted. The grant of a direct contempt power need not be the only answer. It is significant that federal agencies have operated with some amount of efficiency for about seventy-five years since their beginnings without the direct contempt power.

However, the fact that denial of a direct agency contempt power is justified pragmatically, though perhaps not historically or logically, need not create the impression that some method of obtaining compliance swiftly and efficiently is not necessary. Government action, administrative or otherwise, which could be delayed with facility and obstructed with impunity, might well result in inefficiency and unnecessarily excessive costs to the general public. The cost would be in imperfect justice as well as financial waste. The reluctance to grant a direct summary power for constitutional or other reasons has resulted in the development of various indirect statutory methods which apparently were designed to strike some balance between the protection of individual liberties, the maintenance of judicial control over the administrative process, and the preservation of efficiency in bureaucratic government. Whether this goal has been achieved by the procedures developed to that end will be considered next, along with a résumé of those indirect procedures.

ADMINISTRATIVE CONTEMPT AS A STATUTORY CRIME

One indirect method of dealing with contempts of administrative agencies is to consider contemptuous conduct before an administrative agency a misdemeanor. This kind of statute is rarely employed. A typical example of this kind of law provides:

Any person who shall neglect or refuse to attend and testify or to produce books, papers, . . . (etc.) . . . if in his power to do so, in obedience to the subpoena or lawful requirement of the Commission, shall be guilty of a misdemeanor and upon conviction thereof by a court of competent jurisdiction shall be punished by a fine . . . or by imprisonment . . . or by both.[132]

Since the proper preoccupation of administrative agencies with respect to sanctions is compulsion, as opposed to punishment, this kind of statute departs from the more vital needs of the agencies. Moreover, one might quarrel with the policy which considered contempt of agencies a criminal act. Additionally, the practical value to the agencies of this approval is questionable. The delays of prosecution might deter the agencies from using the statutory power; the administrative officials would be kept from their primary work in order to testify at the trials; and the end result might not bring them the compulsion they sought, but would only punish the contemnor.

Though this statutory treatment does have flaws, it is the one step which has been taken away from traditional summary contempt procedures. Its perfection and refinement might well provide the solution to many of the legal and practical problems encountered in this area, and will be more fully discussed in the conclusion of this chapter.

INDIRECT COURT ENFORCEMENT: THE TWO-STAGE PROCEEDING

Here is the scheme most commonly provided for in both federal and state laws for court enforcement of agency orders.[133] This is an indirect method by which the agency applies to the court for an enforcement decree of their (the agency's) order. Violation of the court decree is then punished as contempt of court. For obvious reasons, this procedure has been labeled a "two-stage" contempt process. The first stage is the application proceeding. The second phase is the contempt proceeding for disobedience of the court order. At both levels, the agency is generally the instigating party, though the court could institute the contempt proceeding on its own.[134]

Although this duplex process is provided for in the Federal Administrative Procedure Act (APA) for enforcement of subpoenas,[135] it is not the uniform federal practice. The APA provisions apply only to agencies that have not adopted specific contrary provisions.[136] Few agencies have, however, departed from the APA scheme. The Internal Revenue Service and the Department of Labor are significant exceptions.

While the common two-stage provision has heretofore been used exclusively for enforcement of subpoenas and orders, its broad language would permit its use in "all cases of contumacy." [137] Exactly how it would apply to physical misconduct or verbal contempts is not clear. It is likely that the language "all cases of contumacy" is deliberate surplusage, conveniently inserted to cover any odd or unforeseeable types of contempt which might arise.

Since the earliest days of American administrative law, Congress has provided agencies with this burdensome duplex procedure. The Act of 1887 creating the Interstate Commerce Commission (ICC) contained a provision nearly identical to some found in twentieth-century statutes. The Commission was given the power to require the attendance and testimony of witnesses and to call for and examine books and records pertinent to matters under investigation. To that end it could issue subpoenas. In case of failure to comply with a subpoena, the agency could seek the aid of a United States circuit court in securing obedience. The 1887 statute provided:

[A]ny of the Circuit Courts of the United States within the jurisdiction of which such inquiry is carried on may, in case of contumacy or refusal to obey a subpoena issued to any common carrier subject to the provisions of this act, or other person, issue an order requiring such common carrier or other person to appear before said commission . . . and give evidence touching the matter in question, and any failure to obey such order of the court may be punished by such court as contempt thereof.[138]

This provision was not the first of its kind. In fact, each of two nearly identical predecessor enactments had already been before federal circuit courts prior to 1887. On both occasions they were declared unconstitutional.[139]

The provision in the ICC Act of 1887 came under legal fire in 1894 in the *Brimson* case, discussed earlier. There, an investigation had been begun by the ICC against the Illinois Steel Company and five railroad companies for alleged violations of the

Interstate Commerce Act. In the course of the investigation, William G. Brimson, the president and manager of the five railroad companies, was subpoenaed along with other company officials. They all refused to answer certain questions or to produce certain books and papers. The Commission thereupon petitioned the circuit court for an order requiring compliance with their demands. Among other defenses, the defendants alleged that the part of the Act which permitted court enforcement of the Commission's subpoenas was unconstitutional. Two specific claims were made. First, it was alleged that the statutory procedure failed to present a "case" or "controversy" so as to enable the court to assume jurisdiction. Second, the defendants asserted that such a procedure imposed nonjudicial functions on a judicial body in violation of the separation of powers doctrine.

The circuit court agreed and dismissed the Commission's petition as "nothing more than an application by an administrative body to a judicial tribunal for the exercise of its functions in aid of the execution of duties not of a judicial nature." [140] It ruled that the proceeding did not present a case or controversy over which the judicial power of the United States could be exercised.

However, on appeal by the Commission, the Supreme Court in a 5-to-3 decision, reversed the circuit court decision. Justice John Marshall Harlan spoke for a majority of the court. Justice Brewer wrote the dissent. First Justice Harlan decided that there was a "case" or "controversy" which could properly be heard by the circuit court.

Upon everyone . . . who owes allegiance to the United States, or who is within its jurisdiction, enjoying the protection that its government affords, rests an obligation to respect the national will as thus expressed in conformity with the Constitution. As every citizen is bound to obey the law and to yield obedience to the constituted authorities acting within the law, this power conferred upon the Commission imposes upon anyone, summoned by that body to appear and to testify, the duty of appearing and testifying, and upon anyone required to produce such books, papers, tariffs, contracts, agreements, and documents, the duty of producing them, if the testimony sought, and the books, papers, etc. called for, relate to the matter under investigation, if such matter is one which the Commission is legally entitled to investigate, and if the witness is not excused, on some personal ground, from doing what the Commission requires at his hands. These propositions seem to be so clear and indisputable that any attempt to sustain them by argument would be of no value in the discussion. Whether the Commission is entitled to the evidence it seeks, and whether the refusal of the witness to testify or to produce books, papers, etc. in his possession, is or is not in violation of his duty or in derogation of the rights of the United States, seeking to execute a power expressly granted to Congress, are the distinct issues between that body and the witnesses. They are the issues between the United States and those who dispute the validity of an act of Congress and seek to obstruct its enforcement. And these issues made in the form prescribed by the act of Congress are so presented that the judicial power is capable of acting on them. . . . The United States asserts its right, under the Constitution and laws, to have these appellees answer the questions propounded by the Commission, and to produce specified books, papers, etc. in their possession or under their control. . . . The appellees deny that any such rights exist in the general government, or that they are under a legal duty, even if such evidence be important or vital in the enforcement of the Interstate Commerce Act, to do what is required of them by the Commission. Thus has arisen a dispute involving rights or claims asserted by the respective parties to it. It cannot be that the general government with all the power conferred upon it by the people of the United States, is helpless in such an emergency, and is unable to provide some method *judicial in form and direct in its operation,* for the prompt and conclusive determination of this dispute [emphasis added].[141]

As to the second issue in the case, which was a claim that the circuit court was exercising an act administrative in nature and therefore outside its domain, the Court said:

The duties assigned to the circuit courts of the United States . . . are judicial in their nature. The inquiry whether a witness before the Commission is bound to answer a particular question propounded to him, or to produce books, papers, etc., in his possession and called for by that body, is one that cannot be committed to a subordinate administrative or executive tribunal for final determination. One of the functions of a court is to compel a party to perform a duty which the law requires at his hands. *If it be adjudged that the defendants are in law, obliged to do what they have refused to do, that determination will not be ancillary and advisory but . . . will be a "final and indisputable basis of action,"* as between the Commission and the defendants and will furnish a precedent in all similar cases. *It will be as much a judgment that may be carried into effect by judicial process* as one for money, or for the recovery of property, or a judgment in mandamus commanding the performance of an act or duty which the law requires to be performed, or a judgment prohibiting the doing of something which the law will not sanction. *It is none the less the judgment of a judicial tribunal dealing with questions judicial in their nature,* and presented in the customary forms of judicial proceedings, because its effect may be to aid an administrative or executive body in the performance of duties legally imposed upon it by Congress in execution of a power granted by the Constitution [emphasis added].[142]

Harlan's analysis is cogently stated and logically unassailable. It has withstood the tests of time and application. Criticism was, however, raised with his initial premise that all individuals have a duty to appear and testify before administrative agencies if the requested testimony is relevant and unprivileged. To be sure, he says: "These propositions seem to be so clear and indisputable that any attempt to sustain them by argument would be of no value in the discussion." [143] Though there may be such a recognized duty today, in Harlan's era this attitude was not beyond rejection. In fact the three-judge dissent in *Brimson*, delivered by Justice Brewer, vehemently attacked the premise that such a duty existed. He declared:

It may be that it is the duty of every citizen to give information to the commission when demanded, but it is no more a duty than it is to avoid murder or other crimes; to lead a life of social purity; to avoid fraud in business transactions, or neglect of other duties of good citizenship. Will it be pretended that these obligations can be enforced by the courts through proceedings as for contempt? [144]

But the power and value of the administrative process has long since been accepted, and the corresponding duty to testify long since justified.

If individual rights are not considered to be improperly invaded by compulsory processes in general, a fortiori, there may be no cause to complain where similar invasions of personal freedoms are engendered by equally important societal interests through the instrument of administrative agencies. Certainly an investigation by the Civil Aeronautics Board into the cause of an airplane accident is as vital and consequential to the public as some judicial litigation over the title to a quarter acre of weedy swampland. This is not to say that the aggregate of what individually may seem to be petty legal actions is not equally important to an ordered society as the protection of the vast public interests by the administrative process. But the values which substantiate the rights do apply in both cases with at least equal vigor.

Once having established this legal duty to testify, it is futile to attack Harlan's reasoning. Nor did Justice Brewer attempt this in his dissent in *Brimson*. Instead, he argued that Harlan's decision overlooked the substance of the statutory procedure under attack. Justice Harlan had said: "No question of contempt could arise until the issue of law, in the circuit court, is determined adversely to the defendants and they refuse to obey, not the order of the commission, but the final order of the court." Brewer retorted:

It is no sound answer to say that the court orders the witness to testify and punishes for disobedience of that order. The real wrong is not testifying before the Commission and that is the ground of the punishment. . . . His failure to obey the order of the court is only the nominal, while the failure to discharge the prior duty is the real ground of punishment. No forms of statement can change the substantial fact that the inherent power of courts to punish for contempt is exercised, not to preserve the authority of the court, not in aid of proceedings carried on in them, but to aid a merely administrative body, and to compel obedience to its requirements. It makes the courts the mere assistants of a commission. . . . Why call in the court to act as a mere tool?

Thus, the difference between the majority opinion and the dissent, as drawn by the dissent, is one of substance versus form. However, the majority opinion seems to satisfy both. In theory there is no doubt that the court may be ultimately punishing contempt of its own order. Whether reality conforms to theory is a question which can only be resolved on a case-by-case analysis. If an initial petition for an enforcement order is actually litigated with a full hearing of arguments on both sides, the subsequent decision of the court as to the corresponding rights and duties of the litigants would be no different from that in any civil litigation. Since the court actually made a decision and was wronged, the contempt could truly be said to be of the court. The court's enforcement order in such a situation is analogous to an injunction in a civil action which might be granted as relief for the victorious party. If this "injunction" is then disobeyed the court may punish such noncompliance as a contempt, just as it might in any case where its injunction was violated.

The only objection that an individual could raise would be against the right of a court to punish contempt at all, or its right to do so summarily; but as the law presently stands this objection would be in vain. The individual in this situation has no more complaint than any defendant who loses a civil or criminal trial and refuses to comply with the court order. The fact that some administrative function, rather than some private right, is being aided or vindicated by this statutory process makes no substantial difference. In this sense, the agency is merely a party to a judicial litigation, entitled to no more and no less than a private person in a similar situation.

It is only in those cases where the courts actually become a "tool" or "rubber stamp" of the agency and make no independent decision that the dissent in *Brimson* becomes justifiable. There where the argument is justifiable in fact, the theory is relatively superfluous. If the court merely ratifies the agency order or automatically grants the subpoena and enforces them without a full hearing, in a judicial sense, of arguments on the issues raised by the alleged contemnor, there is no substantial intermediary court order which could later be contemned. The court would be punishing a contempt of the agency order and not its own. This would truly be an unconstitutional exercise of a nonjudicial function and a violation of the federal statute which, by its words, permits courts to punish only contempts of their own authority.[145]

Though in *Brimson* form and substance seemed to have coincided, later cases have questioned whether the same can be said of present day court enforcement procedures. There are criticisms that courts are often acting as "rubber stamps" of agency action,[146] and even if this is not always true, it raises a substantial enough issue to put current practices in constitutional doubt.

AGENCY SUBPOENAS

As a result of several Supreme Court decisions,[147] during the past twenty years, culminating in the recent case of *CAB v. Hermann*,[148] it has been the practice of many lower federal courts to grant enforcement of administrative subpoenas nearly as a matter of absolute agency right. Exalting administrative efficiency above individual rights, the courts often give merely superficial consideration to objections raised by prospective witnesses. The courts are permitted to dispose of claims of irrelevancy by merely "laying the subpoenas alongside the charges in the complaint." [149] If immateriality or irrelevancy is not apparent by that test, the court will go no further and will issue an enforcement order. The individual is thereby deprived of a full court hearing and the opportunity to support his objections by oral argument. While the witness is theoretically still able to raise other objections, like constitutional privileges under the Fourth and Fifth Amendments, such possibilities have little practical value. "Probable cause" is not even a prerequisite to an enforcement order.[150] And, the privilege against self-incrimination is seldom available because it is a personal privilege which is not applicable to the most frequently called for evidence, such as corporate records. In other cases it is unavailable because immunity from subsequent prosecution is commonly provided.

In practice, therefore, the subpoena enforcement order is relatively perfunctory, and may result from a robot exercise of judicial powers. It could be argued that a contempt proceeding which might ultimately follow a violation of that "court" enforcement order could not, except nominally, be for contempt of court.

Unless there is a truly adjudicated intermediary court order there would be exactly the situation which the *Brimson* case implied would be unconstitutional. If there is no full consideration of these issues there is no "case" or "controversy" actually litigated upon which a court order can realistically be based. Without such an order there is no court authority which is being flaunted and, as pointed out before, a court cannot punish contempt of any authority but its own. This procedure is not justified by saying that a defendant has a full hearing when he is charged with contempt. Procedurally, the absence of a real enforcement order gives the court absolutely no grounds to punish for contempt; and one should not be forced this far to get his hearing on his claim.

Agency Orders. What about the determination of whether the order of the court itself was disobeyed? This problem arises in the case of enforcing agency orders, as opposed to subpoenas. Here, the need for an independent judicial finding is even greater. While the courts will review a defendant's case before ordering enforcement of an agency decision, they will usually go no further than determining whether the decision is supported by substantial evidence. This greatly narrows the judicial reviewing function but, nevertheless, involves a close inspection of a record already exhaustively scrutinized by the agency. The significant constitutional question arises in relation to the contempt practice employed in the event of a violation of the court enforcement order.

Whereas the general practice of the circuit courts is to hear all the facts which allegedly constitute the contempt or, in some cases, to relegate the fact-finding job to an impartial master,[151] on occasion the courts have been known to permit the agency prosecuting the contempt charge to make the initial findings of fact.[152] While this is done because of the expertise of the agency and its peculiar ability to deal with technical facts, it is, nevertheless, a practice which places the question of contempt peculiarly within the hands of the agency and for obvious reasons is therefore objectionable. Some federal courts have considered this practice improper.[153] However, in 1953 the Ninth Circuit Court of Appeals sustained the practice against an objection that the agency (in this case the NLRB) was in effect enforcing its own order. The court said: "While we are in accord with the proposition that the Board should, as a general rule, have no part in a contempt proceeding, there should be some flexibility in the rule." [154]

The court went on to say that although such a practice is permissible it is not binding on the court, which should exercise caution in its use. The ultimate fact-finding function must still remain with the court. And, unlike other cases, the court in a contempt proceeding is not bound by the board's finding, even if it is sustained by substantial evidence.[155] Although the court was cautious in reaching its decision, and imparted many admonitions against making a regular practice of submitting the fact-finding duty to the board itself, it could be further suggested that it would be unwise to permit the practice in any case. There is no way to measure the influence of an agency's finding upon the court. The danger in any one case of permitting an adversary party to so influence the court's ultimate decision, especially where one's liberty is involved, should better be avoided. At best this practice is highly questionable and approaches what would essentially be the indirect grant of a direct contempt power to the agencies.

Agency Sanctions. Another objectionable development with respect to this indirect court punishment of contempt of administrative agencies accents the contention that this two-stage procedure is constitutionally questionable.

On several occasions, the Supreme Court has diminished court discretion to infinity with respect to the imposition of sanctions arising out of violations of court orders. In the case of *N.L.R.B. v. Warren Co.*,[156] the Court considered a board claim that it was improper for a circuit court not to have punished the respondent contemnor for criminal contempt as was requested. The Court sustained the board's contention with the following significant language:

> It is the statutory *duty* of the Court of Appeals on petition of the Board to adjudge him [Respondent] in contempt of its enforcement decree. To conclude otherwise would greatly weaken the administration of the N.L.R.B. . . . The granting or withholding of such remedial action *is not wholly discretionary with the court* [emphasis added].

In an earlier case,[157] the Court permitted the Securities Exchange Commission to challenge the circuit court's granting of a criminal contempt citation, when the Commission had requested a finding of civil contempt for coercive rather than solely punitive purposes. The circuit court had fined the respondent a flat $50. The Supreme Court reversed and insisted that some coercive punishment be imposed in lieu of the fine. The Court in effect subordinated the circuit court's contempt power to help fulfill the agency's function. Justice Frankfurter, in a vigorous dissent, urged that in this attitude the Court was approaching the status of a mere automaton and was no longer punishing contempt of its own authority, but was bound by the demands of the agency. He recalled: "The power of Congress to impose on courts the duty of enforcing obedience to an administrative subpoena was sustained precisely because courts were not to be automata carrying out the wishes of the administrative . . . *I.C.C. v. Brimson.*"

Justice Frankfurter's concern seems well justified. If the agencies can dictate what punishment shall be inflicted on a contumacious witness or party, they are in fact, if not in form, directly punishing the contempt of their authority. In such a predicament the court is exercising a nonjudicial function and acting as a mere adjunct to a subordinate administrative agency. It is all the more hypocritical to allow this procedure and, at the same time, call it something less than a direct contempt power.

The legal collapse of this procedure is obviously a result of a designed effort to invigorate the administrative process by providing efficient enforcement of the statutory policies which are placed in the hands of the agencies. While this goal is laudable, it has driven the courts to a position which, as Justice Frankfurter aptly indicated, is inconsistent with the *Brimson* decision. The fact that it is the Supreme Court itself which has weakened the effect of the *Brimson* case does not make the current practice any less defective. A constitutional defect cannot be camouflaged by merely shrouding it in judicial procedure, any more than it should be sanctioned in the name of efficient government.

This procedure could be rationalized either on the theory that any party to a proceeding in court may suggest or request the court to act in one certain way as opposed to another, or that the agency is an adjunct of government and therefore has the peculiar responsibility to advise and provide guidance to the court. The problem with these theories is that the issue is the propriety of the exercise of judicial power and not the right of the agency to argue for or against a particular course of court action. In fact, if the court is divesting itself of some of its discretionary functions by relying on administrative conclusions a constitutional objection exists. This fact is difficult to determine when the advocate is a governmental body itself, and one which has entered the decision-making process in the matter at hand.

Furthermore, it is doubtful whether the desired results have been achieved. The agencies are still crippled to a large degree by delays. In the case last discussed, the contempt proceeding resulted in a four-year delay, which virtually destroyed the effect of the administrative process. Whether this is typical is difficult to determine because of the paucity of intra-agency information of this nature. Nevertheless, it should be evident from the foregoing illustrations that this indirect contempt procedure is one with constitutional and practical difficulties. Though it may be theoretically unassailable, the procedural problems caused by its use make it highly awkward and unusable.

DIRECT COURT ENFORCEMENT:
ONE-STAGE PROCEEDING

The continuous search for an effective method of compelling compliance with agency mandates has led Congress and many of the state legislatures to enact various statutes eliminating the need of intermediate court orders as are required under the two-stage agency court scheme.[158] Under these one-stage proceedings, the agency need only certify to the court the facts which constitute the alleged contempt, and the court can act as if the wrong was a contempt of its own authority. A typical statute of this variety provides:

If any person in proceedings before the Secretary of Labor or his duly authorized representatives disobeys or resists any lawful order or process, or misbehaves during a hearing or so near the place thereof as to obstruct the same, the Secretary or his duly authorizea representative shall certify the facts to the district court having jurisdiction . . . which shall thereupon in a summary manner hear the evidence as to the acts complained of, and if the evidence so warrants, punish such persons in the same manner and to the same extent as for contempt committed before the court, or commit such person upon the same conditions as if the doing of the forbidden act had occurred with reference to the process of or in the presence of the court.[159]

This type of procedure is authorized for the Labor Department and the Internal Revenue Service and is used by numerous state agencies. In the state courts, it has met some opposition and has been invalidated on several occasions on the ground that judicial powers like contempt should be confined to the actual use of the courts.[160] One court rationalized the unacceptability of this procedure thusly: "where an individual is being proceeded against in one tribunal for an act done in the presence and in derogation of the authority of a different tribunal, the ability of the trial tribunal to exercise its proper functions is not involved." [161] In one federal case, a similar statute which required an application of the agency to the court for attachment of recalcitrant witnesses was upheld.[162] However, the actual practice in this situation included an intermediate order upon which the court could base its punishment for contempt of court. The statute was condoned because it provided for an independent basis for the court's jurisdiction. In the absence of such an intermediate order the procedure would be objectionable.

This one-stage procedure includes all the practical values of rapid enforcement of agency mandates, but also all the constitutional defects which arise from the absence of a court order upon which to base a contempt of court punishment. All questions of separation of powers, due process of law, and blind court enforcement of what are truly agency contempts are present in these cases; and these flaws have not been overlooked by the courts. In one state case, a statute which made provisions for an agency to apply to the court for punishment of contempts committed before the board, was held to be a violation of procedural due process. The court said: "Contempt of the investigations cannot by legislative fiat be transformed into a judicial judgment; due process must be observed." [163]

The court continued and determined that due process was not satisfied because there was no violation of a court order, without which there could be no contempt of court. In another case the procedure was objected to on the grounds that:

The power to punish for contempt is not given to the . . . court for the purpose of maintaining the authority of a board upon whom it would be unconstitutional to confer such a power. The men [defendants] are not in contempt of the . . . court; the head and front of their offending is their refusal to give evidence before the Board.

On the other hand, this type of statute has been employed without successful objections in some states. It does contain the advantage of having the contempt charge submitted to a court which is a third, and hopefully, impartial body. This is manifestly more desirable than permitting the agency to directly punish for contempt. Nevertheless, the procedure is laden with the constitutional objections that there is no "case" or "controversy," and that the practice violates strong and long-respected constitutional principles of due process and separation of powers.

RECOMMENDATIONS

For all the various reasons described, there is presently no contempt procedure available to administrative agencies which is practically or legally satisfactory. Various suggestions for change have been made ranging from recommendations for grants of the direct contempt power to particular agencies, to others urging primary contempt jurisdiction within the agencies, subject to subsequent judicial review. These suggestions all presuppose the necessity of broad powers with summary contempt procedures either at the administrative or judicial level. This presupposition neglects the prime and basic issue concerning the conflicts between individual liberty and effective administration of the law. It is submitted that some procedure could be developed within the framework of administrative law which would be more satisfactory to these two competing interests. But even here, no single practice will apply satisfactorily to all problems typically dealt with by current contempt practice. A more versatile procedure would accommodate administrative power to the particular control desired, as well as to the corresponding demands for protection of individual rights.

Recommendation A. If the problem is one concerning a physical contempt through disorderly or disrespectful conduct in or near the hearing room, it is easily remedied by the simple sanction of bodily exclusion. In the case of agency practitioners, suspension or disbarment would be sufficient. In either case, the right to raise on appeal any question of abuse should be preserved for the excluded or suspended individual. Where this practice exists it seems to have worked well. Of course, where the contumacy is of an aggravated nature, and the agency desires criminal punishment of the individual, resort to prosecution under an appropriate disorderly conduct statute should suffice. In any case where *punishment* is the agency's desired end, there are good reasons for not permitting a summary proceeding against the individual by a hearing officer who may be personally offended by the conduct in question. A criminal prosecution before an impartial judge should not be sacrificed for the sake of alleged injury to governmental dignity. Presently, the absence of summary punishment in most agency practice has not interfered with the growth and effectiveness of administrative agencies. This indicates that dignity and authority can be preserved by methods which fall short of actual punishment.

Recommendation B. In the realm of subpoena enforcement or testimonial compulsion the needs are and the remedies must be different. Obviously, exclusion of a noncomplying witness would defeat the agency's purpose and satisfy only the contemnor. Presuming that the agency desires to *coerce* the witness to testify rather than *punish* his recalcitrance, some swift, but procedurally satisfying, method must be found. As we have seen, the existing procedures have in this respect proved to be open to question constitutionally, awkward, and hence inadequate. It is submitted that some hybrid or peculiar criminal proceeding would satisfy most if not all objections to existing methods of subpoena enforcement.

Specifically, refusal to appear or testify pursuant to an agency subpoena could be made a criminal offense, punishable as an ordinary crime, but subject to special priorities on court calendars, and punishable optionally on a determinate or contingent basis. Here, the agencies' objectives could be swiftly fulfilled, and at the same time the procedure would preserve for the individual all the procedural safeguards of a criminal trial. The only differences between this and a regular criminal prosecution for the same conduct would be the immediate availability of a court proceeding (by reason of the calendar priority), and the coercive rather than retributive aim of the punishment. The proceeding would resemble a motion for a temporary injunction where irreparable injury is claimed. The irreparable harm in this case would be to the agency's efficiency and to governmental effectiveness in general.

In many cases this proceeding would probably be no more

than a hearing, with no need for a jury, because only the legal question concerning the validity of a subpoena or some claimed privilege would be in dispute. In this event the suggested procedure would eliminate the intermediate order required in the current indirect two-stage methods required by most statutes, as well as the technical objection to the one-stage process that there is no contempt of a court. Moreover, where questions of fact are in issue, the accused contemnor would be protected from the potential abuses of summary proceedings. He could demand a trial by jury or at least a full hearing, and all other procedural safeguards required in general criminal proceedings.

Recommendation C. The same procedure could be employed for enforcing agency orders. The only difficulty in this regard would be that of submitting highly complex fact questions to an inexpert jury. But with cautious selection of jurors and careful instructions by the judge, these objections could be minimized. This is a commonplace in other trials. At the same time, the long delays which result from the usual series of intermediate hearings and orders by courts in the current indirect enforcement procedures would be eliminated. Likewise, all current constitutional objections inherent in present contempt procedures, would be eliminated.

Although these suggestions are not submitted as an exegesis of the many practical, and constitutional defects in existing procedures, they are offered as a realistic balance of the agency and individual interests concerned.

CHAPTER IV

Limitations on the Contempt Power

Having examined the history, variety, and pervasiveness of the contempt power and having indicated some of the political and nonlegal problems provoked by its application, it is now possible, and hopefully fruitful, to pass to a study of the constitutional issues which arise in contempt situations and those other judicial and legislative limitations which have been imposed upon the power by law. In a government of laws such as ours, it is not unusual for disputes to ultimately be resolved by resort to the most fundamental, enduring, and decisive of our laws, the United States Constitution. Few legal devices find conflict within the pages of our constitution with the ubiquity of the contempt power. These conflicts involve issues concerning the governmental power-structure such as the separation of powers in local and federal governments (which was described in Chapter I as an historical contribution to the establishment of contempt powers), and the delicate balancing of federal-state relations. Beside this, there are civil liberties issues arising out of the conflict between the use of the contempt power and such vital procedural protections as the right to trial by jury, freedom from self-incrimination, double jeopardy, and indictment—to name only the most recurring and polemic examples. Aside from these problems, there are issues of civil rights, such as freedom of

speech, association, and religion, which have been raised by the
exercise of the contempt power. This chapter will deal with
these problems separately, and describe both the past treatment
and the present status of the law in these areas. Since most issues arise out of the procedural implementations of the contempt
power, a succinct statement of those procedures should assist
the summary and discussion which will follow.[1]

The congressional contempt power in America derived from
the Parliament's common-law power. Its adoption was considered necessary, expedient, and innate. The right to punish contempt of Congress was quite automatically assumed by early
Americans, who were as anxious for efficacy and power as they
were intolerant of the unjust practices of their English forebears. Though the Constitution is silent with respect to federal
legislative contempt powers, the Congress acted early, asserting
an inherent right to punish contempts. All contemnors were
allowed to present a defense and be aided by counsel. Procedures were summary; there was no jury; and sentences were
limited in duration only by the extent of congressional sessions.
In 1857, a federal statute was passed which provided a different
procedure for punishing contempts of Congress, but which did
not preclude action under the prior inherent-claimed procedures. Nevertheless, since that time almost all legislative contempt procedures have been pursuant to the statute, which remains the authority to date. The federal statute reads:

any person summoned as a witness by the authority of either House
of Congress to give testimony or to produce papers upon any matter
before either House, or any committee . . . who shall wilfully make
default, or . . . refuse to answer any question pertinent to the matter of inquiry . . . shall . . . be liable to indictment as and for a
misdemeanor . . . and on conviction, shall pay a fine not exceeding
$1,000 and not less than $100, and suffer imprisonment in the common jail not less than 1 month nor more than 12 months.[2]

Section 3 of that statute directs that the presiding congressional officer submit all cases to the local United States Attorney, who in turn will seek a grand jury indictment and prosecute the case in the ordinary way. All the general criminal procedural safeguards inure to the contemnor. The sentencing power is a limited one. Though this power has been exercised in increasing volume, there are fewer procedural problems than in the contempt of court situation. Once assuming the acceptance of some kind of contempt power, one limited in these ways seems at least comparatively satisfactory.

However, the inherent power still exists. Though it is not currently used, and the likelihood of its revival is remote, it is still a shadow in the congressional arsenal of powers. Only recently, certain Senators who were dissatisfied with present judicial review of contempt of Congress convictions threatened to return to the use of the broad inherent power. Justice Clark has expressed a similar sentiment.

The judicial contempt power is procedurally more confused, intricate, and troublesome. The power of courts to punish contempts early became a settled precedent in English common law, though the extent of its application historically is open to question. After a brief colonial use of contempt powers, claimed to be inherent, and some state legislation formally establishing the power, the first federal statute concerning contempt of court was passed in 1789. It gave federal courts the discretionary power to punish contempts as defined by the common law. The statute expressly covered misconduct of officers of the court, disobedience of process, and misbehavior in the presence of the court. No criminal procedural rights were given the contemnor, and the courts were limited in sentencing only by their own conscience. This enactment was followed in 1821 by a second federal statute. That legislation allowed a summary, virtually unlimited power with specific limitations, and covered the same categories of conduct as the prior legislation, except that the controversial words "or so near thereto as to obstruct the administration of justice" were added with reference to the offense of misbehavior in the presence of the court. The present statute reads much the same as the 1821 law. The sentencing power is in many ways unlimited, and the procedures are summary. Through the years, some fear has been expressed about the unlimited nature of the power. Though few have advocated abolishing the contempt power itself, there have been some confinements in its use by both limiting legislation and judicial interpretation.

Limiting Legislation

The Clayton Act of 1914[3] included a provision guaranteeing the right to a jury trial in all criminal contempt cases arising out of willful violations of orders of the district courts. Further conditions required that the contemptuous act must be one listed as a federal or state criminal offense in order to fall within this section, and that direct contempts and contempts arising out of suits brought by the United States be excluded from the statute's coverage. These qualifying conditions sobered hopes that the new law would be labor's Magna Carta, by so circumscribing the jury rights as to prevent their available employment, which it was hoped might be accomplished by the act.[4]

In the next decade, numerous bills were presented to Congress calling for liberalization of the harsh summary contempt procedures, and finally in 1932 the Norris LaGuardia Act[5] was signed into law by President Hoover. This law provided for trial by jury in indirect contempt cases arising out of labor disputes, and disqualification of judges personally involved in contempt actions. When the Supreme Court ruled that legislation like this did not violate the separation of powers doctrine,[6] several of the states followed with similar legislation softening some of their more stringent contempt procedures. Rule 42 of The Federal Rules of Criminal Procedure further refined the accompanying procedures for prosecution of all direct and indirect criminal contempts in matters of notice and hearing.

In 1957, a Civil Rights Act was passed which included certain contempt provisions.[7] This act, the first major attempt to deal with civil rights since post-Civil War times, gave injunctive protection to voting rights, enforceable through criminal contempt proceedings. Use of the contempt power was a pivotal issue in passage of the act, providing as it did a means for governmental protection of rights already existing but lacking enforceability. Contemptuous misconduct under this statute might arise out of disobedience to commission orders or interference with voting rights. The statute grants contemnors a right to demand a jury trial de novo where their sentence exceeds $300 or 45 days imprisonment. Otherwise, it is permissive and in the courts discretion.

A novel situation, therefore, confronts the judge who must try the contemnor. Where the alleged contempt is so serious that if proved it would probably call for a fine or imprisonment in excess of the non-jury maximum, the judge, in order to avoid the duplication of a new trial, would probably proceed before a jury. In less serious cases, the non-jury procedure might be used. Should the statutory maximum then be exceeded, however, the contemnor would probably demand a jury trial, there being slight probability that a jury would recommend an increased fine or imprisonment. The judge trying the case must, therefore, take these factors into consideration in making his initial decision whether to use a jury.

In summary, a jury trial by permission may be given by the judge in any contempt proceeding arising under the Act. However, a jury trial as of right depends on four factors: (1) There must be a contempt arising under the Act, that is, where the original basis of the action was the infringement of a voting right; (2) the contempt must not be a direct contempt; (3) the contempt must be criminal, as distinguished from a civil, contempt; and (4) there must have been an initial trial at which a fine in excess of $300 or imprisonment in excess of forty-five days was imposed.[8]

Notice, hearing, subpoena power, and the right to counsel are also guaranteed by this law. Strong feelings that Southern juries would not convict, at least in part precipitated the fight for the jury guarantee, which the Senate added to the original bill passed by the House of Representatives. Paradoxically, enemies of the bill's purpose were joined in this fight for jury rights by liberals, who found themselves awkwardly between dreams of a good civil rights bill on the one hand, and libertarian claims on the other that the blameworthiness of the contemnors should not warrant their unfair procedural treatment.

Time will show the success of these statutory provisions, but the direction is away from summary procedures—if only in limited situations like those mentioned.

Judicial Limitations

The courts have also shown self-consciousness about the summary contempt power, and at times have limited some of its harshnesses through their power of judicial interpretation. Less direct than legislation, this has often been as effective. For example, it has been noted that strong policy against court control over the press provoked the Supreme Court to interpret the "so near thereto as to obstruct the administration of justice" clause of the federal contempt statute in a way which all but precludes most constructive contempt convictions.[9] This attitude is the antithesis of the English treatment and may be based upon distaste with summary procedures as well as attitudes about the contempt power itself. Another example of judicial conservatism with the applicability of contempt procedures may well be evidenced by their interpretation of the federal statute's words "officer of the court" not to include attorneys.[10] By such an interpretation contempt sanctions are given one less subject, though in every other sense of these words attorneys are officers of the court. Furthermore, courts have created mystic distinctions between civil and criminal, direct and indirect contempts, often to avoid or apply specific procedural protections attaching to those various kinds of contempt, if in disregard of all other legal symmetry. This subject was treated in Chapter II. To that description might be added the observation that many of the tenuous judicial classifications of the contempt power seemed to have been prompted, at least in part, by a desire to avoid summary procedures typical of certain kinds of contempt. In other more isolated instances, courts have gone far to interpret statutes and situations in order to arrive at more just results, where strict contempt law might not have clearly directed such results.

Thus one can note in the present body of contempt law a trend toward limiting in specific instances the harshness of certain typical procedures customarily used in trying contemnors.

Beyond the statutory scheme within which the contempt power is now operative, there are still greater, more taxing, more vital issues concerning the limitations of the contempt power. These controls lie in the basic Constitution of our country, and, in a great many ways and forms, assert themselves to curb or qualify the contempt power. As with so many important legal issues it is crucial to resort to the Constitution, so in this case is it necessary to fully examine those parts of the Constitution which in so many ways bear upon the contempt power.

The Constitution and the Contempt Power: Jury Trial

The most glaring and disputed denial of civil liberties which is featured under current contempt procedures is the denial of the right of an accused to have a trial by jury. Originally, no contempts were tried by a jury. Gradually, American courts and legislatures, while relentlessly holding on to other vestigial common-law characteristics of the contempt power, have discernibly, if sketchily, retreated from an absolute denial of the right to a jury trial. Now, all contempts of Congress are tried by a jury; indirect criminal contempts of court are too, if they arise out of certain labor disputes, if the act constitutes another state or federal crime, or if it arises under the Civil Rights Acts. But all direct criminal contempts, the remaining indirect criminal contempts, and all civil contempts are still punished summarily.

A recent case, *Green v. United States*,[11] clearly underscored both the problem with respect to the right to trial by jury in criminal contempt cases, and a political dilemma which arises out of the judicial dispositions of Supreme Court members, and which affects the law in general, and contempt law more particularly. The case involved two of the men who had been convicted in the celebrated *New York Smith Act* trial for conspiring to teach and advocate violent overthrow of the United States.[12] They were each sentenced to a five-year imprisonment and a $10,000 fine. The court released them on bail, but ordered them to appear on a set date for execution of their sentences. On that date, it was discovered that they had disappeared. They remained fugitives until their voluntary surrender four and a half years later. Then, the United States brought criminal contempt proceedings against them for willful disobedience of the surrender order. This action was tried by the district court without a jury; they were found guilty and were sentenced to three more years imprisonment. The Supreme Court upheld this conviction and sentence, finding no reasons of law, history, or policy which would mitigate the egregious offense of the defendants.

No one would seriously suggest that the defendant's tardiness ought to have gone unnoted. The issue is with the choice of alternative actions which the court made. Justice Harlan, who wrote the majority opinion, disposed of issues regarding the applicability and extent of the contempt power by resort to the accepted history and precedent surrounding the exercise of this power. Conflicting constitutional safeguards were dismissed as simply inapplicable. An existing bail-jumping statute, under which defendants could have been tried in the ordinary way, was deemed irrelevant.

Justice Black wrote a passionate dissent [13] criticizing the summary nature of the contempt power as "an anomaly in the law," ripe for "fundamental and searching reconsideration." He called for judicial action which would reconcile the existence of a contempt power with what he conceived to be basic principles of the American form of government, and our Constitution. His chief complaint about the contempt power is its denial of traditional rights to trial by jury, the democratic element of our law, and, in his words, the "birthright of free men."

This sharp divergence in attitudes of the court emphasizes the vital importance of Supreme Court membership in the resolution of legal, political, and even philosophical problems. Statement of such a conclusion unfortunately comes easier than does accurate and thorough description of the precise sources of the difference. As well as any single legal issue, contempt focuses the existing difference in attitude of the recent court.

The majority disposition is best attributed to Justice Frankfurter's philosophy about the nature of judicial power. For example, in 1924 while a teacher at Harvard Law School, Professor Frankfurter and a colleague wrote an article which unearthed much of the academic misconception about the summary use of the contempt power. The clear import of the article was one of criticism. In fact, in his attack at the historical support for the summariness of contempt procedures, Justice Black referred to that article and noted that the myth of immemorial usage as a reason for continuance of the practice had been exploded by recent scholarship. Yet, Associate Justice Frankfurter concurred in the majority opinion in the *Green* case, which upheld the contempt conviction, for reasons which he has frequently urged. Change, he argued, must come, if at all, from the legislature. Courts are inhibited in this respect, notwithstanding their impressions about the merits or lack of merits of law. He wrote: "The fact that scholarship has shown that historical assumptions regarding the procedure for punishment of contempt of court were ill-founded, hardly wipes out a century and a half of the legislative and judicial history of federal law based on such assumptions." [14] Calling a roll of Supreme Court Justices and lower federal courts who for 150 years approved of the summary use of the criminal contempt power, and admonishing that the court is not a third branch of the legislature, Justice Frankfurter refused "to fashion a wholly novel constitutional doctrine . . . in the teeth of an unbroken legislative and judicial history." [15] Citing former Chief Justice Hughes's words "We do not write on a blank sheet," and never mentioning the merits or demerits of the doctrine at issue, he cast the vote which made the majority decision.

If we compare Justice Black's attitude about those matters deemed crucial by Justice Frankfurter, their difference becomes clear. After stating his fear of the political dangers of the summary contempt power, arising out of their conflict with the Bill of Rights, Justice Black urged that the precedents mentioned by Justice Frankfurter should be rejected because they are wrong. Though sound policy directs adherence to prior decisions, this practice should not be so inflexible as to preclude correction of obvious errors. Justice Black suggested that the prime responsibility of the courts is just this power to reappraise when precious parts of the Constitution are jeopardized. Justice Black is usually characterized as the leader of that school of Supreme Court personnel, loosely but characteristically labeled liberals or judicial activists. Speaking often in dissent, this group is chiefly concerned with the substantial effect of any law upon the sacred rights and liberties of individuals guaranteed by the Constitution in the Bill of Rights.

This attitudinal conflict often reappears in the garb of legal rationales; it has had an enormous impact upon mid-twentieth-century American law and society in general and often lies at the base of the contempt decisions of American courts.

There has been, in the past quarter of a century, an increasing inclination to alleviate some of the procedural harshness of standard contempt procedures. Extension of the right to trial by jury has been a foremost example of this trend. This is at least in part reflective of generally changing attitudes toward the value of the jury method of trial. Like more earthly fashions, the vogue toward the worthwhileness of the jury system has had periods of rising and falling favor. Critics of the jury system in general have been as frequent and as vociferous as have been its advocates. Rather than digressing to enumerate the arguments, it should be only hastily noted that summary contempt procedures are most obnoxious to those who place faith and importance in the libertarian nature of trials by jury.

It could well be suggested that, most peculiarly, in contempt cases the jury has a valuable role. First, it brings the public's attention and interest to a dispute which is usually an official, governmental one. Public enlightenment, even if only through jury representation, has been characterized as an "indispensable element in the popular vindication of the criminal law." [16] This participation hopefully encourages popular understanding and acceptance of the administration of justice. Second, the jury may serve as an insulation between the alleged offender and the offended party, who is sometimes the judge and sentencer. This conservative deliberation in an otherwise unlimited, uncontrolled situation allows the jury to function as a wall against possible abuses by governmental powerholders upon individuals. The general public may look with skepticism upon a judicial process which allows one man to be judge, prosecutor, victim, and jury, but as Justice Black aptly pointed out there is inclined to be less false martyrdom where a jury convicts. Third, there are subtle subversive potentialities in summary criminal proceedings other than the direct issues about who should be the decision-maker and why. The lack of external restraints over the vices of summary proceedings was also scored by Justice Black in his dissent in the *Green* case. The review of a cold record by appellate courts, which are sometimes sympathetic to their brethren of the lower trial courts and are often hesitant to reverse in absence of clear and serious error, is to some viewers an impotent or idle ceremony. Therefore, the original denial of a jury trial is not only a danger in itself but is compounded by being carried up through appellate levels in the form of an often "cold," unreviewable record.[17] Judicial self-restraint, like that voiced by Justice Frankfurter in the *Green* case, compounds the lethargy of appellate judicial scrutiny. This has provoked Justice Black to comment that this offense, which is most inordinately vague and sweeping in substantive scope, is now punished by the harshest procedures known to law and is subject to an unlimited punishing power and a token review.

In Chapter I, the historical causes which resulted in the settled practice of summarily trying contempt cases were described. For better or worse American law has adopted the practice. How then can this practice be rationalized in light of our most basic legal directives—those found in the Constitution?

With respect to the right to trial by jury, article III, section 2 of the Constitution provides that: "The trial of all crimes, except in cases of Impeachment, shall be by Jury. . . ." This particular section was included within the early substance of the Constitution as a reflection of the strong feelings at the time of our national birth that the right to trial by jury was coequal with and essential to a government under law and free from tyrannical abuse. The deprivation of this right was one of the serious grievances which the American settlers held against the King.[18] Specific exceptions to this guarantee were included in the Constitution, so it can be argued that the intent was not to exclude contempt from this coverage since it is not one of those exceptions. This argument is strengthened by the fact that contempt is not listed as a special judicial or legislative power in the enumeration of the granted powers of those governmental branches. Any other conclusion about this aspect of the contempt power is interpretive and based on less evidence. In the *Green* case again, Justice Black noted that, although called upon to present any available evidence of intent on the part of the Constitution writers or expressed at the original state conventions, the government attorneys in that case could find no corroboration for the use of summary contempt proceedings.[19] The cases during this period do not illuminate this uncertainty.[20]

The Bill of Rights twice reaffirms the importance to the people of the right to trial by jury. The Fifth Amendment directs that "No person shall be held to answer for a capital or otherwise infamous crime, unless on a presentment or indictment of a Grand Jury. . . ." And, the Sixth Amendment follows, declaring: "In all criminal prosecutions, the accused shall enjoy the right to a speedy and public trial, by an impartial jury. . . ." The import of this latter constitutional provision was applied to the contempt situation in these compelling words:

> The history which gave rise to the constitutional provisions guaranteeing the right of trial by jury is succinctly summarized in the Declaration of Independence in which complaint was made that the

Colonies were deprived "in many cases, of the benefits of Trial by Jury."

The Constitution provides, "The Trial of all Crimes . . . shall be by Jury. . . ." But those fresh from experiences with tyranny were not content with this general guarantee, and Amendments VI and VII were promptly adopted, the former providing: "In all criminal prosecutions, the accused shall enjoy the right to a speedy and public trial, by an impartial jury. . . ." The concept of a criminal "prosecution" is broader than a "trial" and the addition of the more inclusive term indicates a determination to afford the right of trial by jury to those subjected to prosecution of any sort which might result in fine or imprisonment. The selection of the language of the Sixth Amendment is hardly explainable upon any other postulate.[21]

Nonetheless, contempt has been excluded from these constitutional protections, and disputes with the clear meaning of these words have for the most part prevailed.

In Chapter II, it was shown that the right to a jury trial is dependent upon classification of the contemptuous act as criminal. Writers, judges, and lawmakers have peremptorily brushed aside any argument about juries for civil contempts with total declarations that such procedural provisions simply do not apply to the ordinary contempt situation.[22] Only this and nothing more! Interestingly, even Justice Black has found no fault with summary procedures for civil contempts, though he has suggested that all criminal contempts be tried by a jury. In this former respect, he is not in any minority. Since civil contempts most often arise out of equity proceedings, the Seventh Amendment's guarantee of jury trials in civil matters would by its own terms ("In Suits At Common Law") be inapplicable. So, civil contemnors are between two rules, one providing for jury trial in civil matters arising out of other than equity actions; the other guaranteeing jury trial in criminal cases, a category from which civil contempts have been distinguished, though so many characteristics of criminal treatment are present in these cases.

With these constitutional provisions as well as the judicial and legislative fiats concerning contemporary contempt practice in mind, one can pass to an analysis of the appropriateness of the jury trial. Is contempt a crime? Is it an infamous crime? Are there any valid reasons for applying variant nonjury procedures in this situation?

The Fifth Amendment speaks of "infamous crimes." Like the Eighth Amendment's language about "cruel and unusual" punishments, this phrase too is subject to changing interpretations. In 1884 the United States Supreme Court, drawing from Lord Auckland's *Principles of Penal Law*, attempted to put some substance into the words "infamous crime." [23] Ruling that no United States court had jurisdiction over infamous crimes unless the Fifth Amendment's conditions precedent of indictment and grand jury were fulfilled, the court set up two criteria of infamy. The first inquired whether a conviction for that particular crime would result in impeaching the credibility of the criminal in the future. This is based on an old rule of evidence which dilutes the credibility of testimony given by one who has committed a crime involving moral turpitude or one bearing on veracity. This test for infamy may become circuitous when one presses for definitions of moral turpitude. This legal term of art is often applied as an ingredient or characteristic of more infamous crimes, the kind which would reasonably connote some questionable trait bearing on the probable truthfulness of the criminal. Reasonable as this rule may be, in the present context it leaves one with a formula directing that infamous crimes bear on credibility, and crimes bearing on credibility are infamous. It leaves hazy which crimes are by their nature infamous, or which aspects of criminal behavior bear either upon the infamy of the crime or the credibility of the criminal.

The other criterion, which the court adopted as a guide to determine the infamous nature of a crime, involved the mode of punishment authorized for the particular crime. Here again there is less insight afforded before the fact to establish the nature of a crime than reflection after the crime has been characterized or classified. Since in nonstatutory contempt cases the punishment is unlimited and therefore unknown until it is announced, one cannot determine at a preliminary stage whether or not the crime is infamous. This queer phenomenon accents the inadequacy of the mode of punishment test for classifying criminal contempts as infamous.

The court also mentioned that the nature of the crime, independent of its punishment, determined its characterization as infamous. Therefore precedent is only partly helpful in directing whether contempt or any crime is infamous and warrants Fifth Amendment protection. What was infamous early in English history may not have been so during the period of American colonialism and in turn may or may not be so at the present time. Generally, the decisions have held that the possibility that grave punishment could be inflicted is the test for an infamous crime, and the test of grave punishment is the possibility of being sentenced to hard labor or imprisonment. This over-all Tweedledum and Tweedledee logic is really no more than holding that—an infamous crime is infamous; and that infamous crimes are treated with punishments worthy of infamy; and they are committed by people who are not worthy of belief because of their commission of an infamous crime. This is not really very helpful in cases where there is question: whether a crime has been committed, and what the sentence will ultimately be.

Later cases seemed to adopt the mode-of-punishment test.[24] If a crime can be punished by a sentence including imprisonment or hard labor, it is infamous. Often, a contemnor cannot know that he has committed what a court may later decide was a criminal contempt, or what his sentence will be even if he has some notion of his contemptibility.

I suggest that without employing further semantic niceties, it can be fairly concluded that contempt qualifies as an infamous crime, by any reasonable, fair standard which considers either the nature of the wrong or the usual gravity of the sentence. Twentieth-century America can concern herself with procedurally protecting (as well as prosecuting) people who commit acts for which serious and unlimited prison sentences can be exacted and which are as socially grave as rationales for the contempt power imply. The right to an indictment and a grand jury hearing has already been recognized in limited contempt situations by legislation. Those areas other than civil contempts which are not now embraced by this protection should be. Society is apt to lose less by the minor delays and insignificant expenses of jury trials, than it may from the insecurity which naturally flows from inequitable treatment of its citizens. Cheap or easy convictions are not the aim of the Constitution or the Bill of Rights and, in fact, are a trifling economy in view of the losses likely to result from loose and unrestrained governmental tactics. The conclusion that contempt is a serious crime is strengthened by reference to the statutory definition of a felony (the most serious crime) as an offense punishable by death or imprisonment for a term exceeding one year.[25] Contempt frequently qualifies under this criterion, as well as having all other characteristics commonly attributed to crimes.

The other pertinent constitutional jury provisions allow even less latitude. That there shall be no trial without jury admits little interpretation. But the courts have ignored this constitutional admonition, or shrugged it off as inapplicable to contempt.

As has been described in Chapter II, the distinction between civil and criminal contempt has often been no more than a matter of hindsighted classification of characteristics. The courts are as inconsistent in their conclusions, as they are in deciding upon which characteristics to base their classification. So, while one Supreme Court was saying:

These contempts are infractions of law visited with the punishment as such. If such acts are not criminal we are in error as to the most fundamental characteristic of crimes as that word has been understood in English speech. So truly are they crimes that it seems to be proved that in the early laws they were punished only by the usual procedure. That at least in England it seems that they may be and preferably are tried in that way.[26]

another was asserting with equal authority and vigor that:

If it has ever been understood that proceedings according to the common law for contempt of court have been subject to the right of trial by jury we have been unable to find any substance of it. It has always been one of the attributes—one of the powers necessarily incident to a court of justice—that it should have this power of vindicating its dignity, or enforcing its orders, of protecting itself from insult, without the necessity of calling upon a jury to assist it in the exercise of this power.[27]

And a still more judicious, if not more perplexed, court was saying about the dichotomatic difference between criminal and civil contempts that:

It may not always be easy to classify a particular act as belonging to either one of these two classes. It may partake of the characteristics of both.[28]

The decision last quoted from held that contempt was sui generis, possessing the qualities of both civil and criminal wrongs. Indeed it does. On the authority of precedent alone, that court said that although contempt is criminal in nature, it is not criminal in the sense that the Sixth Amendment envisions. So concluding, it denied the right to a jury trial. This inconsistent, illogical judicial treatment is not unusual in contempt cases. Courts are wont to rationalize their decisions on grounds that contempt is peculiar and subject to novel treatment. Therefore, it may be considered a crime for the purposes of the statute of limitations and the pardon power, but not for the purpose of applying the venue guarantees of the Sixth Amendment.[29] Such *ad hoc* treatment is all too typical. Courts have often dipped selectively into a group of laws, applying some aspects while discarding others, and holding that contempt is what the Constitution meant by a crime in one clause but not what it envisioned in another. All this is done with vision bordering on the clairvoyant, since the authors of the Constitution left no evidence of their intent in this respect.

Through the years, different Supreme Court Justices have commented about the nonjury trial aspect of the contempt power, and their words of caution, if not prevailing as judicial policy, may indicate a growing disposition to change this feature. Justice Jackson wrote in the *Sacher* case that summary punishments must always and rightly be regarded with disfavor. In another case, the court wrote:

It is abhorrent to Anglo-Saxon justice as applied in this country that a man, however lofty his station or venerated his vestments, should have the power of taking another man's liberty from him. Society has always permitted one exception—a limited right of courts to punish for contempt. But that right has been grudgingly granted, has been held down uniformly to the least possible power adequate to the end proposed.[30]

Justice Murphy expressed this hesitancy in these words:

The contempt power is an extraordinary remedy, an exception to our tradition of fair and complete hearings. Its use should be carefully restricted. . . .[31]

And more recently, a federal court reiterated:

the grant of summary contempt power . . . is to be grudgingly construed so that the instances where there is no right to a jury trial will be narrowly restricted to the bedrock cases where the concession

of drastic power to the courts is necessary to enable them to preserve
. . . authority . . . order . . . decorum. . . .[32]

These three values—authority, order, and decorum—are currently tipping the scales away from constitutional protections of criminal defendants, though not without the aid of some judges' thumbs. These are the overriding interests which courts consider eclipse the old and cherished right to jury trial; these, and the reverence of prevailing majorities of the Supreme Court for steady, respected precedent.

This subject was treated long ago by Edward Livingston in his famous work on the penal system of New Orleans.[33] In discussing the contempt power, he noted that all the rationales giving courts broad and indefinite contempt powers are based upon necessity. This is so, even though the power itself is repugnant to all the fundamental principles of criminal justice applicable to other criminal acts. He asked: Just what is the conduct that will secure a man against a vain or vindictive judge? The judicial regard and respect which Blackstone offered as grounds for contempt (the order and respect courts now rely upon as authority for the contempt power) can only be gained by impeccable moral conduct, and not always by that. In response to the claims of necessity, Livingston wrote: "Not one of the oppressive prerogatives of which the crown has been successfully stripped in England but was and is today defended on the plea of necessity. Not one of the attempts to destroy them but was deemed a hazardous innovation." [34]

Justice Black emphasized this same point in his *Green* dissent, pointing out that necessary has come to mean expedient rather than indispensable, and it is applied too loosely to warrant derogation of fundamental constitutional rights. Quoting with agreement the suggestion of Justice Holmes that where there is no absolute need for immediate action contempts should be dealt with like other breaches of law,[35] he added that there is actually more of a need for delay to prepare and prove a case than an urgency to try it immediately, in contempt cases.

Livingston suggested that though courts may have a right of self-defense, only society as a whole has the right to punish offenses. Once the interruption to the court's proceeding ceases, the sovereign should be the only one to punish, and then only according to the procedures set out in the Constitution. It is not for the individual or for the incorporeal body that is wronged to punish. The sovereign which permits such retribution is radically defective because this gives a single party the right to punish. The necessity ends, he pointed out, with its own self-defense. The punishment should be by law only. Though a governmental body has the power of self-defense, the power to punish should be exclusively vested in society as a whole, and not in its individual departments. He compared the practices in contempt cases with the right of individuals to defend themselves against assault. Certainly an individual may defend himself. But once having defended himself, he cannot punish his assailant other than through the orderly processes of law. Livingston concluded that contempt is less a necessity for the exercise of a legal power than an engine for its abuse; and though courts should have the right to dispel interference with the performance of their functions, that power should go no further.

Still others have argued that the summariness of contempt proceedings is necessary because it speeds prosecutions, deters misconduct, avoids delay in the judicial process, and promotes the dignity of the court. True as these observances may be, it is questionable whether in our democratic society these expediences (and this is all that they are) are sufficient grounds to eclipse or ignore important procedural safeguards, such as the right to jury trial, which are so imbedded in the democratic way of life and our system of justice. And, as long ago as 1874 the Supreme Court held that contempt of court is a specific criminal offense, and the fine therefor is a criminal judgment.[36] In 1917 a federal court also ruled that a criminal contemnor can be classified as a convict.[37] Yet, arguments continued, opinions varied, and exceptions were made, so that now there is no clear answer to gain from history.

The constitutional policies are clear. Criminal contempt should be tried as other crimes are—with all procedural guarantees protecting the accused. There should be the right to a jury trial of the charged contempt. The confusion wrought from vague and misleading distinctions between civil and criminal contempts, and the stronger policies of protecting individual liberty, underscore this logical conclusion.

The argument that contempt is of a sui generis nature because it has customarily been treated peculiarly, and that it is treated this way because it is sui generis is of questionable appeal. Clearer, more directly reasoned views, such as Justice Black's comment in the *Sacher* case that "these contempt proceedings are criminal prosecutions brought to avenge an alleged public wrong"[38] are more directly reasoned, if not preferable in substance.

There are instances where an act of contempt simultaneously constitutes another crime. There, by statute, the defendant is entitled to a jury trial. This law was probably passed to avoid the circumvention of the right to a jury trial by hasty or angry judges who might treat a questioned act as contempt instead of whatever other crime it was, in order to apply the stricter contempt procedures. How, it could be asked, can an act be a crime for so many purposes[39] (perjury, bribery, etc.) and sui generis for another (contempt)?

When a man is deprived of his property or liberty as punishment for commission or omission of an act which is proscribed by society for whatever reason, he is treated as a criminal. In these contempt cases, there are no reasons strong enough to override the long- and well-established policies guaranteeing the right to be tried by a jury, after indictment and in the ordinary course of the law. The Constitution is quite clear in its directives in this respect. The policies involved go to support, at least in comparative value, the Constitution's implications.*

In the *Green* case, Justice Black thoroughly articulated the argument for reinstatement of jury protection in criminal contempt cases. With directness and eloquence that should be the standard of all who would follow this view in the future, he wrote:

The power of the judge to inflict punishment for criminal contempt by means of a summary proceeding stands as an anomaly in the law. In my judgment the time has come for a fundamental and searching reconsideration of the validity of this power which has aptly been characterized by a State Supreme Court as "perhaps, nearest akin to despotic power of any power existing under our form of government." Even though this extraordinary authority has slipped into the law as a very limited and insignificant thing, it has relentlessly swollen, at the hands of not unwilling judges, until it has become a drastic and pervasive mode of administering criminal justice usurping our regular constitutional methods of trying those charged with offenses against society. Therefore to me this case involves basic questions of the highest importance far transcending its particular facts. But the specific facts do provide a striking example of how the procedural safeguards erected by the Bill of Rights are now easily evaded by the ever-ready and boundless expedients of a judicial decree and a summary contempt proceeding. I would reject those precedents which have held that the federal courts can punish an alleged violation outside the court room of their decrees by means of a summary trial, at least as long as they can punish by severe prison sentences or fines as they now can and do. I would hold that the defendants here were entitled to be tried by a jury after indictment by a grand jury and in full accordance with all the procedural safeguards required by the Constitution for "all criminal prosecutions." I am convinced that the previous cases to the contrary are wrong—wholly wrong.[40]

* For further discussion, see author's note, p. 333.

The First Amendment

Some indirect ramifications of the exercise of the contempt power cross over lines marked caveat by the First Amendment. All contempts are in the form of speech, writings, acts of expression, or inaction. The First Amendment reads:

Congress shall make no law respecting an establishment of religion, or prohibiting the free exercise thereof; or abridging the freedom of speech, or of the press . . . or the right of people peaceably to assemble, and to petition the Government for a redress of grievances.[41]

FREEDOM OF RELIGION PROBLEMS

The freedom of religion problem arises only in few limited contempt situations. The Supreme Court of Pennsylvania in 1793 reported that in a case which was tried on a Saturday "the defendant offered Jonas Phillips, a Jew, as a witness; but he refused to be sworn, because it was his Sabbath. The court therefore fined him £10; but the defendant, afterwards, waiving the benefit of his testimony, he was discharged from the fine." [42] In a similar case, the Supreme Court, while recognizing an excuse from swearing for Quakers, denied it to a Jew, and found him in contempt for refusing to be sworn.[43] This kind of problem is now obsolete, since affirmation has generally been accepted as a substitute for the court oath.

Another area of conflict, though not yet one of serious proportions, has recently been before the courts. The Iowa Supreme Court in 1956 dealt with this situation.[44] A Protestant woman and a Catholic man married, and had a child. They were later divorced. They agreed that the mother would have custody of the child, and that she would raise him as a Roman Catholic.

Years later the father sought to have the mother punished for contempt because she was raising the child as a Protestant. The trial court decided that the mother was guilty of a contempt, but it suspended her sentence, giving her an opportunity to purge the contempt by rearing the child as a Catholic. This was a civil contempt proceeding to coerce her to act. She appealed to the state Supreme Court on the ground that this treatment violated her First Amendment freedom of religion. That court reversed the contempt conviction, but on the ground that the decree which she disobeyed was too vague and uncertain to warrant a contempt conviction for its breach.[45] The court avoided the constitutional issue raised by the First Amendment.

There is some analogous, though indirect, precedent to support this First Amendment defense. Rearing a child in a particular faith has been held to be the exercise of a religious act by the parent.[46] And the right of custody includes the right to dictate the religious teachings which one's child will receive.[47] No parental agreement about the religious education of a child is so binding that it cannot be changed without legal censure.[48] Those moral inhibitions of personal conscience which may flow from such an agreement have not been considered to be within the control of the law. This judicial attitude is a proper and natural application of the principle of nongovernmental interference with First Amendment rights by courts.[49] This principle is applicable to the states through the controls of the Fourteenth Amendment. So any official judicial enforcement of an agreement about religious participation or upbringing of a child is such state or federal action, as the case may be, as is prohibited by the First or Fourteenth Amendments.[50] The state is secular; and religious practices are separated from state control by the strong policy and language of the Constitution. An absolute wall between the two makes eminently good sense, at least in the context of the contempt problem. Any control or direction by courts over religious matters through the contempt power might tend to convert the courts into ecclesiastical bodies. This is a danger long agreed upon as avoidable. Moreover, a court should not be able to estop or control a right which is for all purposes inalienable. If the power to make such an order does not exist, disobedience cannot be a contempt.

Precedent like this does not and ought not leave the offended spouse without a remedy. The critical issue is with the nature of that remedy. Penal sanctions, such as those implicit in the civil contempt power, are not proper. The frustrated father may still seek the strictly civil, supervisory aid of the courts to protect his rights in ways less drastic than imprisonment of his spouse.

Only the gravest social necessities, those about which all of the secular world would agree, should be deemed sufficient enough to warrant any governmental curtailment of rights of religious participation. Those instances should be strictly limited by the courts to matters involving the utmost social cost.[51] Even there, it is questionable whether the contempt power is the most suitable vehicle of control.

The issue which this last case raised could, under the present unpredictable status of the contempt power, fission into several tangential problems. The matrimonial, surrogate, and juvenile courts[52] are frequently called upon to deal with situations involving questions of freedom of religion. There are countless instances in which these courts might feel compelled to exercise their contempt power. Yet, there is no clear cut resolution of the problems raised by the First Amendment's guarantee of religious liberty by the contempt cases to date. Better reason would suggest abstinence by the courts in this area, at least in so far as their exercise of the contempt power is concerned.

FREEDOM OF SPEECH AND OF THE PRESS

The free speech and press cases in which the judicial contempt power has been questioned might by analogy offer some formula for the First Amendment contempt conflicts. In these cases, the courts have adopted a strictly construed clear-and-present danger test for balancing the exercise of First Amendment rights which are in conflict with other interests which are often augmented by the sanction of the contempt power.[53]

This doctrine gradually evolved from the long-fought battle within the United States Supreme Court concerning contempt by press publications in this country. As detailed in Chapter II, the United States and England have long wrestled with the problem of maintaining a free press consonant with a system of fair trials.[54] Often, the two goals have conflicted, and presently, both countries treat the problem with opposite applications of the same contempt power.[55]

In this country, the contempt-by-the-press problem began as one of interpretation of the federal contempt statute. Courts were given the power to punish contempts in their presence "or so near thereto as to obstruct the administration of justice." The latter clause was first applied in its causal connotation.[56] Application of the contempt sanction was left to the discretion of the judge, who could punish the press if its comments had a reasonable tendency to obstruct justice. This approach was changed in 1940, when the Supreme Court decided that the quoted words from the federal statute should be interpreted in a physical rather than causal context.[57] "Since most press publication occurs neither in the presence of the court nor 'near thereto' geographically, the power to punish contemptuous publications was made ineffectual."[58] Soon thereafter, the Court more directly recognized the First Amendment issues, and adopted and applied Justice Holmes's clear and present danger test[59] to press comments about pending cases.[60] The rule was applied to the contempt powers of both the federal and state courts. Justice Black has referred to the clear and present danger test as "a working principle that the substantive evil must be extremely serious and the degree of

imminence extremely high before utterances can be punished." [61]
The evils envisioned in the contempt by publication cases are
disrespect to the judiciary, and interference with the administration of justice. Through the years, the Supreme Court has not
allowed the exercise of the contempt power in the former instance. Their rationale has been that judges should be above
personal attack, and that popular respect is less apt to be gained
from the exercise of the contempt power than from exemplary
judicial standards subject to free criticism. "The assumption,"
Justice Black noted, "that respect for the judiciary can be won
by shielding judges from published criticism wrongly appraises
the character of American public opinion." [62]

Though recognizing the possibility of contempt treatment in
the second category of press comments (interference with the
administration of justice) courts have been chary to find the
instance where the need to protect the fairness of trials overrode
the value to be gained from allowing free discussion. These cases
indicate that the courts in their decisions are more concerned
with the free press–fair trial civil liberties conflict than with developing a consistent doctrine with respect to the power to punish
contempts by publication on theories bedded in the contempt
power itself. "The Supreme Court's formula seems to grant the
press a virtual immunity from contempt rather than resolve its
historic struggle with the courts. Nevertheless, the actual scope
of the immunity continues to be uncertain." [63]

Though the Supreme Court's majority disposition has been to
thus limit contempt against the press, a minority of that court has
consistently sought a broadening of the scope of the power in
these cases. However, the court has only recognized press abuse
under the due process clause, where press commentary made a
fair trial impossible. Moreover, the clear and present danger test
has been somewhat extended in other than contempt cases by
emphasizing the magnitude of the danger of the evil as an aspect

of its imminence.[64] A change in personnel on the court might tip the balance in favor of the Frankfurter-led minority, who are now disposed toward extension of the contempt power in these cases in emulation of the English courts.

Individuals, on the whole, have not fared as well as the press in avoiding contempt convictions for what might otherwise be considered the exercise of First Amendment rights. In one case, the United States Supreme Court upheld the contempt conviction of an attorney who disobeyed a trial court's admonition to be silent about a certain matter in his summation to the jury.[65] Justice Black, for a four-man minority, wrote in his dissent to that case: "Fisher having been stopped at one point tried another strategy. He was acting the role of a resourceful lawyer. The decision which penalizes him for that zeal sanctions censorship inside a courtroom where the ideals of freedom of speech should flourish." [66]

Another attorney was fined $1,000 and imprisoned by a state court for six months for a contempt which consisted of a series of critical letters and articles about the state judiciary.[67] A television announcer was found in contempt for comments made "over the air" about parties to a pending divorce proceeding.[68] The remarks were in response to personal claims made against him in the divorce action. The trial court exercised its contempt power there because it thought the administration of justice was impaired.[69] A single letter to a judge was considered contemptuous,[70] while an advertisement by an insurance company about excessive verdicts and their economic effect on the public was held not to be a clear and present danger to the administration of justice.[71] The latter case came thirty years after the former, though both arose in California. A more recent case dealt with an avid segregationist who made a rousing speech to 1,500 people, urging disobedience to federal court orders regarding the integration of Tennessee public schools.[72] He spoke in violation of an injunction against interference with the courts' integration order. The court upheld a contempt conviction and ruled that the conduct of the contemnor was not protected by the First Amendment. Since the right of free speech is not absolute, it can be subordinated to legitimate and overriding governmental objectives. The segregationist had created a clear and present danger of public violence, and it was held that the First Amendment did not give the right to incite others to break the law.

The cases in this area are too numerous to list comprehensively. Since most disobedience which would constitute a contempt is involved in some act which might well come within the protection of the First Amendment, the possibilities of conflict are myriad. One can examine any contempt case, and the chances are high that it involves some form of speech when silence was appropriate, or silence when speech was demanded.

This problem is most vexing with respect to the conduct of lawyers in the course of trials. At what point does the proper zeal of advocacy end and contumacy begin? Although, on the one hand, attorneys should be given the broadest margin to advocate their clients' causes effectively, on the other, they are officers of the court with a professional interest in the fair and respectful administration of justice.

There is as yet no satisfactory answer to this dilemma, and courts have treated these situations in an *ad hoc* fashion. Recently, the Supreme Court disposed of two such cases. *In re McConnell* [73] dealt with an attorney who violated a court order to discontinue an offer of proof which the attorney felt in good faith was required by the Federal Rules of Criminal Procedure. The court summarily found him in contempt for obstructing the administration of justice. The Supreme Court reversed the conviction, stating that a lawyer's arguments for his client do not amount to contempt of court unless they so exceed the line of duty as to constitute an obstruction of the performance of judicial duties.

Surely this line of demarcation is so vague and subjective as to provide little if any reasonably foreseeable standard or guide. The second case, *In re Green*,[74] dealt with an attorney who advised a union client to test the validity of a state court injunction because only the NLRB had jurisdiction to issue the requested order. The court found the attorney in contempt without a hearing. The Supreme Court reversed this conviction on the ground that it violated the due process clause of the Fourteenth Amendment and did not reach the First Amendment issue.

The status of the individual who claims that the First Amendment shields him from the contempt power of the courts is less certain than the status of the same person who writes the same comments in a newspaper or magazine. In either situation, the clear and present danger test will usually be applied, but with less certain expectation of sympathetic judicial reaction for the individual. There are no clear policies or doctrines or trends. Analogy with the press cases would indicate a liberal stance since the dangers of true interference with proceedings by the press are greater than those which might be caused by individuals. The courts' leniency in the press cases has been consistent. The lower courts have taken a case-by-case approach in nonpress cases, and no *cause célèbre* or precedent-setting case has reached the United States Supreme Court which might hint of a settled attitude. Nevertheless, though the actual interference with the administration of justice by an individual would, in most cases, be less than that of the ubiquitous and powerful press, the individual's greater susceptibility to contempt conviction is indicated by the decisions. Possibly this is explained by the fact that so many cases of contempt by individuals arise out of personal incidents involving affronts to judges. Though the wrong to society in such a case is unquestionably less than the situation where the press actively invades a trial, the result in terms of responsibility is often opposite. There is a danger that these convictions realistically may be more a result of governmental power being exercised for personal or emotional reasons than a desire to foster the efficient administration of justice. Of course, this is a speculation which can never be proved or disproved. It may, as well, be a manifestation of the long inculcated American attitude favoring judicial power and the necessity of contempt law.

Acceptance of what is now a minority view, that First Amendment rights are absolutes, would clearly resolve all these issues. The wisdom as well as the popularity of such an attitude is open to debate, which it is not the function of this book to include or evaluate, except in so far as it affects the present subject. In the contempt context, it is not unreasonable to suggest a complete First Amendment protection of the press. Since judges may be left to private actions for defamatory criticism by the press and ought to be able to withstand nondefamatory criticism, the principle reason for the constructive contempt power is to protect the fairness of the trial itself. This can be accomplished in ways less calculated to interfere with vital constitutional rights like freedom of the press. In nonpress cases, a more restricted freedom has prevailed, though the power to affect trials is generally less than that of the press. It could be argued that the contempt power should be changed in this respect too. This will be discussed in greater depth in the concluding chapter.

Some distinction between fair comment and other verbal activity might be developed, which would recognize the right of press or individual editorializing or opinion-venturing, but outlaw the kind of speech which is really no more than verbal misconduct of a slanderous or clearly obstructive nature. This, too, provides only a vague standard.

The First Amendment claim for freedom of the press can arise in congressional contempt cases, too. This point was raised in the recent *Russell* case,[75] which involved six contempt of Congress convictions against men of the press who refused to answer questions of a congressional subcommittee investigating Communist infiltration of the American press. Their contempt convictions were reversed by the Supreme Court on the ground that the indictments in their cases failed to identify the subject of the congressional inquiry. Since the history of the congressional contempt power showed that the pertinency of the questions was vital, the indictment had to state the purpose of the question. Otherwise, the defendant would not be apprised of what he must defend against, and the court cannot decide the issue of pertinency.

Although the majority opinion spoke about Fifth and Sixth Amendment safeguards in federal criminal cases, and applied them to contempt of Congress cases, Justice Douglas spoke of the First Amendment in his concurring opinion. He felt that the First Amendment precluded a conviction in this case because Congress' power to inform goes only so far as its power to legislate, and here there was no power to legislate. His opinion raises a difficult point. Does the fact that one is a member of the press absolutely preclude his being questioned by Congress? If Congress is engaged in legitimate fact-finding, it is questionable whether it should be automatically fobbed off because its witness is a reporter or a member of the clergy or a public speaker. The issue is whether the question invades the freedom of the reporter, the freedom of religion of the clergy, or the right to speak of the speaker. It may not. And, if not, the status of the witness should not raise an automatic wall to separate him from any other man properly called as a witness. I should think that this would be a question of fact in each case. Does the question to the newspaperman invade his right as a journalist, or is it a question dealing with matters apart from his freedom to report? In the former instance, there is a First Amendment question; in the latter there is not. And the witness' status as a reporter is not necessarily determinative of this distinction.

The eloquent thought and words of Justice Brandeis, as expressed in his famous concurrence in the *Whitney* case,[76] echo over this issue as they have over other issues in the past. Authority must be reconciled with freedom; order should not be exalted over liberty.

order cannot be secured merely through fear of punishment for its infraction . . . it is hazardous to discourage thought, hope and imagination . . . fear breeds repression . . . repression breeds hate . . . hate menaces stable government . . . the path of safety lies in the opportunity to discuss freely. . . .

Congressional Contempt Cases

"The legislature is free to determine the kinds of data that should be collected. It is only those investigations that are conducted by use of compulsory process that give rise to a need to protect the rights of individuals against illegal encroachment." [77]

The First Amendment has played a vital and changing role in the congressional contempt cases. Here, where the court procedures accompanying statutory contempt of Congress convictions are the same and therefore as fair as those applicable to criminal trials in general, the problem has been more one of quantity than quality. The contempt power has been exercised by Congress with increasing frequency and, indeed, has typified one of the more deep and troublesome political conflicts of the mid-twentieth century—the increase of governmental investigative powers and their effect upon individual liberty and privacy. The issue has manifested itself in the form of several First Amendment conflicts—freedom of association, rights of speech and silence, and even the right to petition. Though the First Amendment issue does not arise in the congressional contempt case as directly as other constitutional issues such as the right to trial by jury, it has been a most asserted claim and has provoked a deep and philosophical contemporary problem.

Who is to prevail when a legislative body in the name of the national interest imposes its questions upon a witness who refuses to testify because publication of his ideas, associations, or politics would violate his personal privacy, or would subject him to serious public scorn, economic loss, or actual personal harm? Where this has been the case, men have sought the shield of the First Amendment, and asserted its protection of ideas, associations, and privacy. Courts have not uniformly agreed who should prevail in these contests, and the result has been claims of abuse by both advocates of greater legislative powers and advocates of broader protections of civil liberties.

THE RISE OF CONGRESSIONAL INVESTIGATIONS

The frequent implementation of the congressional contempt power has been synonymous with a corresponding rise in the activity of legislative investigations in the past few decades. It has already been tellingly illustrated that congressional investigations have drastically changed in both kind and quantity in the past twenty-five years.[78]

The first congressional investigation took place in 1792; it was an inquiry into the failure of a military expedition and the slaughter of soldiers at the hands of Indian tribes of the Northwest Territory. For the next one hundred years in American history, congressional investigations were usually confined to civilian and military operations of the executive branch of the federal government. In the period from 1792 until 1942, there were only 600 congressional investigations and only 108 contempt citations.[79] This means that in the first 150 years of congressional investigations, there was an average of four investigations each year, and an average of less than one citation for contempt each year. However, this conservative average did not continue, but in fact radically changed.

Starting in the 1930s, our country encountered a national economic depression, a catastrophic world war waged in two hemispheres which seriously threatened the nation's security and survival, and finally the rise of Communism and its threats of ideological destruction of all its foes in the free world. No wonder then that national security and the fear of subversion should have become prime concerns of our people and government. Along with prosecutions for subversion, the enactment of loyalty and security legislation, and a general concern for the national welfare came the assertion of greater powers by legislative investigating committees. Few could fairly criticize the purported noble and necessary goals of these investigations. But serious and profound questions can and have been raised about the extent and nature of these investigations and the societal problems they have caused.

In his book *Contempt of Congress*, Professor Beck has shown that in the thirteen years between 1944 and 1957 there were 226 citations for contempt of Congress.[80] The House Un-American Activities Committee alone held 230 public hearings from 1945 through 1957. Three thousand people were called to testify at these hearings, and 135 were cited for contempt.[81] This fantastic increase cannot be wholly due to either a corresponding quantity of new legislative problems and functions or a sudden ill-founded increase in individual recalcitrance. It may as well be an effect of psychological fears and anxieties which have spurred legislative activity either to quiet the fears of the legislators themselves, or to respond to the anxieties of the voting populace. The contempt power has been the wedge with which the legislative investigating committees have been able to force into areas hitherto protected by the First Amendment, if not by individual restraint.

Another difference in the recent congressional investigations, beside their increase in number, has been their change in nature. In modern times, the contempt power has characteristically been used by congressional committees of from one to any number of congressmen. This practice of using committees to conduct congressional work was first applied in 1827, and then only after serious debate within the Congress about its propriety. Indeed, one commentator has written that the British Parliament differs from our Congress in this one tremendous feature: It is in the full assembly of the House, not in its committees, that the center of authority over political principles and action is located.[82] In this respect, there has also developed a difference from the historical American contempt power which was originally exercised by the Congress as a body. The increase and diversity of congressional business has occasioned an era of considerable committee work, and these committees have been vested with the contempt power to assure their effectiveness. However, committee use of the power misses that aggregate and deliberative representational aspect which the contempt power originally included, and is more subject to individual use and abuse by frustrated or angered legislators operating for but out of Congress. Professor Beck pointed out in his study that "of the 226 contempt citations presented to both Houses of Congress by fourteen committees in the period from 1945 to 1957, few were debated in either the House or the Senate and none was defeated; few were even discussed; many were approved en masse." [83] He also concluded that the whole function of contempt convictions has recently changed from coercion of cooperation to punishment.

Still another difficulty in framing the prime issue between contempt and the First Amendment has been the discernment of the proper extent of legislative inquiry. The difficulties encountered in resolving the First Amendment versus congressional contempt problem are compounded by the imprecision of and the lack of agreement about the bounds of either force. It has been written that the limits of legislative inquiry are the limits of legislative powers of contempt.[84] That statement somewhat begs the question of the past few decades, which is what the limit of legislative inquiries should properly be. The limits of

rights asserted under the First Amendment have been so con-
tentiously debated that I, wary of digression, will venture to
offer my specifications only in the context of the instant conflict
between the amendment and the legislative contempt power.

What is the jurisdiction of Congress, and what are the contours of that right of privacy of citizens which the First Amendment keeps free from legislative penetration?

THE LIMITS OF LEGISLATIVE POWERS

The power to legislate was early interpreted to include the
power to obtain information needed for the exercise of that
power.[85] Thus, the contempt power was extended and applied
for the compulsion of both personal and documentary evidence
pertinent to any proper congressional inquiry. As time and
political climates changed, the conceded purposes of the legislature have become threefold: strictly legislative (recommendations for the development, modernization, and implementation of
legislation), supervisory (controlling agencies that administer
laws relating to subjects of legislative concern), and educational
(an informing function, by which areas of national concern are
watchdogged, and the public is kept enlightened).[86]

It is mainly this latter aspect of the legislature's power which
has provoked the recent conflicts with the First Amendment. It
has been vehemently argued that the right to investigate and the
duty to inform should not include the right to expose for mere
exposure's sake. If it did, the argument continues, short-term gains
would be eventually eclipsed by long-term ruin of cherished
American liberties. So, the drastic increase in legislative investigations in the 1940s and 1950s has been accompanied by bitter
criticism. And, the investigating committees have been likened to
"roving satrapies unrestrained" and intruding into "every kind of
public and private business."[87] More extreme and vituperative
epithets have been legion. The contempt power has been the

prime offender in this fight, since without it the problem would greatly diminish, if not vanish. Those who were willing to assist the legislature would; those who did not would not, and would not suffer for their feelings; and the legislative problems that arose from this noncooperation would be resolved in other ways, less destructive of constitutional privileges.

Indications do not point in this direction. Legislative committees have increased and seized upon emotive areas of popular appeal and concern to investigate. Difficult as it is to attack the committee's noble assertions of goals, an era of constitutional uncertainty has resulted, as have a great number of contempt convictions against those who have chosen not to accede to governmental pressures. One federal judge, in discussing the most active and controversial House Un-American Activities Committee, wrote that though "there are no bounds to its exerted and asserted powers" it has nonetheless characteristically "avoided the suggestion of legislation." [88] His dissent to a congressional contempt conviction on the ground that it unconstitutionally interfered with First Amendment rights of speech and expression was forceful and eloquent. The Supreme Court refused to review that case.[89] The same issue was soon again commented on similarly by another federal judge.[90] His dissent came in a case which upheld a contempt of Congress conviction, which dealt with a refusal to deliver subpoenaed organization books to the House Committee on Un-American Activities. In discussing the balance between congressional investigative demands and First Amendment freedoms, he argued that the latter must occupy a preferred position.

LEGISLATIVE CONFLICTS WITH THE FIRST AMENDMENT

This attitude brings us to the opposing interest in this constant legal, political, and philosophical tug-of-war. What is the extent of the protections afforded by the First Amendment? If we agree that rights, which are invaded by a congressional investigation, fall within areas protected by the First Amendment, does it mean that the legislature must automatically step aside; or is the issue one of balancing both the national and the individual rights involved and making case-by-case decisions; or is the national interest so clearly one of primacy that it must prevail in all cases of such conflict?

THE ABSOLUTE RIGHT OF THE LEGISLATURE

Interestingly, the latter course is scarcely suggested even by the most zealous advocates of legislative committees. Yet, one might well hark back to the case of Andrew Jackson mentioned in Chapter I, and repeat his claim that the national security and welfare must prevail in cases of conflict with individuals, for without national security there can be no individual security. This argument could be made on the practical ground that if the country loses a worldwide ideological or physical war with its enemies, or if the legislature is prevented from coping with national domestic problems, none of the Bill of Rights will be worth the paper on which it is written. The theoretical grounds for such an attitude would be that all individual rights in a republic derive from an over-all sovereign sanctity, and interference with the latter necessarily interferes with the former, much in the same way as a pebble tossed in a pond is the cause of all of the ripples which result. Therefore, the national interest is always, of necessity, greater than the individual.

In a recent contempt of Congress case, Justice Black described the reason which may well lurk behind the lack of serious acceptance of this argument. There, he wrote that if all that was required to allow a congressional contempt conviction was some vague claim of a legitimate national interest, no individual would be safe from governmental harassment, because "any first-year law school student worth his salt could construct a rationalization to justify almost any question put to any witness at any time." [91] Though some extremists might defend this attitude of absolute legislative predominance, its general acceptance is remote in the absence of enormous changes in governmental personnel and popular ideals about the extent of the Constitution's protection of civil liberties. Even though some judicial decisions have condoned the broadest legislative freedom, it is still reasonable to assume some legislative self-restraint and constitutional responsibility. One need only look at those totalitarian regimes extant in the world today to recognize the dangers of absolute governmental power.

THE ABSOLUTE PROTECTION OF THE
FIRST AMENDMENT

As there are people who fear that any absolute governmental power will lead to totalitarianism, so are there those who fear that absolute individual freedom would lead to anarchy. So, the attitude that the First Amendment protects absolutely when in conflict with governmental power has not been generally asserted or accepted. Justice Black has been the foremost advocate for the most liberal construction of First Amendment freedoms, but his theories have seldom prevailed. In his dissent to the *Barenblatt* case, Justice Black clearly stated the applicability of this theory to the congressional contempt conflict in these words: "I do not agree that laws directly abridging First Amendment freedoms can be justified by a congressional or judicial balancing process."

His position has been that "there are absolutes in our Bill of Rights, and that they were put there on purpose by men who knew what words meant, and meant their prohibitions to be absolutes." [92] The fact that our Constitution is a single, written document defining and specifically limiting governmental powers, the supremacy of our Constitution over the legislature, the separation of governmental powers along with the system of checks and balances, the creation of an independent judiciary with powers to review legislation for constitutionality—these are the underlying reasons for viewing certain of the Bill of Rights absolute. These, along with the clear language of the First Amendment "Congress shall make no law . . . abridging freedom of speech . . . or of the press . . . or . . . to assemble and to petition" lead disciples of this school of thought to the conclusion that Congress may not punish through its contempt power, if it punishes the exercise of some First Amendment right. These rights should be beyond the reach of the government. If indeed all governmental power was withdrawn from certain areas by the First Amendment, our legal problem would vanish as quickly as it would were we to accept the first position, that all individual rights must succumb to overriding governmental interests. Perhaps the new problems it might provoke would be as great. In any event, we are a far way from popular agreement with this attitude.

A COMPROMISE APPROACH

Perhaps inevitably then, the middle ground "balancing" approach has been adopted by the courts, who, in conflicts like those under discussion, have attempted to strike a balance between the interests of the legislature, on the one hand, and the interests of the individual, on the other. This formulation is to some people a death blow to civil liberties and a poor legal scheme, though it may sound quite sensible and rational in its mere postulation. Justice Black pointed out that under any balancing scheme the Bill of Rights would inevitably suffer, since in times of dire emergencies few would sacrifice the national interest of the momemnt. As hard cases make bad law, he urges that these are the times when the potency of the Bill of Rights must be preserved, if it is ever to be of value.

The balancing approach also revitalizes the legislature's power to a point which the Black school would consider violated our separation of powers doctrine by insulating the legislature from any judicial control. Recent congressional contempt cases indicate that this balancing approach is what is currently most satisfactory, at least to a majority of the present Supreme Court.

It might be questioned whether this approach in effect really recognizes any preferred or sacred aspect of the First Amendment, and if so how that can be judiciously balanced against equally compelling legislative demands. In a recent case, Justice Harlan upholding a contempt conviction, stated that the nature of the activity under legislative investigation establishes the government's overbalancing interest whether or not the particular conduct in question is protected by the First Amendment.[93] This language does not bespeak even a balance, though the court indicated that balancing it was. Moreover, such a balancing approach ignores the weighty interest of the public in the constitutional rights of all individuals, the heart of the philosophy of First Amendment freedoms. This idea will be further explored at a later point.

Granting that almost all conflicts in the congressional contempt cases involve First Amendment claims, where does this balancing approach leave matters? Every case will balance a legislative need with a First Amendment claim, no matter how remote or vital each really is. Every decision will then merely reflect a value preference by a majority of a court. Often one man's set of values will be determinative since a 5–4 majority may prevail. That this is so often the case with constitutional issues before the Supreme Court hardly lessens the dissatisfaction one may have with the results of this balancing approach.

In fact, the balancing approach depends upon little more than the predispositions or working theories of the individual decision-makers. Some judges have ruled that any valid legislative interest outweighs the individual's First Amendment loss. Others have argued that First Amendment rights are entitled to a preferred, more weighty position in any conflict. One is left wondering whether there is any science involved in the balancing approach, or whether it is really anything more than a question of judicial preference of choices, with the weight being heaviest where the weigher wants it. Certainly this balancing approach underscores the political nature of the federal courts, especially the Supreme Court, by which the attitudes of the personnel may alone predetermine the balance which decisions will make.

Justice Black critically summarized the effect of the balancing test upon the congressional contempt conflict thusly:

To apply the Court's balancing test under such circumstances is to read the First Amendment to say "Congress shall pass no law abridging freedom of speech, press, assembly and petition, unless Congress and the Supreme Court reach the joint conclusion that on balance the interest of the Government in stifling these freedoms is greater than the interest of the people in having them exercised." [94]

In a later case, a more frustrated Justice Black said that this balancing test in effect balances away the First Amendment.[95]

THE CASES

Let us now see how these general theories have been applied in the landmark cases which gradually evolved the law with respect to congressional investigations, contempt powers, and the First Amendment.

As all roads are said to lead to Rome, all discussions about congressional investigatory powers must lead back to a common origin—*Kilbourn v. Thompson*. The *Kilbourn* case [96] discussed in Chapter I not only dealt with the historical antecedents of the legislative contempt power, but also set the tone for future debate about the confines of that power. In that case, the oft-quoted statement was first made:

no person can be punished for contumacy as a witness before either house, unless his testimony is required in a matter into which that house has jurisdiction to inquire, and we feel equally sure that neither of these bodies possesses the general power of making inquiry into the private affairs of the citizen.[97]

With gradual changes in the nature of legislative work, this clear and graphic rule sprouted exceptions and deviations, and the law has grown irregularly and unpredictably in its trail. Fifth Amendment cases made inroads on the "outroads" cut by modern legislative activity. These issues will be discussed under a separate section dealing with the Fifth Amendment. The development of First Amendment arguments to meet extensions of legislative activity has evolved gradually and indirectly. After broad judicial condonations of Fifth Amendment defenses to congressional investigations, the active committees altered their tactics somewhat and began questioning witnesses as much about others and organizations as about themselves. Here, the Fifth Amendment could be no defense. Individuals rebelled and groped for some constitutional protection for that which might be termed matters of conscience. The odious stigma which gradually became attached to Fifth Amendment defenses caused those who did not want to cooperate to seek new protections, less loaded with indirect personal injury. Was there some safe place for the individual to seek sanctity from his past? Was there some zone of silence where he could keep his political beliefs private? The turn was to the First Amendment, and its protection of associations, speech, and petition. At first, these arguments were overridden,[98] but forceful dissenting opinions foreshadowed what was to be one of the most volatile and interesting legal disputes of current times—the invasion of First Amendment freedoms by the legislature through use of its contempt power. Recent conflicts have brought the issue more obviously to the surface, and though the cases have not clearly answered the basic question, a consideration of some of these decisions will indicate the current status of the law in this area.

The congressional contempt power, not expressly conferred by the Constitution, was implied for reasons of efficiency and power, but not as a means for punishment of private matters.[99] Legislation and cases following the *Kilbourn* decision further confined the scope of the congressional contempt power. The federal statute describing the power was interpreted to apply against only willful refusal to answer pertinent questions.[100] Judicial decisions soon interpreted these words so that "a witness rightfully may refuse to answer" where the questions are not pertinent to the matter under inquiry.[101] Further, the courts held that the pertinency of the question was an essential element of the offense of contempt of Congress [102] which the government must prove and the witness cannot waive. Other constitutional limitations, such as those within the Fifth Amendment, were also added by judicial interpretation as qualifications of this legislative punishing power.

The spirit of these rules was stated to be such that it behooves courts to zealously protect individual rights in these cases, without fear of interfering with governmental bodies, because of the natural vagueness shrouding legislative inquiries, and the invasionary quality of the power in general.

Gradually, the issues changed from questions about the province of congressional contempt powers to questions about the conflicts between those proper powers and the civil liberties of individuals. As Chief Justice Warren mentioned in one case, the Court's early decisions "defined the scope of investigative power in terms of the inherent limitations of the sources of that power," while the more recent cases have shifted the emphasis of judicial review "to problems of accommodating the interest of the Government with the rights and privileges of individuals." [103]

The applicability of First Amendment defenses to congressional investigations and contempt powers was then firmly stated by the Supreme Court. Chief Justice Warren wrote in the *Watkins* case:

Clearly an investigation is subject to the command that Congress shall make no law abridging freedom of speech or press or assembly. While it is true that there is no statute to be reviewed, and that an investigation is not a law, nevertheless an investigation is part of lawmaking. It is justified solely as an adjunct to the legislative process. The First Amendment may be invoked against infringement of the protected freedoms by law or by lawmaking. [104]

Soon, in another case, the Chief Justice wrote:

It is particularly important that the exercise of the power of compulsory process be carefully circumscribed when the investigative process tends to impinge upon such highly sensitive areas as free speech or press, freedom of political association, and freedom of communication of ideas. [105]

The Chief Justice's dictum in the *Watkins* case was heralded by many civil libertarians as the beginning of a new era for broad judicial protection of individuals at the hands of investigatory bodies. However, a later case quickly changed their hope and praise to criticism and despair.

In the *Watkins* case, the court overruled a contempt of Congress conviction of a labor leader, who was described as being a Communist. Watkins answered the committee's questions about himself, but refused to testify about the political affiliations of other people. The Supreme Court based its decision on narrow procedural grounds. All inquiries must be pertinent to a proper legislative purpose, which purpose must be made crystal clear to the witness in order that he can judge the relevancy of the question before his decision to refuse to answer. Justice Warren, writing the majority decision, included broad language which seemed to sate those of the watching world who desired judicial condemnation of legislative exposure tactics. Prior cases of the Court had indicated that the legislative investigatory power could not be used to delve into private affairs which were not related to proper legislative purposes, nor to extend into areas in which the Congress could not act. Nonetheless, congressional committeemen reasserted the propriety of committee exposure tactics, and committees sometimes acted with that as their primary goal. In *Watkins*, the Chief Justice warned that there should be no unlimited right to expose private affairs by the legislative branch of government.

Many thought, or at least hoped, that Chief Justice Warren's dictum in the *Watkins* case finally resolved the matter. But Justice Frankfurter added a concurring opinion in that case, in which he confined his vote to the limited procedural point which he felt was the nub of the case. In retrospect, his attitude seems to have indicated the change which was to come but a few years later, when, as Professor Gellhorn put it "the Chief Justice's ringing declarations lost some of their ring." [106]

The Supreme Court was called upon in 1959 to review the contempt of Congress conviction of Lloyd Barenblatt, a young teacher at Vassar, who refused to answer questions of the House Un-American Activities Committee concerning his past political affiliations. [107] Barenblatt based his refusal on the First Amendment's protection of his personal and associational affairs. A majority of the court, to the surprise of many who were still elated over the previous *Watkins* decision, upheld the conviction. The legislative purpose, this majority held, was clear when read in the light of the "persuasive gloss of legislative history." The court declined to face the broader issues and claimed that its function was to deal only with the particulars of the individual case and not to pass judgment upon investigating committees in general, the Un-American Activities Committee in particular, the propriety of exposure tactics, or the extent of First Amendment protections (though here the First Amendment was put directly in issue).

The advocates of the seemingly broader *Watkins* rule hardly had time to assuage their wounds or understand the resulting confusion caused by the *Barenblatt* case, before the Supreme Court dealt what may have been an even more severe blow to the critics of investigating committees. This came in the Supreme Court's decisions in the "sister" cases, *Braden v. U.S.*,[108] and *Wilkinson v. U.S.*[109] Because these cases involved most of the basic theoretical First Amendment issues which have been provoked if not raised by many of the congressional contempt cases, their analysis is warranted before undertaking an examination of the constitutional issues themselves. A statement of these cases and an examination of their implications should amply illustrate the status of the instant problem as of 1963.

Carl Braden was a longtime controversial character in Southern liberal movements. In 1958, he sent a letter to the United States House of Representatives, in which he solicited help for the cause of integration and requested that the House Un-American Activities Committee not be sent to the South. His reason for the latter request was that the committee's presence would deter white people from supporting integration for fear of being investigated and labeled subversive. The letter also pointed out several civil liberty problems in the South, and criticized the committee for neglecting them in its investigations of un-American activities. Soon thereafter, Braden was subpoenaed to appear before the House Un-American Activities Committee in Georgia. There, he testified about preliminary matters, but refused to testify about certain matters having to do with his associations. Braden based his refusal to answer this question on the

First Amendment, and the argument that the question was beyond the scope of pertinent investigation.

The key question giving rise to his contempt of the committee was whether he was a Communist at the time he signed a second letter. It is worthwhile to digress momentarily to describe the circumstances surrounding this second letter.

In 1954, Braden was convicted of sedition in Kentucky.[110] The state prosecution was alleged to have been assisted by the same House committee. The charge of sedition arose out of an incident which began with the purchase of a home by Braden in a white neighborhood, and its later resale to a Negro friend. Soon, Braden's home was bombed by members of the irate white community, and when local authorities entered to investigate the bombing, they found a book on communism in his home. This book provided the basis for the sedition charge against Braden, to wit: advocating violent political revolution to modify the United States government and the Commonwealth of Kentucky. After serving some of his sentence, Braden was dismissed because the Supreme Court ruled in another case that national sedition was not a proper matter for local prosecution.

Braden later wrote the letter in question. This letter was sent by him and his wife to unidentified people, between the time of his sedition trial and the date he met the House committee in Altanta, Georgia. The letter opposed certain proposed federal legislation, which was aimed at nullifying the decision of the Supreme Court in the case dealing with state power to punish sedition—the very case which was the basis for his release from prison. The letter expressed the fear that if the legislation was passed giving local prosecutors the power to punish sedition, every unpopular or dissident individual in the South would be at the mercy of these prosecutors, many of whom consider dissident ideas seditious. The letter also pointed out that this legislation would divert and hinder the integration movement in the South.

Did Braden's conviction for refusal to answer these questions violate his First Amendment rights of petition, of association, or of silence? His refusal to testify came at a time after the *Watkins* decision, but before the Supreme Court's decision in the *Barenblatt* case, and was specifically based on the majority opinion in *Watkins*. The Supreme Court upheld Braden's contempt of Congress conviction, stating merely that the congressional inquiry was a proper one, and that the witness had been apprised of the pertinency of the question. The fact that the question related to First Amendment rights, the majority held, should no more protect the witness in this case than did the fact that the question in the *Barenblatt* case related to education, which is also a legitimate activity.

Again Justice Black wrote for the dissenting minority. Again, he voiced his belief that the dangers to democracy are best fought in the free marketplace of ideas, associations, and petitions, and that punishment, directly or indirectly, of these freedoms is the quickest way to national self-destruction. No number of laws, he has said, can have as much effect on a person's political convictions as that which comes from hearing arguments and rejecting them, or from recognizing the worthlessness of tenets once accepted. Criticizing the majority opinion for balancing away the First Amendment by making it a mere avoidable admonition, he dramatically warned: "There are grim reminders all around this world that the distance between individual liberty and firing squads is not always as far as it seems."

Wilkinson was the next witness called by the same committee. He had been identified as a former member of the Communist Party, and he refused to answer the committee's question about this political affiliation. The court, noting that Wilkinson "was not summoned to appear until after he had arrived in Atlanta as a representative of a group carrying on a public campaign to abolish the House Committee," but refusing to condemn the committee's motives, upheld his conviction for contempt of Congress. Harking back to its decision in *Barenblatt*, a majority of the Court held that it is now clear that "the nature of the Communist activity involved, whether the momentary conduct is legitimate or illegitimate politically . . . establishes the Government's over-balancing interest."

Justice Black dissented and summarized the effect of the majority decision as condoning "an attempt by the Un-American Activities Committee to use the contempt power of the House of Representatives as a weapon against those who dare to criticize it." Against such a formidable opponent, he urged, few will have the courage to criticize for fear of intimidation. About the majority's contention that identification as a Communist establishes a proper legislative interest, Justice Black pointed out that this charge is one "so common that hardly anyone active in public life escapes it." And finally Justice Black voiced his ultimate answer to the arguments about national interests in security and well-being: "true Americanism is to be protected, not by committees that persecute unorthodox minorities, but by strict adherence to basic principles of freedom that are responsible for this Nation's greatness."

The *Braden* and *Wilkinson* decisions provoke four general theories which have been advanced against convictions in many of the congressional contempt cases. These issues can be summarized as follows: Does the policy of the First Amendment include some protection of the freedom of silence; the right of spiritual or intellectual privacy; or the tangential interest of the general public in the First Amendment freedoms of all individuals? One other argument is that committee exposure tactics are in effect unconstitutional bills of attainder. None of these theories has been fully accepted or directly rejected. There are only isolated indications of partial acceptance or rejection. Since it has been reported that there were approximately forty similar cases pending review at the time of the *Braden* and *Wilkinson* decisions, the import of these cases is real and far-reaching.[111] The theoretical arguments these cases arouse are likely to be raised again in the near future. These four theories will be discussed separately, with a special accent on the recent Supreme Court decisions which indicate some attitude or disposition toward their acceptability.

THE FREEDOM TO BE SILENT

No matter what the specific decisions have said about the conflict between the freedom of speech and the First Amendment, the issues were at least clearly drawn in the cases where people were punished for contempt because they said something contemptuous. Speech, punishment, the First Amendment—these three follow logically. But the issue is deeper and more difficult to visualize—perhaps more difficult to accept—where the contempt arises out of a refusal to speak when one is ordered to speak by a government official or body. Is there a personal privilege to remain silent in the face of an order to profess? If so, from what constitutional provision does this right derive; and in what instances will the right apply? In many of the recent congressional contempt cases, witnesses have refused to testify and have based their refusal on the freedom of speech provision of the First Amendment. Does the freedom of speech imply a freedom of silence; and does a congressional contempt conviction based on a refusal to speak violate this part of the Constitution?

There have been some isolated cases which have recognized a right of silence.[112] And, by analogy, there have been several recent Supreme Court cases which have recognized and protected a freedom of anonymity implicit in the First Amendment's more direct protection of the freedom of association.

Recently the Supreme Court reversed a state conviction which was based upon violation of an ordinance which forbade public distribution of handbills which did not list the sponsors of the writings.[113] The court acknowledged that the freedom to associate requires freedom of anonymity, and that history has proved the value of encouraging free opinion-venturing and intellectual privacy. This, the court held, should be protected by the First Amendment's freedom of association.

In another recent case,[114] the Supreme Court recognized that "compelled disclosure of affiliation . . . may constitute an effective restraint on freedom of association." In that case, the court concluded that the inviolability of privacy in group association is indispensable to the freedom of association guaranteed by the First Amendment.

Where, one might ask, is the governmental interference with these negative First Amendment rights? The individual is not punished in congressional contempt cases for speaking, but for not speaking. Is it true, as Judge Edgerton has suggested, that freedom of speech means freedom with respect to speech, and includes the freedom not to speak? [115]

A line of cases in the late 1950s has indicated a judicial recognition of the more subtle, indirect dangers of erosion of First Amendment rights. These cases have protected what might be called the other face of First Amendment rights. The Court has said, for example, that First Amendment freedoms are to be protected not only from heavy-handed frontal attack but also from being stifled by more subtle, less direct governmental interference.[116] While punishing speech might be a frontal attack like that referred to by the Court, might not the coercing of speech, with the threat of contempt for refusal, be such a subtle indirect punishment as the Court indicated it would protect? Forcing an integrationist to publicly advocate integration in some Southern cities is an indirect way of punishing the advocacy of integration, much as a statute making such advocacy a misdemeanor would be a direct way. The integrationist in the former case has the choice of publicizing his ideas and running the risk of suffering community reprisals, or refusing to speak and being punished for contempt. Should there be some constitutional protection to keep this man from the "frying pan" of social hostility and the "fire" of contemnor's jail? If so, where does this protection lie?

Indirect interference with indirect First Amendment rights by use of the contempt power has been recently condemned by the Court.[117] The United States Supreme Court overruled a state contempt conviction which was based on refusal of the NAACP to disclose its membership lists. A unanimous court, recognizing that "effective advocacy of both public and private points of view, particularly controversial ones, is undeniably enhanced by group association," and that "compelled disclosure of affiliation . . . may constitute an effective restraint on freedom of association," struck down the contempt conviction. Privacy was recognized as essential to free association.

Does an investigation which subjects one to embarrassment, social and economic harassment, or any unofficial but well-calculated and ascertainable damage unconstitutionally burden free speech and association? An interesting question arises out of the conflict which this issue has raised. Recognizing, first, that the *Fifth* Amendment precludes a contempt conviction for refusal to answer questions which would subject one to *formal* governmental punishment,[118] and, second, that courts sometimes will protect individuals from indirect, nongovernmental punishments of social sanction, could it then follow that the *First* Amendment is to these *informal* punishments as the *Fifth* Amendment is to *formal* governmental punishments? If courts will protect against these "nonfrontal" nongovernmental perils as they have in limited cases, it might well be that this defense to contempt cases arising out of exposure by legislative committees' pressures would provide that element of protection of individual privacy which has recently caused this troublesome issue in government-individual relationships.

These recent decisions make a realistic appraisal of social facts-of-life, in recognizing the likeliness that restraint of speech will follow from public pressures upon those whose only wrong may be the admission of nonconformity.

Many contempt cases deal with punishments based not on acts done but upon refusals to act. And, to make matters more difficult, many of the acts would not themselves be formally punishable even if they were done, though their noncommission and privacy has been deemed contemptuous. Acts, in this sense, are those of speech as well as physical acts. Should the First Amendment forbid Congress from burdening expressions which it may not punish? And if Congress may not restrain, or punish in the ordinary sense, may it do so indirectly through exposure? Exposure of certain opinions which they deem inimical is the admitted purpose of the committee under whose work most of these conflicts have arisen.[119] If the effect of this practice is to inhibit dissident advocacy or association by subjecting it to non-official punishment, though it could not be formally punished and might be more successfully defeated by counter-advocacy, then resort to the First Amendment would not be inappropriate.

Some have replied to this argument by stating that many liberal causes, which all are free to advocate and promote, are adopted by those who would use these subjects to agitate and accomplish other evil ulterior motives. This may well be true. However, a distinction could be made between fascists advocating Fascism, and fascists advocating for or against integration. The history of our First Amendment supports freedom in the latter instance. For example, as little as I like to hear Mr. Rockwell and the members of his American Nazi Party speak against Jews, I realize that he is less apt to prevail in his views in a country like America where the stupidity of his argument can be simply displayed. And if he advocated strict immigration laws (a legitimate point of view) as a subterfuge for his views about genocide (certainly a point of view subject to governmental control), would we not be reducing ourselves to his despicable level by punishing him for this?

Justice Rutledge has forcefully argued that society can best protect itself by prohibiting only the substantive evil itself and relying on a comparatively free interchange of ideas as the best safeguard against demoralizing propaganda.[120] If he is right, a contempt power may be not only superfluous but in a sense even incompatible to our government's functioning. Judge Edgerton in one of his opinions concluded that "Congressional action that is either intended or likely to restrict expression of opinion that Congress may not prohibit violates the First Amendment. Congressional action in the nature of investigation is no exception. Civil liberties may not be abridged in order to determine whether they should be abridged." [121]

The contempt power has been one of the few methods by which Congress has been able to pry into these private areas of First Amendment rights. Through its exercise, resistance to investigations may be punished. In some cases, this leaves these alternatives: perjury or profession of ordinarily protectible ideas and consequent social stigma and reprisal. The question whether Congress is acting in an appropriate legislative area then seems somewhat less troublesome or important than whether it should punish an individual, who will not cooperate, by forcefully ventilating his opinions and ideas and revealing his associations if they themselves are not punishable.

THE RIGHT OF PRIVACY

Another theory, which could be offered in these cases, is that congressional investigations unduly violate some privilege of privacy which individuals may properly assert as a First Amendment right.

Long ago, Louis Brandeis, later to become famous as a Supreme Court Justice, wrote an article about the right of privacy.[122] That article, now a Harvard Law Review classic, expressed for the first time the importance of the individual's right of self-determination concerning the communication and publication of his thoughts, sentiments, and emotions. "It is certain every man has a right to keep his own sentiments, if he pleases. He has certainly a right to judge whether he will make them public. . . ." [123]

The right of an individual to prevent public portraiture is now recognized.[124] Should this right of physical privacy be extended to protect one's intellectual personality? Is forcing one to profess, under the threat of a contempt conviction for refusal, an intrusion on that intellectual privacy? Should one's insistence on privacy constitute contempt? Our government functioned and thrived for many decades without maintaining a legislative "bloodhound." In fact, even today the greatest majority of legislative investigation is conducted without need for recourse to the contempt power. Could it be that in this fractional percentage of cases, individual privacy of ideas and associations might be maintained without suffering the legislative branch of government to compromise or ineffectiveness? Individuals are generally ready to cooperate with their government, as is exemplified by the miles of testimony compiled in recent years by legislative investigations without resort to coercion or punishment. Would it be unreasonable to exalt the privileges of privacy of those who for reasons of principle or personal fear want to be left alone? In these exceptional cases, is there as much to be gained from protecting individual security and constitutional rights, than there might be lost in legislative dexterity? All that would be lost in the sacrifice would be what is to many an unjust and ignoble legislative punishing power.

Putting the argument in more dramatic language, could it be

said that our country may face a clear and present danger of losing conscience because of the stigmatizing and fear-instilling effect of many congressional investigations? Or could it be that these investigations themselves are not so much the cause of the problem, as is the contempt "hatchet" which the investigators may now wield? Abolition of these committees need not be the answer. This is a more drastic cure than the wrong may require. But the contempt power might be limited in such a way that legislative work could go on, but in a manner more consistent with individual freedom. There is a greater need to curb the abuse than to curb the investigating power itself. This thought will be explained in the concluding chapter.

As long ago as 1929, one lawyer, distressed by the conflicts between congressional investigations and individual liberty, predicted that less wrong was likely to arise in America from any possibility of anarchy that would result from emphasizing individual liberty, than would result from an annihilation of individual rights by government itself.[125] That admonition still rings true though some innings have passed in the battle he foresaw. Time enough has gone by for deliberation, working out, and observation, but still the problem exists and a satisfactory solution is wanting. Perhaps the right of privacy, which may be implied from the language and spirit of the First Amendment, is an answer.

THE PUBLIC'S INTEREST IN FIRST AMENDMENT FREEDOMS

Any balancing approach in congressional contempt cases, which overlooks the interests of the general public in each man's First Amendment rights, does not fairly weigh one of the scales on the balance. Certainly, no one would deny that the investigating committee's interest in these cases is bolstered by the weight of the national purpose inhering in the work of the legislature. A contempt of the type under consideration here is not necessarily a dispute between lone committees and equally alone individuals. As the committees represent the legislature and thereby the nation, so individuals, in asserting First Amendment rights, represent the general community's right to speak, hear, join, quit, petition and respond. The denial of one man's freedom to speak may interfere with all other men's freedom to hear, and to know, and to decide. It may inhibit another's inclination to speak.

Many years ago, the Supreme Court recognized that the far limits of the First Amendment covered more than each man's singular right to speak or associate or petition. In 1946, the Court ruled that the balancing in First Amendment cases must give weight to society's interest in being subjected to speech and advocacy.[126] In his dissent to the *Barenblatt* decision, Justice Black pointed out that balancing the interests of the legislature with Barenblatt's freedom to associate "completely leaves out the real interest in Barenblatt's silence, the interest of the people as a whole in being able to join organizations, advocate causes, and make political mistakes without later being subjected to governmental penalties for having dared to think for themselves." In the *Watkins* decision, Chief Justice Warren iterated the idea that interference with one individual's First Amendment rights has subtle and immeasurable negative effects upon those who might tend to adhere to unorthodox or controversial views. In the *Braden* case, Justice Black wrote: "Liberty, to be secure for any, must be secure for all—even for the most miserable merchants of hated and unpopular ideas." This probably states as clearly and directly as anything written, the fear of many people that the greatest danger from committee exposure tactics is not the injury to the individual involved as much as it is the broader general social stultification or freezing of dissent, learning, questioning, and intellectual freedom which is liable to result. This attitude is untenable unless one can accept the basic premise that by meeting talk with talk, ideas with ideas, only force with force, and acts with punishment, democratic ideals will sooner win out than by fighting dissent or unorthodoxy with punishment. The idea is no more than the libertarian principles of Locke, Milton, Jefferson, Madison, and those others whose ideas formed so much of our national ideology. Any unacceptability of this idea is less attributable to basic American notions of freedom and justice than to current American fears, anxieties, and politics.

BILLS OF ATTAINDER

Another argument which has been made in some of these congressional contempt cases, though not a First Amendment issue, has been that investigations whose ends are exposure amount to unconstitutional bills of attainder. Though this is somewhat out of place in a review of the First Amendment, the argument is posed here because it has typically been thrown into the hodgepodge of constitutional arguments against this aspect of legislative investigations, and might add some weight to the First Amendment arguments, which must ultimately succeed or fail in the clash with the congressional contempt power.

The Constitution proscribes legislative bills of attainder and guarantees thereby that all men shall not be punished except by the judicial process.[127] This provision was included in the Constitution to protect against legislative abuses, which odiously lingered in the memories of our country's Founders.[128]

Some congressional investigations have been likened to bills of attainder because in effect they intentionally caused punishment in the form of loss of employment, opprobrium and ostracism, and loss of reputation, without the usual constitutional safeguards and procedural criminal standards.[129] The Constitution forbids any bill of attainder. Exposure is punishment for past acts, though the purpose of legislative investigations is supposed to be to forestall future conduct. Though exposure undoubtedly assists the legislature, it could be questioned whether there are not other ways, less violative of First Amendment rights of speech and association, by which proper congressional goals can be accomplished and vital security areas policed?

This defense to contempt action has not been seriously accepted by the Supreme Court, though Justices Black and Douglas have consistently raised the point in dissent. In one case, Justice Black wrote: "Legislative acts, no matter what their form, that apply to easily ascertained members of a group in such a way as to inflict punishment on them without a judicial trial are bills of attainder prohibited by the Constitution." [130] Only by recognizing informal, nonofficial governmental sanctions in the form of exposure to community wrath as punishment, as the Court has been willing to do in some recent cases, can this defense be made to contempt convictions. Its application to the contempt situation is more remote than the argument that contempt directly violates the First Amendment, and is less likely to be the successful constitutional law from which any solution will derive in this perplexing conflict. But recognition of the spirit of this law should add to the weight of the First Amendment arguments previously discussed.

Around this issue has been fought one of the most perturbing political disputes of recent times. It has been a conflict not reserved to lawyers alone. Because of the philosophical and social ramifications of the problem, the press and the public have shown keen interest, and have been active participants in the debates that have ranged. The more notorious names in this battle are familiar to all who can hear or read—Uphaus, Pauling, Trumbo, Miller, McCarthy, Walters, Dies—the list is a long one.

The problem is perplexing not only to witnesses but to Congress, too. Sincere congressmen, interested in the dispatch of their important business and in avoiding legal disputes with the well-intended exercise of their power, have proposed legislation to ameliorate the present awkward, often doubly-defeating, and confusing status of the law in this area—but to no avail.[131]

The legal answers are unsettled, the policies undefined. A definite trend is not even visible. Where precisely is the point where individual freedom and governmental power stop irritating and begin accommodating one another is a question about which people seldom agree. Some advocates for change have suggested procedural refinement to curb the committee's zeal.[132] Lawyer advisory committees,[133] codes of fair procedure,[134] and revitalization of constitutional safeguards [135] have been suggested as answers to the conflicting interests of man and committee—First Amendment freedom and legislative power. Other views have been that one must be consistently suffered to the other, or that a balance should be struck by which individual value judgments could be made and specific decisions issued therefrom. As much as anything else, the resolution of the value, extent, and limitations of the contempt power should supply some answer.

The Fourth Amendment

Like the religious clause of the First Amendment, the pardon power, and the punishment provision of the Eighth Amendment, the defense of the Fourth Amendment in contempt cases is one which has infrequently and only indirectly been raised, has caused little serious conflict, and has been consistently construed by the courts. The Fourth Amendment of the United States Constitution reads:

The right of the people to be secure in their persons, houses, papers, and effects, against unreasonable Searches and Seizures, shall not be violated, and no Warrants shall issue, but upon probable cause, supported by Oath or affirmation, and particularly describing the place to be searched, and the persons to be seized.[136]

The moving spirit of this constitutional provision was the protection of individual privacy from governmental trespass,[137] or, as one court put it, to protect against autocratic and despotic action under color of national authority.[138] The amendment was written in response to an unhappy English and colonial experience with general warrants and writs of assistance [139] and was aimed at protecting the interests of individual liberty from governmental overbearing.[140] In words peculiarly applicable to the contempt situation (though not so intended), one federal court interpreted the policy of this amendment to mean that expediency in law enforcement must yield to the necessity of observing individual freedom.[141]

It is now settled that Congress and courts may compel unwilling witnesses to disclose facts essential to proper governmental inquiry and, to that end, may enforce the attendance of witnesses and the disclosure of evidence, through their subpoena and contempt powers.[142] In this, they are limited only by the general laws of procedure and the Constitution. Where an individual asserts his prerogative not to cooperate, these governmental bodies may exercise their contempt powers to punish him or to try to coerce his cooperation. The Fourth Amendment issue may arise where an individual claims that compulsion of his testimony or securance of his property amounts to a search or invasion of privacy which the Constitution prohibits.

The key issue in Fourth Amendment contempt cases has been whether the amendment's protection is one aimed at physical, trespass-like interferences, or whether the scope of this law is broad enough to cover indirect psychological interferences such as those described in the section of this book dealing with the First Amendment defense to congressional contempt convictions. In this sense, the inquiry is directed beyond questions about the procedural application of the contempt power and is addressed more to the substantive effect of its use upon rights of privacy in general. Is the amendment aimed at physical searches and seizures only, or is it broader, encompassing an intangible right of personal security—some privacy of person and property?

In contempt cases where direct physical interference is involved, the applicability of Fourth Amendment defenses is clear, even if it is not tenable under the circumstances. For example, a contempt of court conviction, by which judges and clerks concerned with a state election were punished for misbehavior in office, was upheld by the Illinois courts over the objection that the trial court violated defendant's Fourth Amendment rights by opening ballot boxes and examining tally sheets which were used as evidence against them.[143] Here, the assertion of the Fourth Amendment defense is obvious. The government physically took things which were used as evidence against a defendant. Although the court did not uphold the defense, its assertion was appropriate, and typical of search and seizure cases in general.

The more indirect effects of the contempt power upon Fourth Amendment rights are more obscure; the issues less clearly defined.[144] What, for example, is the effect of the threat of a contempt conviction upon the freedom of choice in relation to cooperation with governmental inquiry? A recent federal case dealt with such an issue.[145] There, the defense was made that the fear of the contempt power nullified the voluntariness of the submission of incriminating evidence by an accused. Called before a Senate investigating committee, defendant was threatened and led to believe that he must either testify and incriminate himself or be convicted of contempt for his refusal. The defendant surrendered a drawer full of papers and books, and was thereafter convicted of violation of the lottery laws based at least in part upon the evidence he submitted. On appeal, defendant claimed that he did not understand his true alternatives, and therefore his presentation of the incriminating evidence was really involuntary and, therefore, was a violation of his Fourth Amendment rights.

On appeal, the circuit court ruled that "Nelson's freedom of choice has been dissolved in a brooding omnipresence of compulsion. The Committee threatened prosecution for contempt if he refused to answer, for perjury if he lied, and for gambling activities if he told the truth." The court went on to say: "Courts and committees rightly require answers to questions. But neither may exert this power to extort assent to invasions of homes and to seizures of private papers. Assent so extorted is no substitute for lawful process."

Concluding that the evidence was illegally seized in violation of the Fourth Amendment, the court reversed the conviction. The dissenting judge believed that the situation was one of proper compulsion, a sound feature of the judicial process, and not an illegal coercion, and that this did not violate the Fourth Amendment.

A more recent case allowed a motion to quash a subpoena *duces tecum* improperly issued, before the evidence was received.[146] This is an eminently more satisfactory procedure for questioning an investigative power than reliance upon a constitutional defense to a later contempt conviction for outright refusal. That case adopted a test for consideration of the reasonableness of searches and seizures which was based upon a realistic appraisal of all conduct, its fundamental fairness, and the balance between proper governmental ends and protectible individual rights.[147]

The most profound issue raised (thus far unsuccessfully) concerns judicial interpretation of the outermost reaches of the Fourth Amendment and the extent of the amendment's protection of the right of privacy, and its defensive application against investigating committees. Does the Fourth Amendment protect against infringements of a physical nature alone, or does it go further to protect individuals against invasions of personal thoughts, associations, and property, and from public scrutiny and exposure? The defense that use of the contempt power violates the right of privacy, guaranteed implicitly by the Fourth Amendment, has not, so far, met with success.

The issue came before the Washington state courts in 1950.[148] There, the defendant was convicted of contempt of a state legislative committee on un-American activities. He based his refusal to cooperate, and his defense to the contempt conviction, on the ground that forced disclosure violated his right of privacy as guaranteed by the Fourth Amendment. The court did not accept this defense because it felt that the governmental interest in information was greater and more direct than the defendant's claim of constitutional protection. The court reasoned that investigations are matters of the country's survival and, therefore, may properly invade an individual's personal affairs to the extent that it is necessary to a proper legislative purpose. Individuals have constitutional rights, the court held, because they are citizens of this country, and, to the extent that the country needs information, they can be investigated even as to their own private matters.

The United States Supreme Court and the lower federal courts have also disposed of similar claims in like fashion. In the *Sinclair* case, the Supreme Court considered but did not apply the rule of privacy deriving from the Fourth Amendment as a defense to legislative investigatory powers. Recognizing that the Fourth Amendment includes a right of personal security from physical attack and inspection and guarantees some element of personal sanctity and privacy, the court ruled that where the legislative subject of inquiry is a proper and relevant one, it is not inhibited by the Fourth Amendment. In such a case, the inquiry does not relate solely to the personal affairs of the citizen.[149]

The Federal Rules of Civil and Criminal Procedure provide for contempt proceedings in case of failure to obey subpoenas.[150] It is conceivable that the thinking expressed in Fourth Amendment defenses raised in congressional contempt cases might prompt the assertion of a similar defense to a contempt of court conviction. The congressional contempt decisions portend similar disposition of possible contempt of court defenses alleging that forced disclosure or surrender of evidence violates a right of privacy protected by the Fourth Amendment.

At times it has been argued that the investigative and enforcement powers of administrative agencies violate the unlawful search and seizure clause of the Fourth Amendment. The courts have tested this claim on the basis of the reasonableness of the subpoena in question and upheld the administrative power as not violative of the Fourth Amendment, so long as the agency demand was reasonable.[151]

In the recent flood of congressional contempt cases, where all constitutional defenses have been raised in defense to committee exposure tactics, the lower federal courts have consistently followed the *Sinclair* decision.[152] The mere fact that an individual's private affairs are subjected to the public gaze has not been considered sufficiently serious to bar an otherwise proper legislative inquiry.[153] Still there has been no clear-cut decision by the Supreme Court dealing specifically and solely with the Fourth Amendment defense to a contempt conviction arising out of a congressional investigation. This defense is often made among the gamut of other constitutional defenses which have been typically raised in these cases. The federal courts have usually either denied the defenses *in toto* or upheld the defense on narrow procedural grounds or on the basis of limited interpretations of a specific amendment other than the Fourth. The applicability of the Fourth Amendment defense to congressional investigations is closely linked with arguments about the exposure function of legislatures and the general rights of individuals to resist inquiry into personal matters, exposure of which would subject them to unofficial public punishment or condemnation. To this extent the defense has been thrown into what at times has been a hodge-podge of constitutional arguments, all amounting to the position

that "you can't do this to me"—"there must be some constitutional provision to protect me." This has caused some clouding of
the constitutional picture of the Fourth Amendment's contours.
Though the argument, in general, against legislative infringement of conscience or intellectual privacy is compelling, the legal
rationale is less clearly attached to Fourth Amendment principles
than relevant to First Amendment protections of privacy, already
discussed. Rights of privacy implicit in the Fourth Amendment
differ from those guarded by the First. In the former, the invaded
privacy is one deriving from a trespass of subtle though physical
means, such as secretly wire-tapping or televising speech or conduct. However, that right of privacy which properly protects
people from public ventilation of spiritual or intellectual ideas is
more suitably derived from First Amendment freedoms of speech
and association. To this extent, it would seem that right of privacy
defenses in the Fourth Amendment cases have been ill-advised.

The Fifth Amendment

"No person shall be held to answer for a capital, or other infamous crime, unless on a presentment or indictment of a Grand
Jury . . . nor shall any person be subject for the same offense
to be twice put in jeopardy of life or limb; nor shall be compelled
in any criminal case to be a witness against himself; nor be deprived of life, liberty, or property, without due process of
law. . . ." [154]

INDICTMENT BY GRAND JURY

The first clause of the Fifth Amendment, requiring a presentment or indictment by a grand jury prior to trial for criminal
offenses, has been mentioned briefly in this chapter in connection
with the right to trial by jury. The guaranty is long-established;
it is based on the idea that one should not be put on trial until

a jury of his peers finds probable cause.[155] As such, it is predicated on the positive theory that this is a right men are entitled to before they can be tried. It is another constitutional insulation from hasty or overbearing governmental action.

Justice Gray, while a member of the United States Supreme Court, elaborated on the purposes of the Constitution's grand jury requirement,[156] though not with specific reference to the contempt situation. He said that "whether a man shall be put upon his trial for crime without a presentment or indictment by a grand jury of his fellow citizens depends upon the consequences to himself if he shall be found guilty." [157] By this standard, contempt would certainly qualify for grand jury protection, since the consequences of contempt convictions could be and often are serious and grave. Justice Gray went further, stating that no congressional declaration could defeat this safeguard.[158] The purpose of the clause was to limit the legislature as well as the prosecuting officers. Of course, the grand jury provision of the Fifth Amendment applies only to the federal government, and not to the states.[159] However, most states have similar requirements in their own laws.

The Constitution specifically excludes certain classes of cases from the protection of the grand jury provision.[160] If contempt was meant to be excluded, it is conspicuously absent from any specific manifestation of historical intent—in the Constitution or elsewhere.

Surprisingly, though intermittent volleys of criticism have been fired at most other contempt procedures, the denial of grand jury rights has provoked little attention or comment. This may be because the broad criticisms made of other contempt procedures implicitly include this argument. For example, if a right to trial by jury was allowed, indictments of some kind would probably follow a fortiori. If not, some of the dangers of its absence would be rectified by the jury trial itself. "Sui generis" rationales which are used in answer to other, often stronger, complaints about summary contempt procedures would undoubtedly be offered in response to arguments that the contemnor should be indicted by a grand jury.

Now, all contempts of Congress are presented to grand juries for indictment. And, undoubtedly, the prime reason why contempts of court are not presented is because they are not offenses defined by a criminal statute as are other crimes. Contempt is the statutory creation of a power, not an offense. Furthermore, habit and the summary nature of the power, which has been uniformly claimed and which appears so appropriate, has undoubtedly preempted any inclination on the part of district attorneys to present contempt matters to grand juries. There have been cases where presentments were made for contempt committed before the grand jury itself.

However, it could be argued that contempt is just that kind of offense which warrants the interposition of a grand jury as a kind of referee between the particular official and individual in the dispute. For example, most contempt of Congress cases arise in the District of Columbia, where Congress sits as a body. Since contempt of Congress is a statutory crime now, all cases must be commenced by a grand jury indictment. In the period from 1950 to 1959, eighty-three contempt of Congress indictments were returned by District of Columbia grand juries; seventeen proposed indictments were no-billed. This means that about 20 percent of the total cases were refused by grand juries. It should also be noted that of those indicted, thirty were convicted; forty-seven were acquitted. And fifteen convictions were reversed on appeal; nine are pending appeal. This indicates that there is room for disagreement between what Congress considered contemptuous conduct and what others in the legal process have felt should be punished.

In contempt cases arising out of disobedience to orders of a

court, it is not an unusual procedure for the action to be commenced by an order to show cause. Some courts have held that
the particularity required of an indictment is not necessary for
an information charging contempt, and that technical accuracy
is not required.[161] In one case of contempt, which arose out of
the carelessness of a sheriff which enabled the escape of his pris-
oners, the contemnor argued that the charge was not sufficiently
made out in the information against him. The court, applying an
exception to the general rule requiring particularity of indictments, denied the defense and approved a fair notice standard
for the indictment requirement.[162] But, even these cases, which
allow a casual treatment of indictments, impliedly conform procedurally to the constitutional directive that there be some form
of indictment or information.

No case has specifically challenged the constitutionality of the
practice in direct contempt cases of deeming the personal knowledge and action of the offended judge sufficient satisfaction of
the indictment-by-grand jury requirements. In certain cases of
indirect contempt and with a contempt of Congress, there is no
problem because the customary grand jury procedure is required
by statute. But in cases of direct contempt and in those cases
of indirect contempt where the proceedings are commenced by
the court sua sponte or by a show cause order or similar procedural means, there may be a proper constitutional objection. Of
course, civil contempts are excluded from many Fifth Amendment protections because they are not crimes. Civil contempts
are commenced spontaneously and are part of the original action
out of which they arose.

The contemnor may well be apprised of the proceedings
against him, even where summary procedures are applied. Under
the present Federal Rules of Criminal Procedure, indirect criminal contempts are prosecuted by an order to show cause or an
arrest order, and notice and hearing are guaranteed. However,

pleadings may be based on information and belief. Direct criminal contempts are prosecuted on a certified order of the judge.

On the other hand, that policy of the Fifth Amendment's indictment clause, which aims at insulating the individual from his government by interposition of a popular group of his peers, is ignored by the present practice. This right was adopted from the common law, and is a mandatory rule in normal federal prosecutions, intended as an intervention and substantial safeguard against oppressive or arbitrary proceedings.[163] The contempt situation involves exactly the kind of summary punishing power which this provision should cure. It is one of the few situations where our government has acted in violation of this constitutional provision. To allow this clear constitutional mandate to be circumvented here, on grounds of expediency, or speed, would be to condone the first chunk to be cleaved from one provision of the Bill of Rights which has been the cause of comparatively few civil liberty problems in American history. There is no counterbalancing governmental need to warrant ignoring this constitutional right, except that which would call for faster-moving litigation. It could certainly be argued that the part of the scale which holds respect for the law and the liberty of the individual outweighs in value the counterbalance which embraces the speed of trials. Hurried justice may not be justice at all.

DOUBLE JEOPARDY

The policy of the double jeopardy clause of the Fifth Amendment may conflict with the contempt power to cause any one of several difficult, mathematical-like, problems. The double jeopardy problem can arise in two situations—the crossfire and the reiterated contempt.

The crossfire situation arises where one act constitutes both contempt and another crime, either in the same or another jurisdiction. For example, in the case of an attempted bribe of a witness in a law suit, the briber could be found guilty of contempt and of subornation of perjury or perjury if he was successful in his attempt. The same wrongful act could then be punished twice. This problem is compounded in a case where the act of contempt is not a second crime in the jurisdiction where it is committed, but is a separate crime in another jurisdiction. From this possibility of crossfire of prosecutions derives issues of dual sovereignty, immunity, and double jeopardy.

The second situation is one of multiplied pressures, in which the contemnor is forced to reiterate his act of contempt after he has been punished for the first act; or where one contempt is multiplied by reiteration of the same or a similar situation as resulted in the first contempt, and the separate punishment of each repeated contempt is immediately sought. The first situation could occur where an individual refuses to testify before a legislative committee or a grand jury, is sentenced for contempt, and after serving his sentence is recalled before the same body, asked the same question, and again sentenced for his second refusal. The other situation arises where a witness is asked a series of related questions, refuses to answer any of them, and is punished separately for each contemptuous refusal. In these cases, a persistent inquisitor could punish a persistent contemnor indefinitely.

In considering the applicability of the double jeopardy clause to contempt practice, it should be noted that the constitutional provision is worded in terms of "offenses"—"nor shall any person be subject for the same offense to be twice put in jeopardy." Though decision-makers have sidestepped or passed over other constitutional protections in contempt cases on the ground that contempt is not a crime, not an infamous crime, nor the like, no one has gone so far as to suggest that the unique act of contempt is not even an offense. In fact, "offense" is the word usually used to describe contempt. Beginning at least beyond that hurdle, one can penetrate to the substance of the clause.

Justice Brandeis dealt with the crossfire situation in a case decided in the last century.[164] There, a convicted contemnor argued that his conviction for contempt of Congress was improper because the same act of contumacy was made a crime by a special federal statute. The offense in that case could have been punished twice—once for contempt, and again under the statute which made refusing to answer questions or produce papers before either House a misdemeanor. Justice Brandeis dismissed the argument that the defendant was immune from one punishment because of the existence of another. He wrote that "Punishment, purely as such, through contempt proceedings, legislative or judicial, is not precluded because punishment may also be inflicted for the same act as a statutory offense." [165]

An earlier Supreme Court, expressing faith in the conviction that this power would not be used cumulatively, had previously upheld a conviction under a federal statute which made refusal to testify before a Senate committee a statutory misdemeanor, even though the contemnor was subject to punishment for contempt of Congress as well.[166]

At that time, Chief Justice Fuller wrote,

it is quite clear that the contumacious witness is not subjected to jeopardy twice for the same offense, since the same act may be an offense against one jurisdiction and also an offense against another; and indictable statutory offenses may be punished as such, while the offenders may likewise be subjected to punishment for the same acts as contempts, the two being *diverso intuitu* and capable of standing together.[167]

The theoretical ground for this practice, which seems to condone precisely those results which the double jeopardy clause sought to prevent, is quite well settled. Where one act is both a contempt and another substantive crime, it is an offense against judicial authority on the one hand, and against the state in general on the other. One punishment then is for violation of the law created by the legislature, and the other for an offense against the judiciary.[168]

Another judicial attitude, by which double jeopardy objections are avoided, was enunciated in the *United Mine Workers* case,[169] in 1946. There, the Supreme Court avoided charges of duplicity by classifying one contempt as criminal and another as civil. The rationale for this approach was stated, though not in a contempt case, in 1955.[170] "Congress may impose both a criminal and civil sanction in respect to the same act or omission; since the double jeopardy clause prohibits merely punishing twice, or attempting a second time to punish criminally, for the same offense." [171] So again, by its power to classify contempts, a court may avoid double jeopardy problems by characterizing one of the contempts as civil, though effectively treating it as a criminal offense.

Under the Brandeis-Fuller rationale or by application of some civil-criminal distinction then, a sovereign can avoid the constitutional objection that its prosecution violates the double jeopardy clause by punishing contemptuous conduct twice.

The more difficult state-federal problem also arises in the context of the contempt and double jeopardy conflict. By early authorities, one criminal conviction would not bar later prosecution for the same offense in another jurisdiction. Similarly, contempt actions are not precluded merely because the very same act constitutes a crime such as perjury, bribery, or insubordination in a second jurisdiction. Here, the individual is subject to double punishment for his one act. The misconduct is single; the offense to society is single; but the sanction is multiple.[172] Recent statutes have granted the right to a jury trial in some instances where one act is both a contempt and another crime.[173] These statutes, while preventing the conviction-minded from circumventing a jury trial by treating an otherwise ordinary crime as a contempt, do not satisfy the double jeopardy problems.

One rationale for allowing double punishments in these cases is that the protectible social interest which warrants legal sanction is different in contempt cases from that which might justify such action in the case of another crime. Even though the wrongful act is singular, the antisocial elements may be multiple. Contempt sanctions are aimed at misconduct which interferes with governmental work. Whereas, kidnaping a witness, for example, is misconduct toward the person of an individual; it may also be an interference with government and therefore constitute a contempt. The wrong is the same, but the interests to be protected are different and, it is sometimes argued, warrant separate and individual treatment. The standard explanation for allowing separate prosecutions in separate jurisdictions is, however, that the classic thought behind the double jeopardy clause was to prevent one sovereign from twice punishing the same act. It never was meant, so the argument goes, to preclude a second action by a second sovereign. So, one state may prosecute although the federal or another state government has already prosecuted.

THE REITERATED CONTEMPT

The second problem area is the reiterated contempt. Assuming that all other aspects were proper in a given contempt situation, could the punished contemnor be repunished if he was adamant in his disobedience to the same, though later, order? If the underlying justification for contempt convictions is the punishment of affronts to judicial authority, then a second contempt is a separate offense to that authority, though it be predicated on exactly similar facts. There would be no legal problem. However, if the reason for using the contempt power is to coerce cooperation or deter interference with government bodies, then a repeated incident comes closer to the double jeopardy prohibition. Although it might be argued that continuous punishments for interference would tend to increase the coercive or deterrent force of the particular government body, the second punishment really borders on the overbearing power against which the constitution admonishes in the double jeopardy clause.

The reiterated contempt focuses, perhaps more clearly than any of the other contempt procedures, on the truly political and philosophical implications of this power. Congress may want information. An individual wants privacy, or at least constitutional protection in proceedings against him. The two forces press against one another causing great social friction of not little political consequence. How far can and should government go in pressing its legitimate will on the uncooperative but free-willed individual? Even assuming that government can punish an individual's obstructiveness, ought it be able to repunish for continuance of individual adamancy, when that individual has already been once punished for that same characteristic? When the contemnor has served a year in jail for refusing to answer a question, ought the governmental officer be able to ask the same question again, and punish a second refusal? And if so, when, if ever, is the government estopped in its insistence? The issue is one of policy which should be reflected in the way in which it is resolved by the law.

By the preponderance of judicial authority, the power of a prosecutor to initially multiply contempts by reiterating similar questions has been limited.[174] In the *Yates* case, the defendant was charged with violation of the Smith Act. After waiving her privilege against incrimination, she refused to answer eleven questions put to her on cross-examination. The trial court treated each refusal as a separate contempt and sentenced her to one year in prison for each contempt. Under such a system, the only thing between Yates and a one-hundred-year sentence was the stamina of the prosecutor. Fortunately, our system of justice is based on sounder criteria. The Supreme Court said that her refusals constituted only one contempt.[175] Refusal to answer many questions within one area of refusal, it held, constitutes but a single offense.[176] This concept has been applied in some state court decisions and ignored in others.[177] Though lower federal court decisions had similarly lined up on both sides of this issue,[178] presumably this final decision of the Supreme Court will resolve the matter. Where separate questions seek to establish one fact or relate to a single subject of inquiry, only one penalty for contempt may be imposed for refusal to answer all questions.

The recently notorious *Uphaus* case [179] involves the other side of the same problem. Once acknowledging that the government may not cause repeated contempts by repeating its questions, may the frustrated government officer await the fulfillment of sentence for the first single contempt by the contemnor, and then greet him with the same question, threatening another contempt conviction if he persists in his refusal? The federal cases have not answered this perplexing question. In the *Uphaus* case, the defendant refused to answer certain questions before a one-man state investigating committee. He was committed to jail for one year. As the anniversary of his imprisonment approached, the contemnor and the contemned both indicated that they would repeat the incident. The viewer could only hope that one would relent. Neither did, and as his final act in office, the Attorney General moved for the unlimited confinement of Doctor Uphaus. Judge Grant, who ordered the first commitment, denied the motion, and Uphaus went free. Interestingly, the contempt of Uphaus was called civil throughout all the proceedings, and it arose out of a legislative investigation by an executive officer, who upon encountering the contemnor's refusal, went to the court for an order, which resulted in a contempt of court conviction.

Analogy with past rationales would probably have allowed the second conviction. Good reason and mercy would not. Once having suffered the punishment for his strong and sincere convictions or for his wrong, the individual ought not to be sacrificed again to overbearing officialdom. The *Yates* decision adds weight to this attitude, as does the legislative policy implicit in the law allowing jury trial where contempt is also another crime.

Still, in a 1963 case, the New York Court of Appeals held that one rule does not follow the other in the reiterated contempt situation.[180] The New York rule is the same as the federal *Yates* rule, that one cannot be forced into numerous different contempts by repeating questions in the same proceeding. However, the court upheld a second contempt conviction where a witness was requestioned a second time by the same body about the same thing after serving his first contempt sentence for the same contemptuous refusal to answer. The court's rationale was that subsequent requestioning about the same matter is not the same as successive questioning about the same matter in one proceeding. The former was a new contumacious act, and therefore a separate offense. That decision is in accord with the rule in other states. I suggest that the distinction is fatuous, and the practice should be unconstitutional.

The double jeopardy problems indicated herein can be readily resolved either by the liberal construction of the policy of the double jeopardy clause or by the adoption of some new manner of treating the contempt problem as a whole. Such a plan will be offered in the chapter to follow.

THE PRIVILEGE AGAINST SELF-INCRIMINATION

Once having defined the contours of legislative jurisdiction in the *Kilbourn* decision, the courts were still to mark the areas within that jurisdiction where constitutional principle or some strong policy forbade use of the contempt power. The Fifth

Amendment's self-incrimination clause was one of those further confinations.

The Fifth Amendment directs that no one be forced to testify against himself if his testimony would subject him to a criminal prosecution.[181] Though this amendment's privilege relates solely to federal actions, all states have adopted it either by their constitution, statutes, or judicial decisions.[182] In the contempt context, problems may arise in one of two ways. First, an individual charged with the commission of a contempt may refuse to testify on the issue of his contempt at the contempt proceeding. Second, one may refuse to testify in a noncontempt proceeding about another criminal matter, and this refusal itself may be considered a contempt.[183] This latter situation arises where one's testimony would subject him to criminal action either in the instant jurisdiction or before another jurisdiction. This latter problem is akin to the crossfire situation discussed in the double jeopardy section. The first class of cases deals with the assertion of the privilege in contempt cases. The second category concerns the convertibility into a contempt of the invocation of the privilege in a noncontempt case.

THE PRIVILEGE IN A CONTEMPT CASE

Again one is left to wonder how our judges will classify contempts for the purpose of this provision. This section of the Fifth Amendment is worded in terms of a "criminal case." Enough has been written about the important ramifications of a judicial classification of a given contempt as criminal or civil to warrant only its briefest mention again here. Better reasoning dictates agreement with Wigmore that the policy of the self-incrimination privilege should apply to the contempt situation.[184] The possible legal consequences in the form of punishments of fine or imprisonment are reason enough to afford this constitutional protection. Wigmore concluded (and I suggest correctly) that distinctions

between civil and criminal contempts should not be the criteria
for allowing the assertion of the privilege in cases of such basic
importance. The applicability of the privilege should better rest
on its own policies and logic.

Most states have held the state-established privilege against self-
incrimination applicable to contempt cases. One California court
stated that "it is fundamental that requiring a defendant in a criminal case to testify violates his constitutional privilege against self-
incrimination," and that "it is likewise a violation of this privilege
to compel a defendant to testify in a contempt proceeding." [185]
The court resolved the classification problem, thusly:

> Contempt of court is a specific criminal offense . . . punished some-
> times by indictment and sometimes in a summary proceeding. . . .
> In either mode . . . the adjudication . . . is a conviction . . . the
> proceeding to punish . . . is in the nature of a criminal prosecution.
> Its purpose is . . . to vindicate the dignity and authority of the
> court. It is a special proceeding, criminal in character. . . .[186]

In the *Gompers* case,[187] the Supreme Court ruled that, in a
federal criminal contempt case, the alleged contemnor is entitled
to the protection of the privilege, but it avoided approval or rejection of the applicability of the privilege for civil contemnors. By
analogy, the courts have held that the privilege is available in
certain civil proceedings like deportation,[188] and at least one
writer has concluded that "a defendant in a contempt case, *either
civil or criminal*, is entitled to claim the privilege against self
incrimination, and to require that the contempt be proven against
him by other witnesses. . . ." [189]

NONCONTEMPT INCRIMINATION IN THE
SAME JURISDICTION

In the category of cases where testimony would subject the
individual to incrimination for another crime in the same jurisdiction, the courts have allowed claims of the constitutional protec-

tion—with respect to defenses to charges of both contempt of court and Congress.[190]

With the tremendous increase in legislative investigations and the adamant response of individuals in recent times to congressional exposure tactics, the Fifth Amendment's self-incrimination clause has been invoked by many individuals as a shield from what they felt was committee harassment.[191] Since, the contempt power was then subject to judicial review, the federal courts' interpretation of the Fifth Amendment was crucial to the resolution of this individual-legislative committee conflict. Originally, these cases turned on procedural points such as whether the privilege was properly asserted, whether it was waived, what is incriminating, and whether the witness was apprised of his rights and the committee's purpose. The Supreme Court went far to extend the applicability of the Fifth Amendment in those cases to reflect a policy sympathetic to the protection of individuals. Still, Professor Carl Beck, in his study of the congressional contempt power, concluded that the vitality of the Fifth Amendment in congressional contempt cases was, as a practical matter, limited. Its broad application, he concluded, did not "presage any significant substantive limitations on the investigatory power," and its application carried "an aura of skepticism toward the innocence of the persons who sought recourse in its protections." [192] Perhaps this provoked the gradual turn to the First Amendment as a surer protection from exposure and harassment, as suggested in the section on that subject. In any event, a review of some of the leading Fifth Amendment contempt cases will be appropriate in understanding the background to the recent First Amendment era.

The general rules of immunity and waiver were held to apply to contempt cases as well as to any other offense.[193] The rule, allowing assertion of the privilege where the testimony sought would only indirectly tend to incriminate, has also been applied in contempt cases.[194] The same rule applies to contempt cases arising from the assertion of the privilege before grand juries. The breadth of the protection of the privilege in these cases has been broadly extended by the Supreme Court. Not only will the privilege against self incrimination protect against answers that would in themselves support a conviction, but also to those which would furnish a link in the chain of evidence needed to prosecute the claimant for a crime.[195] Any language reasonably indicating that the privilege is raised will be sufficient to invoke its protection: "No ritualistic formula or talismanic phrase" is necessary.[196] And committees must clearly apprise individuals about the risk of possible prosecution for contempt if they do not cooperate,[197] in order to be able to later secure a contempt conviction.

NONCONTEMPT INCRIMINATION IN ANOTHER JURISDICTION

Susceptibility to a noncontempt criminal prosecution in another jurisdiction has not been accepted as a basis for protection under the privilege. Therefore, refusal to answer questions on the ground that the answer would subject the witness to prosecution for a crime in another jurisdiction would constitute a contempt.

In 1892, the Supreme Court in broad language ruled that the self-incrimination clause of the Fifth Amendment precluded forced incrimination in any criminal proceeding.[198] "This provision," the court said, "must have a broad construction in favor of the right which it was intended to secure." [199] The court held that the object of the self-incrimination clause was to insure that a person could not be compelled to be a witness in any investigation where his testimony tended to show that he committed a crime. Immunity legislation cannot avoid this constitutional privilege, unless it is so broad as to have the same extent in scope and effect as the privilege. The court held that "no statute which leaves the party . . . subject to prosecution after he answers the criminating question put to him, can have the effect of supplanting the privilege conferred by the Constitution." [200]

That court ruled that only a grant of absolute immunity would suffice to preempt this constitutional privilege.[201] This decision could have been literally construed to mean that immunity must be absolute in order to do away with the self-incrimination privilege. However, the quoted language has been restrictively interpreted, by resort to its peculiar facts, to apply only within one sovereignty and not to preclude later prosecution in a different jurisdiction. Cases since that time have limited the immunity rule to apply only to prevent later prosecution in the granting jurisdiction. In one case,[202] a man was punished for contempt of a federal immigration inspector. He based his refusal to respond to questions on the ground that his answers would expose him to federal and state prosecutions. The Circuit Court of Appeals remanded and instructed the lower federal court to advise the witness which of his answers would incriminate him under federal law, and then to allow him to refuse answering these, free from contempt sanctions. However, those answers which would subject him to possible persecution under state laws were not covered by the privilege, and unless he purged his offense in this respect, he could be punished for contempt. This holding is consistent with a long-noted and recently accented trend to reduce the circumferential protection of the privilege in deference to the independence of sister sovereigns in matters of criminal justice. This policy was thoroughly treated in a recent article, where the author convincingly concluded that such a restrictive policy cannot avoid "enervating the principle embodied in the privilege." [203] However, the policy is not without respectable and persistent authority.

One device often used to override the assertion of Fifth Amendment defenses has been to grant the witness immunity from prosecution and then demand his testimony. A current immunity statute was passed in 1954.[204] Its use causes a perplexing problem to the witness, whose Fifth Amendment claim is defeated by a grant of immunity, which does not bind a second jurisdiction from prosecuting him on the basis of information elicited by the jurisdiction which granted the immunity.[205]

The problem of self-incrimination, immunity, and the contempt power, as affected by the dual sovereignty concept was recently before the Supreme Court.[206] A prisoner was called before a federal grand jury and offered immunity with respect to questions which the federal government wanted him to answer. He refused, urging that his answers would subject him to state criminal prosecution. The district court had found him in contempt of court, sentenced him to two years imprisonment, and included a sixty-day purge clause.[207] Both the district court and the court of appeals approved the contempt conviction on the ground that federal immunity need only extend to susceptibility to federal prosecution, and this it did in the instant case.[208] The Supreme Court was faced with the contention that older precedent,[209] to the effect that the immunity only extended to the granting sovereign, should be broadened to cover any later prosecution for the particular crime in question by any sovereign. The court avoided this broad issue and decided the case on the ground that the particular immunity statute under scrutiny should be interpreted as covering both state and federal prosecution.[210] A dissent noted the admixture of civil and criminal aspects of the lower court's contempt citation and the absence of criminal procedural safeguards.

In another case, which questioned a contempt conviction of a state court, based on defendant's claim that state immunity did not protect him against later federal prosecution, the Supreme Court adhered to the concept of federalist division between state and national governments and upheld the conviction.[211] A dissent criticized the uncertain posture in which Supreme Court decisions left American prosecutions, noting that the current status of the incrimination clause is such that "a person can be whipsawed into incriminating himself under both state and federal law even though there is a privilege against self-incrimination in the Constitution of each."

A witness who is called before a state or federal agency and ordered to testify is in a desperate position. He can testify himself into the jail of another sovereign, commit perjury, or remain silent and run the risk of imprisonment by the immediate sovereign for contempt.

This trend has been vigorously attacked and has often prevailed only by a one-man majority of the Supreme Court. The theory that the immediate and potential evils of compulsory self-disclosure transcend any difficulties that the exercise of the privilege may impose on society in the detection and prosecution of crime seems more compelling than historical or academic arguments about the original intent of this clause.

A nuance of this state-federal dichotomy is the situation where the work of one governmental agency invades the province of another. This situation arose in a typical case which involved a federal Senate investigation of organized crime. Senator Kefauver's committee questioned a defendant about his alleged violations of state laws. The defendant's refusal to cooperate was based on the Fifth Amendment's self-incrimination clause. He was adjudged in contempt. The Ohio District Court ruled that defendant was entitled to immunity against disclosures that might incriminate him under state *or* federal laws.[212] The Fifth Amendment precludes a federal contempt conviction where the federal investigation overlapped into state provinces.[213]

Still another problem was noted by Chief Justice Warren in a recent case.[214] In *Hutcheson v. U.S.*, the Supreme Court upheld a contempt of Congress conviction which arose out of the McClellan hearings into corruption in the area of labor and management. The majority pointed out that no claim could be made that this committee's purpose was solely exposure. Its origins and the products of its endeavors disprove that. Moreover, the committee assured Hutcheson that it would honor his Fifth Amendment privilege. However, he explicitly avoided asserting the privilege because he was under indictment in a related matter in the State of Indiana, and in that state the assertion of the privilege is a fact which can be used as evidence against a defendant. Chief Justice Warren, in dissent, stated that this conviction for refusing to answer questions, under these circumstances, was unconstitutional.

The conclusion from these cases can be stated thusly: In a contempt case, the privilege may be raised as a defense to testifying, where the testimony would incriminate the individual in a criminal contempt. It would seem that the privilege may be successfully raised to avoid testifying on the issue of a civil contempt, as well. An individual may also refuse to testify about matters which would subject him to a noncontempt criminal prosecution in the same jurisdiction, and this refusal will not be deemed a contempt. However, where testimony would subject him to noncontempt criminal prosecution in another jurisdiction, his refusal on self-incrimination grounds will be contemptuous. Yet, where one inquiry solicits testimony relating to incriminating incidents in two jurisdictions, a defendant may refuse to testify about any of the incidents or demand absolute immunity from later prosecution in either jurisdiction.

The essence of the self-incrimination clause is that incriminatory evidence forced from an individual is both unreliable, and unconscionable, and therefore should be constitutionally protected. This policy seems to be dissipated by that trend of cases which allows prosecutions in a second jurisdiction, based on evidence which would be unconstitutional if used in the jurisdiction wherein it was secured. This kind of judicial reasoning allows individual rights to be subjected to circuitous if not devious prosecution tactics. If the self-incrimination clause is to be given more than ceremonious respect, the rule in contempt cases ought to be brought in line with the rule which prevails within each separate jurisdiction. Otherwise, intergovernmental cooperation could defeat the vital purpose of this constitutional protection.

Like the double jeopardy situation, the self incrimination problem is aggravated in contempt cases. The evidentiary problem of sovereign crossfire of prosecutions arise in search and seizure cases, double jeopardy cases, and self-incrimination cases. This is presently one of the most litigated and argued about problems of constitutional law and political power. The interjection of the contempt power adds another pressure to an already explosive situation, by aiming punishment at the individual, who, not knowing which way to turn, elects to stand still.

DUE PROCESS OF LAW

"Summary punishment of contempt is concededly an exception to the requirements of due process. Necessity dictates the departure."[215]

The due process of law clause is one which is doubly difficult to define. It is uncertain semantically, as it is as a direction of legal consequence. Its history has been one of redefinition according to the dictates of changing times and attitudes. Generally, if vaguely, it is a requirement for some standard of comportment in governmental proceedings equivalent with contemporary concepts of fairness and justness. The discussion of the requirements of notice and hearing and representation, in the section to follow, concerning the Sixth Amendment, establishes that many of the specific procedural guarantees in that amendment have been deemed applicable to the contempt situation, but under due process rationales.

In the *Cooke* case,[216] the court wrote: "Due process of law, therefore, in the prosecution of contempt, except of that committed in open court, requires that the accused should be advised of the charges and have a reasonable opportunity to meet them . . . this includes the assistance of counsel . . . the right to call witnesses. . . ." [217] Indeed, several of these rights are now incorporated in the Federal Rules of Criminal Procedure, lest there be any uncertainty in constitutional interpretation with respect to the contempt situation.[218] However, there are other aspects of contempt procedures which still raise serious due process questions.

One of these problems is the requirement of proof of contempt. Civil wrongs are characteristically proved by "a preponderance of evidence," while crimes demand proof "beyond a reasonable doubt." However, the Supreme Court has again applied a variant formula to the contempt case, and likening civil contempt to fraud cases, has called for a requirement of "clear and convincing evidence," exceeding a mere preponderance,[219] but something less than the reasonable doubt test of criminal cases. In the case of criminal contempts, proof beyond a reasonable doubt is required.[220] These two criteria have occasionally been applied by federal courts, which have been astute about the rules, but confused about the proper classification of the contempt.[221] Again, classification of a contempt is the key to an appropriate decision.

In a recent case, the Supreme Court dealt with this problem. In the *McPhaul* case,[222] the court was called upon to review a conviction for contempt of a congressional committee. The defendant's claim was that there was insufficient proof that subpoenaed records of the Civil Rights Congress (an organization alleged to be subversive) were: relevant to the committee's inquiry; in existence; or in his possession and control. The trial court refused to instruct the jury that they must find these three facts to be proved beyond a reasonable doubt. Instead, the court instructed the jury to ignore these facts "because if the defendant had legitimate reason for failing to produce the said records he should have stated the reason for non-compliance with the subpoena." [223] In other words, the court gave defendant the responsibility of coming forward with exculpatory evidence. On certiorari,[224] the majority of the Supreme Court, following certain past decisions,[225] upheld the contempt conviction. Relying on analogous precedent that records kept in a representative rather than a personal capacity are not subject to the personal privilege of the self-incrimination clause,[226] as well as the primacy of the House of Representatives' committee work, Justice Whittaker, for the majority, agreed that the defendant should have, in effect, proved part of the government's case against himself by cooperating in the gathering of evidence for his own future conviction. The Chief Justice and Justices Black, Douglas, and Brennan dissented on the ground that the majority's decision "marks such a departure from the accepted procedure designed to protect accused people from public passion and overbearing officials." [227] The presumption of innocence is shifted by giving defendants the burden of proof on the issue of the willfulness of his refusal.

This point was recognized in an earlier federal case.[228] Dealing with exactly similar facts, the court there overruled a contempt conviction, pointing out: "The defendant can here legally be jailed only for a contempt in failing to produce the sought-after books when they are fairly shown to be presently within his power and controls. He cannot legally be jailed for contempt for invoking his constitutionally protected privilege not to be a witness against himself." [229] Admonishing that this case was a step backwards, the minority in the *McPhaul* case warned: "when it comes to criminal prosecutions, the government must turn square corners. If Congress desires to have the judiciary adjudge a man guilty for failure to produce documents, the prosecution should be required to prove that the man . . . had the power to produce them." [230]

The case, though turning on what appears to be a narrow question of statutory interpretation, really underscores the very basic implication of the contempt power—that is, the constant tug between governmental power and individual freedom, a philosophical and political problem recurring again and again in the garb of legal decisions about the contempt power.

The case above deviates from past federal court treatment of this problem. As far back as 1894 one federal judge wrote: "Accusations for contempt must be supported by evidence sufficient to convince the mind of the trior, beyond a reasonable doubt, of the actual guilt of the accused, and every element of the offense." [231]

Yet, where a direct criminal contempt is committed, the defendant may be convicted upon the sworn statement of the judge alone.[232] That statement, it has been held, "imports absolute verity." [233] The import and gravity of this procedure is compounded by the fact that the appellate courts have no record upon which to base any review and therefore usually uphold the trial court's discretionary conduct.

Congressional contempts are now all prosecuted pursuant to a federal criminal statute and as such must be proved beyond a reasonable doubt, as is the case with all other crimes. The general civil-criminal distinctions are made concerning proof of contempts of court. However, these situations are muddied by interpretations like that in the *McPhaul* case, and by odd classifications of civil and criminal contempts, as well as the special way of proving direct and civil contempts.

THE JUDGE

"A fair trial in a fair tribunal is a basic requirement of due process. Fairness of course requires an absence of actual bias." [234]

Another aspect of contempt procedures which would seem to conflict with due process protection is that whereby the judge in a summary proceeding acts as judge, prosecutor, jury, and sentencer. Often he was personally the subject of the contempt. This anomalous procedure derives from old English practices which were not, and still are not, looked at askance. We have seen that some of these practices have been proved to be based upon shaky historical foundations. Strictly a product of the common-law system, this procedure is astonishing to subjects of the civil law tradition. It is astonishing to some common-law lawyers, too.[235] Justice Black wrote in the *Green* case:

When the responsibilities of lawmaker, prosecutor, judge, jury and disciplinarian are thrust upon a judge he is obviously incapable of holding the scales of justice perfectly fair and true and reflecting impartially on the guilt or innocence of the accused. He truly becomes the judge of his own cause. The defendant charged with criminal contempt is thus denied . . . an indispensable element of the due process of law.[236]

Now, the Federal Rules of Criminal Procedure provide that: "If the contempt charged involves disrespect to or criticism of a judge, that judge is disqualified from presiding at the trial or hearing except with the defendant's consent." [237] A similar requirement was included in the Clayton Act. But in some existing contempt situations the judge is still not disqualified.

These provisions, though they apply only to indirect, criminal contempts, are eminently proper so far as they go. Federal Rule 42 was based on the observations of Chief Justice Taft in the *Cooke* case.[238] There, he noted the delicate balance which individual judges must strike in these cases between any impulse toward reprisal and such leniency as would injure the authority of the court. He suggested substitution of another judge wherever possible. Obviously concerned with this problem, Chief Justice Taft in an earlier opinion had offered this inequity as another ground for extending the pardon power to cover contempt convictions.[239]

The Supreme Court has often noted the human qualities of

judges, by which they, as others, are subject to such fallibilities and frailties as anger, petulance, and even vengeance. Whether judges are made of sterner stuff than other men and are consequently better able to withstand the natural evocations of human emotion, has been debated many times and in many contexts.[240] Though variant opinions abound, and the problem may never be adequately resolved, it is not too heretical to suggest that a shift in personnel is more calculated to insure fairness in the trial of contempt cases, and that the mere donning of judicial robes and the consciousness of an oath long ago taken may succumb to more immediate emotional demands. In a case in which he discussed this issue, Justice Frankfurter wrote: "These are subtle matters, for they concern the ingredients of what constitutes justice. Therefore, justice must satisfy the appearance of justice." [241]

Though one can never know the mental processes by which a judge has acted, it seems more reasonable to conclude that the impersonal authority of law is better guarded and applied by one who is not himself personally involved in a given conflict. Perhaps the most glaring example of this problem was made by the New York Communist trials in 1949. There, Judge Medina and counsel for the defense wrangled, spewed, and fought for nine months during a heated, protracted trial in a celebrated political atmosphere.[242] At the conclusion of the trial, Judge Medina summarily sentenced his contemnors to six months imprisonments. The Supreme Court upheld the conviction,[243] but Justice Frankfurter wrote a dissent in which he deplored the trial judges' conduct.[244] He included in his opinion an appendix of quotations from the trial record which indicated the open hostility and distaste which the judge and contemnors had for one another. It would have taken godliness in that case for the judge to have acted impartially and with proper detachment. Several of Justice Frankfurter's brethren felt that Judge Medina had shown somewhat less than that.

The alternative to this summary procedure is not indefensible judicial proceedings. It is merely the interposition of another judge who is not a party to the dispute in question. Whatever inconvenience this may be is overcome by advantages of moral rightness and fairness that would be likely to inure.

Greater expansion upon the demerits of judging a cause in which one is personally interested begs the very obvious. The axiom that no man should judge his own cause was one early accepted in American law,[245] and with good reason. This was later applied so that a "direct, substantial, pecuniary interest" [246] would preclude judicial action. Professor Edmond Cahn recently noted the anomalous position which would have a wealthy judge disqualified on the basis of a minor or remote pecuniary interest in a cause before his court, while allowing him to decide a case which involved matters of the deepest, most profound effect on his emotional attachments.[247] Not only would his interest be likely to effect the issue of innocence or guilt of the contemnor, but it might also bear on the degree of sentence exacted as punishment for the contempt.[248]

The due process inhibition on judges who are interested in proceedings applies to state officers as well, by application of the Fourteenth Amendment.[249]

Still the Supreme Court has not gone as far as it could. It has not ruled that as a matter of due process of law a judge cannot sit in a case in which he is personally affected. It intimated so in the *Offutt* case,[250] but that decision was based on the court's supervisory authority over the administration of criminal justice in the federal courts, not on due process grounds. This leaves less liberty-loving judges able to distinguish away what could have established a right rule.[251]

The Supreme Court has upheld a summary conviction for a direct contempt which arose out of an altercation between a trial judge and defense counsel in a case before that judge.[252] Recognizing the difficulty appellate courts have in reviewing such cases, yet upholding the conviction, the majority of the court agreed: "In a case of this type the transcript of the record cannot convey to us the complete picture of the courtroom scene. It does not depict such elements of misbehavior as expression, manner of speaking, bearing, and attitude." [253] Justice Douglas felt that the majority opinion deprived defendant's constitutional rights of freedom of speech; Justices Rutledge and Murphy dissented too, but on due process grounds.

Of all the complaints about the summariness of contempt procedures, the argument against having an insulted or at least interested judge preside over the proceedings which adjudge and punish the misconduct requires the least support. Its moral and reasonable sense should not be open to legal distinction. Contempt is the only instance where such an anomalous practice occurs, though there is less reason there than in any other case. This injustice is already recognized in judicial decisions and by legislation. To the extent that these authorities do not prevail, some relief should be afforded. This too will be discussed in the following chapter.

The Sixth Amendment

The jury trial provision of the Sixth Amendment is not the only aspect of that constitutional provision which is pertinent to this review of contempt practices. The Sixth Amendment more fully reads:

In all criminal prosecutions, the accused shall enjoy the right to a *speedy and public trial*, by an *impartial jury* of the State and district *wherein the crime shall have been committed*, which district shall have been previously ascertained by law, and to be *informed* of the *nature and cause of the accusation;* to be *confronted* by the witnesses against him; to have *compulsory process* for obtaining witnesses in his favor, and to have the assistance of *counsel* for his defense.[254]

VENUE

In addition to the issue of whether contempt proceedings are criminal prosecutions and as such merit jury trials, which has already been mentioned, and passing to the following section of the Sixth Amendment, the problem of venue is also noteworthy. Where is the "crime" committed? Again, the decision-maker is initially belabored with the recurrent problem of whether contempt is a crime, as envisioned by that section. If it is not, of course, there is no constitutional venue problem. Assuming that it is, as good sense and reason would indicate, the venue problem may, in a given case, be one of constitutional magnitude.

In 1924 the Supreme Court addressed itself to the problem of ascertaining the proper venue for contempt proceedings.[255] There, the defendants had violated a court decree of one district court, by contumacious conduct in another district. At trial, the defendant objected to the contempt jurisdiction of the first court, on the ground of the Sixth Amendment's direction that crimes be tried in the district where they are committed. The court held that contempts are sui generis, not "criminal prosecutions" within the Sixth Amendment, and that the conviction was therefore proper. This authority has been followed[256] on the theory that the court whose order was disobeyed would not have the power to punish the offense if a contempt had to be tried where the act was committed.[257]

This venue provision of the Sixth Amendment is now embodied in the Federal Rules of Criminal Procedure, as well.[258] The Federal Rules of Civil Procedure specify that civil actions will be tried only in a judicial district where all defendants reside, subject to certain qualifications not important to this review.[259]

These are logical rules since in both civil and criminal contempts, that wrong which is committed is directly or indirectly one to the court controlling the main action. In cases of contempt by publication this rule could become awkward. Take, for example, the hypothetical case of a California newspaper which publishes a contemptuous article about a pending New York proceeding. The New York court having plenary jurisdiction over the subject matter, must have the controlling power elsewhere, as well. The contempt is to the New York court, although it might seem that the offensive act really took place in California.[260] This problem has arisen most often in injunction cases, where court orders were violated in different districts from that of the court which issued the order. The decisions have uniformly upheld the power of the first court to deal with the contempt. As it was written in the *Dunham* case:

A proceeding for contempt springs out of a litigation instituted in a particular court. . . . Its principal object is to secure obedience to the orders of that court, by punishing as a contempt disobedience thereof. It is the court whose judgment or order has been defied which must try the contempt and pronounce judgment. . . . If the place of the trial for a criminal contempt must be in the district where the acts constituting it were committed, then where such acts were committed in a different district than that of the court whose order has been contemned, such court would be powerless to deal punitively with the violation of its injunctive orders, and the trial and punishment of such contempt would have to be by a different court than that whose order had been defied. This would clearly be an alteration of the entire idea of a contempt, and in derogation of the power of a court to deal with violators of its orders.[261]

The principal policy of the venue section of the Sixth Amendment is to guarantee that a person charged with the commission of a crime will be tried by his neighbors who are familiar with the setting and the facts, rather than by strangers who may not be appreciative of local problems, customs, and values. This central idea is maintained in the contempt venue situation, though for slightly different reasons. Since a contempt conviction is designed to punish ramifications of an act (like judicial indignity or inconvenience) rather than the act itself (such as writing a letter to a judge, or failing to produce a book), it is sensible to conclude that the wrong took place where the particular ramification resulted and not where the act which initiated that result was committed. A local court or jury of residents of the area in which the affected court presided would be attuned to the problems presented by the case and aware of the effect of the offense.

SPEEDY TRIAL

The first section of the Sixth Amendment also speaks about the right to a "speedy trial." Is there some statute of limitations governing the contempt action? This problem was dealt with in the famous *Gompers* case.[262] There Justice Holmes wrote an opinion which discussed the time limitations for contempt actions, in a case involving the conviction of a celebrated labor leader. Gompers defended on the ground that a general statutory three-year time limitation for all noncapital offenses implicitly barred his conviction for contempt. Justice Holmes ruled that the statutory period was appropriate, and that formal or rigid legal formulas for statutory interpretations were to be avoided in such vital proceedings. Dismissing an attempt to avoid the application of the statute or the Constitution by classifying contempt as a sui generis "offense" not quite within the terms of the statute, he wrote:

provisions of the Constitution are not mathematical formulas having their essence in their form; they are organic living institutions transplanted from English soil. Their significance is vital not formal; it is to be gathered not simply by taking the words and a dictionary, but by considering their origin and the line of their growth.[263]

"Indeed," he continued, "the punishment of these offenses peculiarly needs to be speedy if it is to occur." He said by way of dictum that it was well that some rule be set out dealing with the punishment of this crime, by the courts if not by the legislature.

The power to punish for contempt must have some limit in time, and in defining that limit we should have regard to what has been the policy of the law from the foundation of the Government. By analogy if not by enactment the limit is three years.[264]

Holmes's basic reason was that allowing an action to be commenced at any time "would be utterly repugnant to the genius of our laws." [265]

In a later contempt case, Justice Douglas affirmed the three-year statute of limitations enunciated by Justice Holmes, and refined it by ruling that the statute began to run from the time of the contemptuous act of misbehavior and not from the time of the last act by which the misbehavior was consumated.[266] A five-year period of limitations for the commencement of criminal contempt actions is now guaranteed by a federal statute.[267] A sister statute limits the time to one year in cases where the contemptuous act also constitutes another crime.[268]

We have already seen that a civil contempt, by its very nature, becomes extinguished at the termination of the action from which it arose.[269] Judge Magruder has said that a district court which issues a compensatory civil contempt order may, as part of that remedial process, later commit to prison where the order is not obeyed.[270] However, acts violative of a decree, and thereby contemptuous, but occurring after the date of the final decree, can be punished as a contempt only so far as they violate terms of that final decree. Another court has gone further, and held that it is "within the power of the court to order punishment for such [civil] contempts whenever the proof was brought to its attention . . . whenever it learns of acts which constitute such contempts." [271] This language sounds unduly broad. Suppose the court learned of the contemptuous conduct long after it was committed, and after the main action from which it arose was completed. A civil contempt citation would not only violate the policy against the revitalization of stale claims but also would have no relation to the purpose of civil contempt—coercing a certain lawful result. In fact, this would seem to be a criminal contempt sanction.

NOTICE AND HEARING

The general trial procedures which govern contempt proceedings are less than uniform and depend again upon a prior classification of the particular contemptuous act—here, as direct or indirect.[272] This distinction was drawn by the Supreme Court in 1888, in a case which involved a determination of the proper procedures for a contempt committed in the presence of the court.[273] The court first stated the proposition that proceedings without notice and hearing are not judicial or worthy of respect. It then expounded a special rule "of almost immemorial antiquity, and universally acknowledged," vital to personal liberty and ordered society, and applicable to direct contempts. The court then adopted this rule, which it felt was based on precedent and necessity, that notice and hearing are not required, and imprisonment may immediately follow. It states:

it is a settled doctrine in jurisprudence both of England and of this country, never supposed to be in conflict with the liberty of the citizen, that for direct contempts committed in the face of the court . . . the offender may, in its discretion, be instantly apprehended and immediately imprisoned, without trial or issue, and without further proof . . . such power, although arbitrary in nature and liable to abuse, is absolutely essential.[274]

In a later case that same year, the court articulated the rule for indirect contempts.[275] Citing the earlier opinion and its rule for direct contempts, the court distinguished indirect contempts, holding that "whereas, in cases of misbehavior of which the judge cannot have such personal knowledge, and is [only] informed thereof . . . the proper practice is . . . to require the offender to appear and show cause why he should not be punished." [276]

At this proceeding, the accused should be given notice of the charges made and an opportunity for explanation and defense.[277] The particular manner of the proceeding, though, is a matter for judicial regulation, "so long as not oppressive or unfair." [278] Thirty-six years later, the Supreme Court ruled that these Sixth Amendment procedural rights were equally protected by the due process clause of the Fifth Amendment.[279]

> Due process of law, therefore, in the prosecution of contempt, except of that committed in open court, requires that the accused should be advised of the charges and have a reasonable opportunity to meet them by way of defense or explanation. We think this includes the assistance of counsel, if requested, and the right to call witnesses to give testimony.[280]

And so the Sixth Amendment's rights of notice, hearing, and counsel were applied to indirect contempts, though direct contempts were still allowed to be treated summarily, in order to avoid a feared demoralization of the court's authority. The balance again was judicially tipped in favor of judicial security and efficiency over personal liberty and procedural safeguards.

The problem arose again in 1947.[281] The Supreme Court was called upon to review a contempt conviction arising out of a secret one-man grand jury proceeding, held pursuant to a Michigan statute. The court reversed the conviction on the grounds that the Fourteenth Amendment's due process protection included such procedural rights as public trial, hearing, notice of charges, examination of witnesses, and representation by counsel. Although the court divided its opinion, the majority held that these procedural rights bound the states as well as the federal government, even in criminal contempt cases.[282]

These rights are now all covered by federal statute in most situations. For any contempt of Congress, the accused is allowed all rights guaranteed by the Sixth Amendment. For an indirect criminal contempt of court, he is guaranteed a speedy, impartial hearing. For direct criminal contempt of court or civil contempt of court, exceptions are made. I suggest that these exceptions are, as a matter of policy, unnecessary, and as a matter of law unconstitutional. The reasons advanced in support of these exceptional deprivations of procedural rights are historical precedent, judicial self-defense and respect, and efficiency. Any legal proceeding, in which an individual may be imprisoned (whether for a specified and limited time or more especially where the duration is unlimited), or deprived of his property in a penal sense, as is the case in all present contempt situations, should be treated as a criminal prosecution as contemplated by the Sixth Amendment. All rights warranted by that constitutional provision should be available to the accused contemnor. Any loss to society through judicial embarrassment, inconvenience, or delay would be far outweighed in social values by the added dignity of individual freedom, and the greater respect which would derive from a system which consistently recognized these constitutional liberties. This is the liberal essence of our constitutional government; the essence of our philosophy of the relation between men and law and government.

The Eighth Amendment

"Excessive bail shall not be required, nor excessive fines imposed, nor cruel and unusual punishments inflicted." [283]

Justice Black's sweeping condemnation of contempt practices in the *Green* case also included a criticism of the open-end sentencing procedure available in many contempt situations. He wrote:

as the law now stands there are no limits on the punishment a judge can impose on a defendant whom he finds guilty of contempt except for whatever remote restrictions exist in the Eighth Amendment's prohibition against cruel and unusual punishments or in the nebulous requirements of "reasonableness" now promulgated by the majority.[284]

And later in that opinion he noted:

its subversive potential . . . appears to be virtually unlimited. All the while the sentences imposed on those found guilty of contempt have steadily mounted, until now they are even imprisoned for years.[285]

This constitutional clause has been infrequently applied and strangely interpreted.[286] The phrase "cruel and unusual punishment" first appeared in the English Bill of Rights in 1688. Thereafter, it appeared in early legal declarations in the United States and finally was adopted as part of the Eighth Amendment to the United States Constitution. All state constitutions have similar language. Courts, though infrequently visited with Eighth Amendment issues, have not always agreed upon the true meaning or application of the clause. Although there is common agreement that the original purpose of this provision was to allay fears of governmental intrusion upon personal liberties by providing some constitutional check, modern courts are less than clear about its interpretation: what is cruel, what is unusual, what constitutes punishment, or whether civil sentences are covered. The predominant view is that the clause is aimed only at preventing barbaric, torturous punishments. Modern interpretations have occasionally gone further, holding that it could be used to relieve sentences whose durations were cruel in proportion to the wrongful act as well as in the mode or nature of the punishment itself. It would be this aspect of the clause which might be relevant in contempt cases.

The Eighth Amendment promises little shelter to the contemnor who feels that his sentence is onerous. Primarily, there is serious question about the applicability of the amendment in civil contempt cases. The clause speaks of punishments, and the argument can be made that civil contempt sentences are remedial civil devices, not punitive sanctions. In a legal sense, punishments are imposed for the commission of crimes. In a literal sense, punishment is a penalty, retributive suffering, pain, or loss. Civil contempt sentences are punishments in the latter sense, but not necessarily in the former.

Occasionally, the point has been litigated. In a New York case,[287] a husband was imprisoned for failing to pay alimony to his wife. He had suffered financially from the depression, and his wife was childless and earning her own living. After two years and seven months of helplessly floundering in jail, he applied for discharge from imprisonment. The court, facetiously nominating him "the senior inmate of the sheriff's alimony colony," released the contemnor, noting that the state's cruel and unusual punishment provision need not be limited to "barbarities," but should be construed as a "forward-looking and progressive declaration of principle." Critical of the rule which would confine the merciful application of the clause to criminal contempts, while denying it in harsher civil contempt cases, the court wrote:

Under these sections if an intruder disturbs the serenity of a courtroom . . . the limits of judicial displeasure are circumscribed by statute. . . . However, let a waspish woman pluck the sleeve of the judicial gown . . . and this temperate restraint is immediately cast aside, and the delinquent spouse faces the possibility of unending imprisonment. . . . This carries the supposed rights of women to absurd . . . lengths . . . there are those who doubt the expediency of its extension into a form of petticoat justice.[288]

The good sense of this reasoning has not prevailed. The cruel and unusual punishment provision has generally been held relevant to situations arising out of the more traditional criminal punishments, and civil contempts have been consistently differentiated from this class of cases.

Not long ago, the New York newspapers reported, with proper indignation, the confinement of an eighty-year-old lady for civil contempt of a surrogate court. She had languished in prison for over three years before the same judge who had committed her ordered her release. At the time of this writing, she is still in contempt of that court and conceivably could be sent back to prison. Her contempt was more a result of a naïveté and ignorance of probate proceedings than a corruption of the administration of justice and her prolonged confinement was preposterous. The severity of the law of contempt upon little old ladies has dramatically frustrated the courts of England, too. In 1886, Maria Annie Davies was imprisoned for contempt.[289] She had been unsuccessful in attempts to get legal title to some houses and property to which she claimed ownership. She had to be enjoined from forcefully possessing them. When her endeavors were not deterred, she was incarcerated for contempt until she would conform to the court's order. She remained adamant, in jail. Two years later, an embarrassed court discharged her from custody, lamented their position, and hopefully ordered her cooperation. In its opinion, the court voiced regret that this annoying, though not serious, offense was punishable by imprisonment at all.

Justice Rutledge defined what he thought to be the mandate of the Eighth Amendment, in his dissent to the *United Mine Workers* case. There, he wrote:

The law has fixed standards for each remedy, and they are . . . for damages in civil contempt the amount of injury proven and no more . . . for coercion, what may be required to bring obedience and not more, whether by way of imprisonment or fine; for punishment, what is not cruel and unusual, or in the case of a fine, excessive within the Eighth Amendment's prohibition.[290]

The realities have not always meshed with his articulation of policy.

In the civil contempt cases, there is often no relation between the sentence and the coercion necessary to compel obedience. In cases where the contemnor does not cooperate on grounds of moral indignation or principle or impossibility (as in some alimony cases), there is no calculable relation between the punishment and the goal sought. Unfortunately, this often results in harsh waiting-out periods, where the prisoner sits in jail indefinitely. Moreover, in fact, civil contempts are sometimes civil in name only, entailing what are in reality criminal punishments.[291]

There is equal question about the realism of the Rutledge formula in criminal contempt cases. Most criminal contempt sentences are something short of cruel or unusual, though they may at times be viewed as harsh, more than necessary, or overly strict.

In the *Green* case, the convicted Smith Act defendants were given an additional sentence of three years' imprisonment for "jumping bail" in contempt of a federal court order to appear for sentencing. The maximum sentence under the bail-jumping statute was five years. But, indictment under that statute would have guaranteed a jury trial before a disinterested judge. Such a severe sentence (and at that the judge was limited only by his good will) is not unusual in contempt cases.

Another Smith Act defendant was found guilty of criminal contempt and sentenced to imprisonment for four years.[292] He failed to obey a district court order to surrender, and was apprehended two years later. The Second Circuit Court of Appeals considered this sentence "well within a reasonable exercise of discretion by the trial judge, obviously . . . not violating the Eighth Amendment."

The casebooks abound with further examples. A Kentucky circuit court fined a man $5,000 for contempt. After the state court of appeals affirmed the fine, a kindly governor pardoned the offender.[293] That case was in 1908, when $5,000 was a considerable fortune. Two years earlier, the Kentucky courts issued a contempt sentence of $3,000 and two-years imprisonment against a codefendant in the above case.[294] The act which constituted the contempt in that case was attempted bribery of a juror. Punishment for that could have arisen only after trial in the ordinary fashion and with all procedural safeguards. Earlier, I mentioned a nine-year civil contempt sentence for refusing to answer questions.[295]

In the *Toledo Newspaper Co.* case [296] the publishers and editor of a local newspaper were fined $7,500 for their constructive contempt of a pending judicial proceeding. Their offensive conduct consisted of no more than editorializing about a disputed street railway franchise in the city of Toledo. More vitriolic comments have gone unpunished since then because of Supreme Court reluctance to include press comments within the wording of the federal contempt statute.

In the sensational *United Mine Workers* case,[297] John L. Lewis, the famous union leader of the mine workers, was fined $10,000 and his union was fined $3.5 million for contempt. Their contempt involved disobedience of a court order restraining interference by the mine workers with temporary governmental operation of the mines during the conciliation of a labor-management dispute. The Supreme Court upheld Lewis' fine, but reduced the union fine to $700,000, conditioned upon its subsequent compliance with the same order. In a separate opinion, Justices Black and Douglas criticized the excessive sentence. They pointed out that the same interference during wartime would have been governed by a $5,000 maximum fine under the War Labor Disputes Act. The equities in that case were compounded by the fact that the defendants felt, in good faith, that they were acting within their legal rights. Lawyers and legal scholars have differed in their interpretations of many laws similar to the one that gave rise to the contempt in the *Mine Workers* case, and of the sweepingly broad language of the contempt statute itself, and even the Supreme Court has not been able to clarify this muddled area of the law.

Regardless of how onerous sentencing for contempt may become, present indications point to little solace from the Eighth Amendment's protections. That amendment was originally included in the Constitution to protect citizens against those horrid and barbarous punishments which the history of man had seen inflicted and which shock the conscience of modern civilized society.[298] By interpretation, however, American courts have restrictively construed this potentially merciful legal vehicle to the point where its usefulness is minimal. Capital punishment by gas, hanging, and electrocution have been considered neither cruel nor unusual. Prolonged imprisonments and, sometimes, capital punishment have been imposed by less progressive states for relatively insignificant crimes. A $3.5 million fine for contempt was based upon a persistent but mistaken interpretation of the law—in the mid-twentieth century. When John Kaspar, a despicable racist, flaunted a court order and attempted to provoke interference at Clinton High School with the Supreme Court's segregation decision, he was sentenced to one year's imprisonment.[299] The federal court which reviewed that contempt conviction disposed of the defense that the sentence violated the Eighth Amendment. Punishments are cruel and unusual, the court held, only where they are "so greatly disproportionate to the offense committed as to be completely arbitrary and shocking to the sense of justice." What criteria or what sense of justice, the court did not indicate.

Another federal court has held that the words "cruel and unusual" are to be considered in light of developing civilization, not what was so in the eighteenth century.[300] But courts have given little attention to this constitutional problem, even philosophically. In a California case where policemen pumped a man's stomach to retrieve evidence which was later used against him at trial, the Supreme Court could not muster approval.[301]

They reversed the conviction because these tactics were too close to the rack and screw for American justice to tolerate. In discussing the meaning of "liberty" under the due process clause, the Supreme Court has spoken of those fundamental rights basic to fair play upon which our concepts of justice are founded. And, in 1959, the Second Circuit Court of Appeals, while recognizing that the unlimited contempt power exists, remanded a case for redetermination, because among other things a contempt sentence was so inordinately harsh as to be onerous.[302] There, a defendant was fined $1,500 and sentenced to imprisonment for six months. He had been summoned in California to appear before a New York grand jury. He sought a temporary adjournment but was refused. Though he failed to appear on the date required, he did appear voluntarily soon thereafter. He offered to purge his contempt and testify before the grand jury, but the government officials refused and prosecuted the contempt instead. These sporadic opinions have not coalesced to form a definite Eighth Amendment philosophy.

At another time, the Supreme Court offered a vague formula, for considering the cruel or unusual quality of punishments, which sought to strike some balance in the relation between the crime and the punishment.[303] In discussing the cruel and unusual punishment provision, one state court judge wrote:

It is regarded as primarily relating to the kind and character or method of punishment, referring to inhuman or barbarous treatment or punishment unknown to the common law or which has become obsolete with the progress of humanitarianism, rather than to the severity in the amount or duration. But it would seem that most of the courts hold it covers that too.[304]

The examples presented in this section would indicate either that the last sentence of this opinion is inaccurate, or that this author's concept of what is excessive in amount is a value judgment which is at odds with the views prevailing amongst others.

In a recent contempt case,[305] a federal court sustained a fifteen-month sentence on the ground that it was reasonable when viewed in the light of other similar convictions of eighteen months,[306] or three and four years.[307] The Supreme Court upheld that decision. The lower federal courts have "considerable latitude" [308] in sentencing for contempt. Compounded by the minimal trial record in contempt proceedings, and the reluctance of appellate courts to overturn the decisions of lower courts, this discretion is tantamount to total license. In the *Brown* case mentioned above, an aggressive district attorney asked the judge to mete out a substantial sentence, to omit a standard clause by which the contemnor might purge his offense, and to deny bail. The judge did all three, in his discretion.

To summarize, the situation is presently thus: For contempt of Congress there is a one-year maximum sentence. The Eighth Amendment would not prohibit this severity, but might possibly apply in cases where successive convictions were sought for the same but repeated act of contumacy. For certain specific cases of contempt of a federal court there are statutory limitations. Many situations find the courts with unlimited discretion in their sentencing powers. Only three states have no statutory maximum punishment for the contempt power.[309] Sixteen states have a maximum for contempts committed outside the court, but none for direct contempts. Twenty-nine have over-all maximums. Nine have maximums of six months; one has a three months maximum; and the rest have thirty-day limitations.[310]

The cruel and unusual punishment provision of the Constitution, though indicating a policy against excessive sentencing practices, actually operates only against barbarous, Draconian punishments. While contempt sentencing practices do not fall into this category, they may occasionally be viewed as more harsh, more extensive, less aimed at purposeful, judicious goals than they might be. Some alleviation, at least, is merited. The chances would appear to be better that this relief will be arrived at through avenues other than the Eighth Amendment. Someday, courts may decide that current contempt practices improperly result in cruel punishments. Then, the versatility of the Constitution, through the elastic powers of judicial review, may be brought to surface. Courts with this sensitive interpretative power can alter the depth of constitutional provisions to high water marks or low, and thereby make the philosophies of time and place consistent with basic concepts of government and law.

Beyond this possibility, some trend can be sensed in recent years in which contempt sentences have occasionally been limited by statute. These legislative maximums have been realistic, and are the best answer to this problem for two reasons. A statutory maximum sentence apprises the potential contemnor of the likely consequences of his wrongful conduct before he acts. It would also limit the power of judges to exaggerate the gravity of punishments in cases where they might otherwise be so inclined. This is a far clearer method of controlling sentencing powers than the vague, varying, and often unusable protections of the Eighth Amendment, or the equally impractical recourse to judicial interpretations of excessiveness or unreasonableness.

Some all-embracing statute, under which all criminal contempt situations are clearly defined and their punishments appropriately limited, would best avoid the dangers and possible abuses of current contempt procedures. Civil contempts, which are sometimes punished more severely than criminal contempts, warrant individual treatment. This will be discussed in the concluding chapter.

The Tenth Amendment: Federal-State Relations

The Tenth Amendment to the United States Constitution reads: "The powers not delegated to the United States by the Constitution, nor prohibited by it to the States, are reserved to the States respectively, or to the people." The powers of the federal government were early interpreted to include those rights specifically granted to it in the Constitution and all powers necessarily inferrible from those specific constitutional grants.[311] These latter so-called implied powers have been the source of heated political and social conflicts from earliest times. One of the most volatile parts of our Constitution, which touches sensitive areas of local chauvinism and power, is the Tenth Amendment. It has caused debate about both the content of state and federal powers and the conflicts between those same powers. Which powers are to be left solely to the control of the states, and which to the national government? And, how does one determine which should prevail where both, properly asserted, conflict? Into this struggle, the contempt power enters only indirectly and infrequently.

In re Comingore [312] illustrates the basic problem. In that case, a collector of internal revenue for the federal government was questioned as a witness in a state civil proceeding. He refused to provide certain information which was demanded from him, on the ground that a federal regulation of the Secretary of the Treasury forbade such disclosure. He was fined and imprisoned for contempt and brought habeas corpus proceedings. The federal district court held that the state had no authority over property or archives of the United States Government. The state imposition through the medium of the contempt proceeding was therefore improper. The court further held that though this might not be the case with respect to the federal government's access to *public* records of states, or vice versa, there was no corresponding right to demand information about *nonpublic* matters.[313] If the latter pertained to internal governmental conduct, which policy demanded be kept from the public, no right of inspection would exist. "The state has neither occasion nor right to call upon the United States nor her officers for reports made under the administration of its laws in order to enforce the collection of state revenue. Nor would the United States have the right to call upon the state." [314]

In *U.S. v. Owlett*,[315] the power of a state committee to investigate intrastate work of the federal Works Progress Administration in that state was questioned. The United States objected on the ground that this interference would obstruct proper federal governmental functions. The federal court enjoined the disputed investigation, holding that it was beyond the jurisdiction of the state of Pennsylvania, and an interference with the established immunity of federal agencies from state control. Since this was not a proper area for state legislative action, the state was enjoined from acting.

The recent conflict between the New York–New Jersey Port Authority and the Celler House Judiciary Subcommittee gave added notoriety to this problem.[316] The New York–New Jersey Port Authority is an interstate municipal agency created by state compact for joint development of transportation and commerce. The defendant, an officer of the Authority, was subpoenaed to appear and testify before a subcommittee of the Judiciary Committee of the United States House of Representatives. The subpoena called for production of all minutes, reports, and even office memoranda, day-by-day working papers, and trivial internal file material of the Authority. The governors of New York and New Jersey requested a delay to look into what they felt was "a novel intrusion by the federal government into areas reserved by the Constitution to our respective states." The request was denied. The defendant appeared before the committee at the appointed time and offered to testify without limit. However, in obedience to instructions of Governors Meyner of New Jersey and Rockefeller of New York, he refused to produce the voluminous informal papers subpoenaed, but he did produce all official minutes and reports. He was ruled in contempt of Congress, denied an opportunity to seek further instructions from his superiors, and was indicted for criminal contempt under the contempt of Congress statute.

The defense to the indictment was based primarily on the argument that federal investigations into areas of state concern unconstitutionally interfere with the federal system of government as established by the reservation clause of the Tenth Amendment. There was no overbalancing federal interest, the defendant argued, to warrant this interference into matters of the internal administration of state affairs. In the context of the congressional contempt power, the problem was novel, and analogy with the few pertinent decisions only vaguely presaged the ultimate outcome.

The assertion of states rights arguments to uphold civil liberties is itself interesting. Lately, "states rights" has been frequently argued in behalf of the causes of conservatism, in conflict with certain libertarian causes. Yet, it may be that contempt convictions, arising out of state interference with federal governmental bodies or agents, violate the Constitution, and that the reverse might well be true unless some broader province is given to the powers of the federal government in the conflicts of dual sovereignty. Perhaps, the broad judicial condonations of legislative investigatory powers in recent times warranted the prediction that the Judiciary Committee would be upheld in its dispute with the Port Authority. A contemporary article implied that conclusion, pointing out that "The theory that state documents are sacrosanct when dealing with wholly internal matters was recently rejected." [317] That conclusion was drawn primarily from a lower federal court decision which upheld a claim by the Civil Rights Commission to voting records of the State of Alabama. The federal court ruled that Alabama's claim of sovereign invasion had to yield to proper exercises of congressional powers.[318]

Judge Youngdahl's opinion in the *Port Authority* case was careful, thorough, and well-reasoned. Ruling in favor of the congressional committee, he found that the inquiry was authorized, the demanded information was pertinent, the legislative purpose clear and prevailing, and that the other defenses of the Authority were unpersuasive. With respect to the Tenth Amendment, he was more judicious. Obviously influenced by recent First Amendment-congressional contempt cases, he refashioned the balancing test. Confining his decision to the unique facts of this case and warning that in different cases the factors would have to be weighed afresh, he found that the impediment to national interests caused by the Authority's failure to cooperate outweighed the state's interest in sacrosanct administration of its internal affairs.

But, he cautioned, the balance need not always tip in favor of the federal government. "If possible, attempt should be made to accommodate conflicting powers which overlap before it is decided that one must yield absolutely to the other." He suggested, "Honest and vigilant administration of the balancing test by the courts can accomplish this result. The federal system is itself the product of accommodation between the need for central direction of affairs affecting the entire nation and the desire to prevent overcentralization."

However, this recognition of state rights was minimized by his incorporation of the Madisonian philosophy that "Interference with the power of the States was no constitutional criterion of the power of Congress. If the power was not given, Congress could not use it; if given, they might exercise it, although it should interfere with the laws, or even the Constitution of the States." In other words, once a proper federal legislative power is discerned (in this case Congress derived its power from the compact clause), it can be used even if it interferes with state interests. The implication is that once the federal interest is established, it will prevail in a state-federal power conflict.

The court of appeals reversed the contempt conviction,[319] but did not answer the Tenth Amendment issue. Using judicial contortions, typical in reviewing congressional contempt cases, to avoid passing on the constitutional question, this court reversed the conviction on the ground that the subcommittee's authorization was not broad enough to warrant the inclusive subpoena in this case. Lamenting the position of the defendant who was forced to test civil and jurisdictional questions at the risk of a criminal conviction if he turned out to be wrong, the court wrote: "A contempt of Congress prosecution is not the most practical method of inducing courts to answer broad questions broadly. Especially is this so when the answers sought necessarily demand far-reaching constitutional adjudications." [320]

The practice of punishing men for contempt when they, in good faith, raise constitutional objections to congressional investigations and are not upheld by the appellate courts was properly criticized by the circuit court in its decision. Additionally, the court referred to Judge Youngdahl's opinion and agreed that this problem is even greater where the conflict is between two sovereigns or different governmental units.

Testing the constitutionality of congressional demands at the risk of a criminal contempt conviction puts a witness in an obviously difficult position. This predicament is often unsatisfactory to the congressional committee, as well. "The limitations inherent in a criminal contempt proceeding may prove burdensome, both to the witness, who must wager his liberty for the privilege of testing his belief that the committee is wrong, and to the committee, which must depend on the vagaries of a criminal action to establish its right to needed information." [321]

An extreme example of the explosiveness of the Tenth Amendment problem can be seen in the recent dispute in Mississippi between the governor of that state and the federal courts and Department of Justice. The *Barnett* case glaringly exemplifies the deep-rooted emotional content of Tenth Amendment conflicts.

Moreover, no better proof could be offered of the importance of the contempt power than its use as the focal point for so important a current issue as race relations and education in the Deep South.

The case also predictably posed an interesting paradox. Which way will the liberals on the Supreme Court turn should they be faced with deciding the constitutionality of contempt of court practices which deny the right to trial by jury? This faction of the court has been as critical of this aspect of criminal contempt practice as they have been active in securing the rights of Negroes to equal protection and due process of law.

The *Barnett* case also highlights the versatility of the Tenth Amendment argument to potentially thwart any federal action with which a state may disagree.

The *Barnett* case and the *Port Authority* case were both nurtured in notoriety, and characterized by adamant conviction on the part of the states and the federal government. The ultimate effects of these cases should be doubly interesting. Most controversies caused by the use of the contempt power involve the rights of government clashing with those of the individual. Here, the conflicts concern two sovereigns in dispute, and the issues of appropriate power and freedom are as perplexing as they are far-reaching.

This chapter provides only a panoramic view of the constitutional problems provoked by the application of the contempt power. Even that view should indicate the present constitutional maze created by the frequent implementation of a legal devise which has many anomalous characteristics. A unique body of law has developed and left a wake of strange and difficult problems—many of which remain unanswered.

CHAPTER V

Conclusion

The contempt power is a rich example of a legal device which raises questions that are at the core of mid-twentieth-century political thought. Should there be a crime based on interference with government? If so, should it be confined to serious crimes like treason or sedition, or should it embrace relatively lesser wrongs such as disorder in a courtroom, or being insolent to a congressman? In our development of democracy, how much freedom is guaranteed the individual? Which individual freedoms, short of absolute license, ought to be limited for the betterment of society? Does the contempt power go too far or not far enough toward maintaining the proper line between order and liberty? Where is that line? Which instances of stubborn protest and individual assertion are part of our proud inheritance, and which are part of a present ignoble characteristic? Should contemptuousness be left a matter of personal morality, or is it a characteristic which government should control?

At a second level, one may question whether any power which is granted to deal with these wrongs should be summarily exercised, without customary procedural protections. To grant such an implementation is to make contempt akin to the rare summary police powers ordinarily reserved for extreme and unavoidable situations.

The preceding chapters show that contempt is a legal power of frequent use, some historical confusion, often inconsistent classification, and a peculiar legal stature. Yet, its minor alterations in the face of sometimes strong criticism and its long and recently accelerated use might indicate that it is nevertheless a doctrine generally satisfactory by current American standards. No one has seriously raised the broad question of its worth and future. Having laid an informational foundation, I should like to raise the question. Is the modern American contempt power worth maintaining; and, if so, with what, if any, modification?

The alternatives are these four: First, the contempt power should be kept unchanged. Second, it should be maintained, but procedurally altered. Third, it should be substantively changed. And, fourth, the power should be eliminated.

The Status Quo

For those who disagree with the criticisms of the contempt power or who, while agreeing with some of the criticisms, feel that they are outweighed by other positive values, this book could end here. Certainly, something like the contempt power is consistent with political philosophies of an ordered liberty, which balances the interests of government and individuals, and prefers one to the other as particular exigencies and interests demand. Our political and legal system has survived a long life with the contempt power, and notwithstanding occasional difficulties they seem to have been compatible, at least to the extent that major conflict has been avoided. Whatever injustices may have resulted could be written off as manifestations of a less than perfect world and a less than utopian legal system. At worst, they are injustices which depend upon judgments of opinion, and they have been considered not unjust by many. Why then, it might be asked, risk the possibility of governmental failure to accommodate a conjectural anxiety?

On a more philosophical level, why subordinate public welfare to private freedom? Is individual freedom not, in a social world, less than absolute? Can the individual rise higher than his State in our scheme of competing values? Is not the exaltation of private freedom, implicit in a lessening of the contempt power, a derogation of an order of many represented, private freedoms? Would even the unruled man find comfort in a society of equally irresponsible individuals?

The fear of change, in the context of the future of the contempt power, is one of compelling force, grounded as it is in the faith in a social order which has government. Government, in its primary definition, is the exercise of authority, management, or control—it is governing! Therefore, is it not a wrong, over which society should exercise sanctions, for an individual to impede governmental functions by recalcitrance or insubordination?

Could it not be argued that while abuses are inevitable results of power, in the contempt situation the abuses are atypical? Is there some middle ground to the oft-quoted aphorism of Lord Acton that power corrupts and absolute power corrupts absolutely? If so, could it lie in Justice Johnson's criterion for the contempt power—the least possible power necessary for the end desired? [1]

Procedural Change

The critic who sees the need only for procedural change might take his cue from the statutory treatment of the congressional contempt power. Issues which have been taken with the judicial contempt power have been directed at the manner of its exercise —the procedural way it should be used. By comparison, the main issue which has been stressed about the statutory congressional contempt power has been not the manner but the extent of its exercise. Thus, some broader scheme could be conceived by which all those acts which are now treated as contempts would remain substantive wrongs, but would be prosecuted with the procedural protections of jury trial before a disinterested judge, after fair notice, and with prescribed limited punishments.

Such a preference is, to a great degree, based upon a faith in the unprovable value of procedural due process. One can only guess whether convictions would decrease or sentences be less severe, when the decision-making process was circumscribed by our constitutional safeguards of criminal procedure. However, a comparison with experiences in totalitarian states makes such a guess an educated one and a pointed one. Moreover, a spreading of responsibility into more popular channels is consistent with the ideal of a government which is as much of and by the people as for them. The cliché which enjoins that justice must include the appearance of justice is more than the hollow hypocrisy it may resemble. Procedural formalities may be as much of an un-provable deterrent to any autocratic tendency as they may some-times seem to be merely a rote ceremony.

Supposing this attitude, then, to be the most considered or the most desirable one, legislation would be necessary. Specifically, the courts could "judicially legislate" by extending current con-stitutional law to include procedural due process in contempt trials. To the extent of federal practice, the Supreme Court might be able to assure procedural rights in contempt cases through its rule-making power over the federal court system. It could promulgate a rule which would guarantee procedural protections in all contempt cases in the federal courts. Congress could act more directly by passing a law which made such procedural protections as the right to trial by jury, counsel, disinterested court, and the others already discussed mandatory in contempt trials. The latter would be preferable, clearer and more imbued with popular sanction.

Such an approach would certainly be consistent with the noble American attitude that government should not stoop to conquer. Aggressive prosecution of antisocial conduct and such punishment as may be necessary to effectuate that prosecution is fine, so long as the "deck is not stacked" against an accused. Government is legitimized and the innocent best protected when fair play guides prosecution. In this manner, contempt would be recognized as a crime but the contemnor would be treated in the same fashion as all others accused of crimes.

Substantive Change or Elimination of the Power

For the individual who feels that the American experience with the contempt power portends philosophical or political danger, substantive change or outright repeal may be a better solution. Such an attitude must include two implicit judgments: one, that our experience with the contempt power has indicated a predominance of bad over good results; and, another, that the proportion of this predominance is so serious that positive limitations are warranted.

Should this be the case, the most severe change would be complete elimination of the contempt power. Would this cause the collapse of government? What indeed would be the case if cooperation with and obedience to government was at the caprice of the individual citizenry? Long, almost rote, acceptance of a contrary presupposition would almost surely dictate the response —anarchy! But would this really be the case?

The Executive Power

The executive branch of government has, for the most part, no contempt power. Yet, this situation has proved to be workable enough. What then about the gamut of acting quasi-executive officers of government such as marshals, notaries, and the like? Does it seem imminent that this class of governmental officers would be emasculated in their work without the contempt power? Their minimal use of this power, along with the comparatively minor part it has played in the actual workings of these officers, might indicate that the difficulty would not be serious, let alone crucial.

The Administrative Power

Administrative agencies have infrequently resorted to the labyrinthal contempt techniques presently at their avail. However, there is good reason to believe that the situations which gave rise to those instances would be increased were the deterrence of the omnipresent contempt power eliminated. Also, at the times of need, no matter how few, the agencies would be rendered impotent without at least some coercive power like contempt. The issue then must be to balance the problem likely to result from a withdrawal of the power with the good which might be accomplished in terms of the exaltation of individual freedom which would follow that withdrawal. Again, one returns to the value judgment. In this case, we cannot be taught from experience, though possibly we may learn by comparison. Our country has always had a contempt power. Other countries have not. The freer-wheeling, looser procedures by which civil-law countries have progressed governmentally is some proof of the fact that the absence of the contempt power of American law need not be equivalent with the collapse of order. Administrative work would be, in certain instances, more cumbersome and, in others, possibly defeated. However, this difficulty would not necessarily leave no alternative. It would, in these limited cases, take the power problem away from the administrative agency. Since these agencies, at best, are not independent, the problem would not have to end with their impotency. So, total failure of the administrative process need not be the result of withdrawal of administrative contempt powers. Only their utility as adjuncts of the legislature or the judiciary would be impaired. Government would be forced to seek or provide some sanction elsewhere, but need not necessarily be without one.

I have discussed this subject with a number of the federal administrative agency attorneys who are experienced in the contempt work of their particular agency. It seems that contempt is resorted to relatively infrequently. For example, in the twenty-seven years of Securities and Exchange Commission experience, there are only twenty-four cases of contempt proceedings for violations of injunctions obtained by this agency. Indeed, there have been additional instances of contempt based on violation of agency subpoenas and civil contempts, as well as some other miscellaneous contempt actions. But these have been few—approximately one or two a year. The National Labor Relations Board has about twenty-five criminal contempt cases extant each year, but only five or so go to the point of actual litigation. Ordinarily, the contempt is purged once the court affirms the agency position. The problem from the agency standpoint is the frustrating delays occasioned under the present practice. The Federal Communications Commission resorts to more indirect powers of control, such as licensing attorneys who practice before the commission, though contempt procedures are available. They are rarely used, since they are rarely needed and are so cumbersome and self-defeating. Moreover, it has recently been noted that some operating agencies do not have the subpoena power, for example, the Post Office, the Federal Reserve Board, and the National Maritime Board. Others, like the Tariff Commission and Veterans Administration, which have the power, do not use it. One author recently remarked: "I wonder if agency investigators truly have demonstrated either a dependence on

compelled testimony, or a gain from such testimony that anywhere near offsets the dangers that lurk in powers to compel." [2]

The Legislative Power

What of legislative bodies? Is thorough and effective legislative
activity possible without a contempt power? Here, the answer is
less obvious, though analysis of the history of our federal legislature and its contempt power offers considerable insight.

Originally, the Congress used an inherent contempt power infrequently, and for the purpose of coercion. More recently, a
statutory power has been used frequently, and sometimes under
circumstances which indicate punitive motives. Accompanying
this change in the nature of the power has been a change in the
areas of legislative activity. Most recent congressional contempt
cases arose out of investigations of subversion or criminal activity—areas ordinarily policed by the executive arms of government. Hence, withdrawal of legislative power in these areas
would only return to the prosecutive officers that which has customarily been theirs. It is doubtful that the executive branch
would be grateful for the return, since legislative cooperation in
these areas is undoubtedly helpful. Still, executive government
should be prepared to deal with these problems which are not
novel to it. Nor need such an exchange cripple legislative dexterity. Only coincidentally and infrequently have congressional
contempt cases arisen out of situations directly related to Congress' interest in lawmaking. More often contempt cases arose
from legislative exposés. The exposure function of Congress has
been debated, and is not so settled or absolutely necessary as to
forebode over-all legislative failure should the contempt power
be withdrawn.

Very much tied up with the ponderous question of the need
for a congressional contempt power is the one suggested in Chap-

ter IV concerning the propriety of Congress' exposure tactics. On one side is the argument that "only the pitiless light of the public glare"[3] will prevent certain unalterable harms to the nation. On the other side is the equally forceful feeling that Congress is out of bounds legally and morally by undertaking a job not constitutionally nor necessarily theirs. And, as a matter of public interest there is a further issue which could be taken with the legislative exposure tactic. In 1954, a panel of psychiatrists concluded and reported that the tendency of repressiveness, fostered by such tactics as official inquiries into the associations, pasts, ideas, and attitudes of individuals, must inevitably effect the national psychic health adversely.[4] Moreover, beyond the anxiety which would be caused in individuals, there would likely be deeper cultural harm to the ego (that aspect of the mind which deals with the object world, and pleasurably entertains the adventure idea), and the super-ego (which can best develop in a free democratic society). In plain terms, as one author pointed out, "If you enslave a man, he will develop the psychology of a slave. If you exclude a man from free access to the benefits of society, his human quality will be materially diminished."[5] This idea is a more scientific way of arguing, as Justice Black often has, that legislative exposés tend to freeze the individual curiosity, daring, and ingenuity so essentially a part of our national characteristic. Justice Douglas has also warned against the creation of a climate or a tendency which would incline one to intellectually adjust to submission and to fear dissent.[6] I believe this philosophical attitude is what is behind his judicial dissents to many congressional contempt cases.

Ours has traditionally been a government of cooperation between Congress and the people. The ordinary representative or senator who seeks legitimate information directly relevant to his legislative work can usually get it without force. Most often, he need only ask to be given zealous, popular assistance. Even in the two areas of greatest conflict, crime and subversion, there is reason to conclude that Congress might have done all it did (possibly more) without the contempt sanction. Most people simply cooperate. In Chapters I and IV some statistics were quoted concerning congressional contempt cases which arose out of subversion cases before the House Un-American Activities Committee and the Senate Internal Security Committee. Here, the extreme recalcitrance of certain involuntary witnesses was but a grain in the sands of people who appeared voluntarily and testified. Those who would not voluntarily cooperate rarely changed when met with the force of the contempt power. The effect of contempt treatment was not to the encouragement of the legislature. Though perhaps more dramatized, Congress was no more informed, and certainly was not precluded from its lawmaking work. What punishing they did could be questioned policywise, and at least could have been done through that branch of government authorized to seek punishment for crimes—the executive. In those cases where the executive could not punish, the argument is stronger for keeping Congress from doing it instead. Even the protracted and extremely volatile McClellan committee hearings concerning crime and labor were such that its counsel, and now the United States Attorney General, reported that "Hearings were conducted over a period of 2½ years and included over 500 open hearing sessions. During this time we heard 1,525 sworn witnesses (343 of whom took the Fifth Amendment) give testimony that filled 50 odd volumes and totalled more than 14,000,000 words." [7] Every committee has miles of testimony and evidence concerning its prospective legislation, most often from voluntary and cooperative experts who are anxious or happy to assist. An argument could be made that there is always a fringe of people who cooperate only because they fear contempt punishment for refusal, and who, in the absence of that fear, would not cooperate. Though this is speculative, it is undoubtedly true to some extent. However, these cases would probably not be so numerous as to warrant disbelief in the general conclusions that people do cooperate with Congress out of duty, pride, and a sense of public spirit, and that Congress could function well without the relatively few whose cooperation must now be coerced.

The congressional contempt power and the congressional investigating power are usually considered together, in claims both for and against contempt convictions. Perhaps a better perspective is one which appraises the two separately, individually. To eliminate the congressional power to investigate because it is subject to abuse when it includes the contempt power would mock the adage of throwing the baby out with the bath. Without an investigating power Congress would be deeply weakened for no good reason. The issue, as I see it, has been with the power to punish contempt of a congressional investigation. While Congress would be seriously hampered without an investigatory power, it need not be without a contempt power or with a limited one. For this very reason, I disagreed with critics of the House Un-American Activities Committee, who recently argued for abolition of the committee because they felt it abused its powers. Clearer thinking would direct criticism at the cause of any fault. Destroying the power of the legislature to meet an avowed national danger because it may have been abused would be self-defeating. A better reform would be one aimed at the abuse.

The Judicial Power

Resolution of the pros and cons of the judicial need for the contempt power is certainly the most complex and trying aspect of any argument for absolutely extinguishing the power. Our government has no substitute for judicial power, and the function of courts would be seriously handicapped without such a power as contempt. The previous argument that people are cooperative is less pertinent, though to a degree still applicable, to judicial proceedings where personal interests are more directly in jeopardy. The dutiful citizen who witnesses an automobile accident may be anxious, if not amenable, to appear in court and give evidence. Not so the drunken driver who caused the accident. Even less so the man charged with evading his income tax. Moreover, once in court a witness or party may find that his civic responsibility is in conflict with his greater interest in privacy about matters sought by the judicial process. If he could refuse to cooperate at any point, the rest of the work of the court would be a futile waste. This fear is greater where a litigant has strong reasons for refusing to comply with the final court adjudication, and chooses to defiantly render the perfection of litigated rights meaningless by failing to cooperate.

The judicial need for a power like contempt will differ in trial and appellate courts, being, I suggest, less compelling in the latter. The problems most dependent upon coercive power arise peculiarly in the trial courts where witnesses and evidence are demanded, histrionic and passionate advocacy are most typical, and orders are initially issued. While appellate courts will encounter situations where the force of sanction is necessary to perfect the judicial process, these instances are fewer, and provoke less taxing problems.

It could be argued that there is a unique quality in the nature of the judicial process which requires some executing power like contempt. The courts are arbitral bodies of last resort; they are the official governmental decision-making organ through which the wisdom and reason of society are applied to the conflicts of men. But, judicial power differs from the more self-executing power of executive or legislative government. Where there the legislature has provided a way to fruition of litigated rights, the problem is considerably less than the case where a court order is all one can rely on (not backed by a contempt power). Take, for example, the case of a civil trial which results in a judgment that John must return a car to Tom. If John refuses, and there is the usual prevailing execution statute, Tom can have the sheriff garnishee, or attach, the car to carry out his litigated right. However, where the judgment is one which orders John to do something for Tom's benefit, and there is no execution statute, all Tom can resort to for fulfillment of his rights, short of personal force, is the court's power to order John to comply, and to coerce his response through contempt proceedings.

At this point the distinction between civil and criminal contempts becomes more important and, since it will affect any decision about the judicial need for the contempt power, warrants individual consideration. I suggest that the typical civil contempt power could be completely eliminated without loss of judicial efficacy, and that the criminal contempt power should be redefined, limited, and thus maintained.

Civil and Criminal Contempt

In Chapter II, I endeavored to show the confusing and unsatisfactory distinction which has continuously been and is presently applied to the ordinary contempt case. Now, I should like to extend my discussion by suggesting a change.

A distinction should be made between the true contempt situation and that which is no more than a civil device for execution of judicial judgments—between what are now classified as criminal and civil contempts. Contempt should be strictly construed to be what it has historically been—a criminal wrong to government manifested through an act of disrespect or disobedience. Contempt should not be generally extended to cover, as it has been, situations where the only aim is to perfect a private litigated right. To do so results in a theoretical bastardization of the true contempt and often an unfair misapplication of penal powers. Only when all methods of ordinary civil execution have failed, and an individual's recalcitrance has gone to the point of positive interference with government, should the broad and powerful contempt sanction be applied. Then it would be a criminal interference with government, and more than a personal dispute between litigants. Of course, the dividing line is hard to draw.

The ordinary civil contempt arises in the situation where an individual refuses to cooperate with the final order of a court in a civil matter. For example, a man may be ordered to pay money or to give something or someone to another. Imprisonment in civil matters such as these is generally unavailable in Anglo-American law, except in those civil contempt cases where this is typically done. Such an extraordinary and often unnecessary measure is not needed. In fact, I suspect that recourse to the contempt device is had in these cases often because it is the only allowable way of bringing retributive punishment upon an individual, even though the law forbids such action in all other similar instances. This suspicion is clearly illustrated by a conversation which I had with an attorney who had recently handled a civil contempt case. After explaining his situation (his client sought custody of her children from her husband—she had a court decree to this effect which he refused to obey), he remarked, "I didn't want a criminal contempt order, because then he could have served his sentence, and still refused to give up custody. *I wanted the more punitive civil contempt order so he could be imprisoned indefinitely.*" This attitude makes good pragmatic sense, but does havoc to certain basic principles of criminal law and justice which have been long accepted in the American sense of values. First, it deprives the individual of the right to trial by jury precedent to his imprisonment. Second, it allows indefinite imprisonment for an undefined offense. Third, it allows imprisonment in a civil matter. Finally, it is often unnecessary since the aim could be accomplished by other available methods short of imprisonment. This extraordinary departure from general principles of criminal law is not made any more appropriate by magically dubbing this peculiar device a civil contempt.

Alternatives to Contempt

One final point should be explored further, as the argument could be more broadly made that in many criminal as well as civil contempt cases there are efficient alternatives to the use of a contempt power. These alternatives are less loaded with constitutional objections than is the contempt power. A hypothetical and admittedly extreme example will illustrate a case which includes almost all of the ordinary contempt situations, and the typically available alternatives to the use of a contempt power. Suppose H and W secure a divorce before Judge J. In the divorce decree, H is given custody of the children, and W is given certain of the joint property. Both H and W are annoyed by the court's order and decide not to obey it. H secretes the property to which W is entitled, and W takes away the children. Each refuses to give in to the other. A newspaper man, R, learns of this situation and, using it as a focal issue, writes scathing articles critical of matrimonial law and Judge J's handling of the H v. W case. J orders H and W into court. H appears; W does not. A citizens' league, whose prime interest is broken homes, marches on the court and, using this case as a cause célèbre for their political interests, causes a great disturbance in the courtroom and the general area surrounding the courthouse. H takes the stand but refuses to testify. When J orders H to testify, L, H's lawyer, leaps to his feet and engages in a histrionic harangue.

Seven examples of typical contempts were committed in this hypothetical case. Examination of each indicates that there are readily available, suitable alternatives to summary or indefinite imprisonment.

H's refusal to give the property to *W* is a contempt of the court's order. So is *W's* failure to give up custody of the children. In both examples, the prime interest of the court is satisfaction of its orders; the sole interest of *H* and *W* is to get that to which they are entitled. Imprisonment of either need not lead to that result, and in fact may only satisfy the animosity of the parties. However, the law can and should seek nobler, better-directed purposes. The court is in a position requiring power. But power need not be in its most brute form. In cases like these, all the court's powers of execution should be used to carry out its judgment. This may be done without imprisoning the recalcitrant party and thereby risking the possibility of defeating the power to carry out the very order for which enforcement is sought. A better way would allow the court to order the sheriff or marshal to take and pass possession of the property or the children. If the subject of an order is out of state, available interstate cooperation should be employed; and where it does not exist some compact should be created whereby the order of one state court could be executed by the sheriff of another state, or by the sheriff of the first state acting temporarily in the second state. This scheme seems too sensible to require elaborate defense. The goal would be most directly sought. Whatever extra expense the court might be put to economically should be borne by him who occasioned it. The deterrent power of the court would be manifest. Yet, civil problems would be handled through civil powers. Wronged litigants and a defied judicial tribunal would be aided by direct and forceful governmental powers. Dispensation with the contempt power would not lead to judicial collapse but would in fact focus on the areas where strong and effective powers of execution are lacking. These powers of execution, like garnishment, levy, and attachment, should be perfected so that a recalcitrant witness could not simply and frivolously defeat proper court orders. Where he attempts to, the court could act directly with the subject of the recalcitrance, not the person of the contemnor. Only when the recalcitrant witness goes so far as to make normal execution by the court impossible should personal action against him be taken, and then it would be for a true contempt of court, a criminal interference with government. After trial for this offense, the contemnor could be imprisoned for a definite period. But, where civil execution (against the recalcitrant witness' will) is possible, this should be the course. He should be personally responsible only for the extra costs occasioned by his obstinacy. Where insufficient powers of execution exist, the legislature should provide adequate machinery.

In the next example, R could be punished for contempt arising out of his publications concerning a pending trial. Whatever wrong this may be need not be corrected by recourse to the summary contempt power either. If the publication is libelous, libel laws are available to the judge or offended party. If the publication is not libelous, it ought to be protected by the First Amendment's policy of encouraging criticism and the espousal of points of view. Whether publications like these affect the fairness of trials is debatable. Whether publicity in fact prejudices jurors is questionable; whether this prejudice is greater than all others occasioned by the frail imperfections of the ordinary-man juror is also open to dispute. Whether the First Amendment should elevate the rights of the press above its wrongs is a question of the interpretation of competing values. Recent Supreme Courts have made that judgment in favor of the press, and I suggest properly so. In any case, the answer to this question involves more than a single judgment about the contempt power, but includes issues like the rights and responsibilities of the press, the value of the jury system (for it is the jury which is said to be that part of the trial which is injured by publicity), and the American adversary method of trial. Since the value of a free press is demonstrable and well inculcated in American social action, the difficulty of this hypothetical case is better met through other means than contempt punishment.

In a recent article, I suggested that both the freedom of the press and the fairness of trials could be maintained without a doctrine of contempt by publication.[8] This could be done by perfecting techniques for filtering the elements of nonjudicial publications from trials, or by the use of alternatives to the ordinary jury trial in extraordinary cases. As a middle-ground compromise conclusion, I suggested in a second article,[9] a special press contempt statute which narrowly proscribed specific abuses that might best be subject to contempt sanctions and which were circumscribed by ordinary criminal procedural protections for the contemnor. The distinction there made was between publications of matters protected by judicial discretion, such as confessions, previous criminal records, or pictures where identity is in issue, and publication of opinions, descriptions, or editorials. If any, only the former group warrants inroads upon the right and duty of the press to report, unfettered, the facts of life. I can see no value to further compromises with freedom of the press.

The physical disturbance caused by the march of the political group upon the courthouse is easily rectified short of contempt punishment. Courts and any other governmental agency should have plenary summary physical control of their proceedings. This control is necessary as a matter of self-defense and common sense. A bailiff or sergeant at arms is always available to clear from the court any disturbing influences. The problem ends with ejectment. Any person wishing to peacefully protest by some form of picketing which does not physically disturb the trial ought to be left alone to do so. Physical disturbance is only an occasional problem, and one easily manageable by ejectment from the precincts of the trial room. Then the court's interest and control should end.

H's refusal to testify is an example of one of the few situations where a contempt power may be the only recourse of an effective court. The judicial function, more than the executive and legislative, requires some artificial power to execute its decrees. Still, in the hypothetical situation, a partial alternative is available. Where two competing parties are involved in a judicial proceeding, courts do have an effective power over the matter of the litigation, short of imprisonment and perhaps as effective as conditional civil contempt imprisonment. The parties themselves usually have the sole interests in the outcome of a case. Why not then imply a condition precedent of cooperation to a party's right to the use of the courts. When a party refuses to cooperate with the court, he could be estopped from using the court to perfect his rights. The only case where this device might not be sufficient would be where there is a substantial societal interest in the outcome of the trial beyond that of the party involved, or where the particular party has no stake in the proceeding. Here, the party's recalcitrance has effects beyond his own, and such a scheme as the one suggested would not suffice.

The case of the impolite or miscreant attorney is also easily handled without the power to imprison for contempt. Attorneys are officers of the courts and usually the other governmental bodies before which they perform, and have always been held to high responsibilities of conduct. The attorney who abuses his unique position by contemptuous conduct can and should be censured by the bench or bar to whom he owes allegiance and upon whom his privilege to practice depends. The attorney who properly fights his case should in no event be censured or punished. In professional disciplinary proceedings, the lawyer has his opportunity to argue his position and be judged by impartial detached peers. This is far better than the summary contempt procedure before a judge who himself may have provoked or been involved in the incident which gave rise to the contempt action against the attorney.

So, there may well be suitable and sensible alternatives to control the problems hitherto resolved exclusively by the courts' contempt power. And, it is submitted that these alternatives, if not a better solution to the problems, are certainly more directly related means-to-ends and less fraught with constitutional invasions, than is the current contempt power.

For the critic of the contempt power these would be the arguments for complete or near complete abolition. But, I suggest that this position is too extreme, and should better be tempered through some compromise solution like the following, which grants a power, but limits it substantively and procedurally.

Recommendation

Abolition of the contempt power is not the answer, no matter how compelling one may view the criticisms that can be validly made of certain of its aspects. Moreover, to suggest complete extinction, even if one wished such a change, would be naïve. Those in whom the contempt power resides would have to agree to implement such a change, and the chance of that happening is infinitesimal. Second, whatever may be wrong with the contempt power is certainly not so wrong as to be likely to provoke great enough popular demands for absolute change to force the officials of government to act against their own interests and intuitions in this regard. I also feel that change in so broad an area of the law should come gradually and be tested for workability. Alternatives should be tried before complete abandonment. Finally, there is a need for control of certain contemptuous conduct.

Some contempt power is necessary for courts in a democratic

government under law, operating with an adversary trial system. Legislatures might well do without a contempt power, though there are some limited situations where some power like contempt, but carefully guarded procedurally, is sensible and quite necessary. Administrative agencies could function with a contempt power limited as I suggested in the conclusion of Chapter III. Executive officers have rarely had such a power, and in view of the minor values to be added by a grant of the power compared to the gamut of problems which would be likely to arise if it was added (one need only recall the issues caused by the courts' and Congress' use of the power), affairs might then better be left unchanged. However, to cover some peculiar situations where certain officials act in executive or quasi-executive capacities and reasonably require a power analogous to that granted to other governmental officers, some special and limited application could be provided for.

The treatment of these wrongs should not continue in the present form and manner. There is much disagreement about which acts before which bodies constitute contempts. Many provisions for punishment are indefinite; some unlimited. Summary procedures prevail. These aspects of the present contempt power should be changed.

The generality and breadth of contempt law is open to legal criticism. This quality, which leaves undefined to potential wrongdoers both the acts which are forbidden and the punishment which may be exacted for their commission, violates a basic accepted legal principle. In criminal law, it is the statute, not the later specific accusation under it, that prescribes the rule to govern conduct and warn against transgression. Enunciating this law, the Supreme Court has noted its underlying democratic policy which directs that no one be required at the risk of his life, liberty, or property to speculate about the meaning of penal statutes.[10] One is entitled to be clearly informed of what a criminal statute commands and forbids. A step in this direction was taken with the passage of the current contempt of Congress statute. But contempt of court practice is not so clear and not so consistent with settled law and attitudes of fair play in this respect. We have reached in fact, though not in practical recognition, the point where contempt is a crime. It is punished as a social wrong. Yet, we often treat this criminal in a more sweeping, unguarded manner than all others. The catchall description of the proscribed act and punishment is another of the peculiar qualities, which, along with the denial of general rights of criminal procedure, makes contempt law so peculiar.

A better scheme could be created by a statute defining an offense (as distinguished from creating a general power) called "misdemeanor to government." This statute would sanction a criminal penalty for conduct which injured or destroyed the proper functioning of a governmental body or official. It would be applied as all other criminal laws, consistent with guaranteed rights of criminal procedure. In those cases (and they would probably be many), where an act conflicted with this statute and another, the wrongdoer could be punished under either statute, but never both. Thus any inclination to punish the same offense twice, once under the particular and again under the general statute, would be avoided. The ability to abusively punish under a broad general catchall law, as contempt now is, where a conviction could never be had under ordinary criminal processes, would also be avoided. Under this statute, the accused would enjoy all of the protections that our Constitution and sense of fair play assures accused criminals in all other cases. Beside aiding the individual, such a scheme would ennoble and legitimize governmental power now sometimes under criticism not for its existence so much as for the manner of its exercise.

Along with such a statute should also come the demise of the innate contempt power as we now know it, and a change in the civil-criminal distinction which is now made. The statute would cover those contempts now classified as criminal, and some aggravated contempts now called civil. However, the typical civil contempt case should be dealt with through other devices than a contempt power, except, as I have suggested, where the contempt goes so far as to become a wrong to the court itself, and is of such a nature as to defy any other alternative treatment than criminal sanction. Such a statute could read as follows:

Misdemeanor to Government

Any person, whether as an individual or in a representative capacity, who *willfully* does an act or omits to act, in such a way as to *substantially* obstruct a governmental agency's legitimate work, without a legal *right* to so act or omit to act, is subject to a fine of from $100 to $5,000, an imprisonment of from one day to one year, or both. Where the act proscribed by this section is also prohibited by any other penal law of the United States, the offender may be punished under either statute at the election of the United States, but *never* may be prosecuted under both that statute and this statute. Action under this law must be initiated by the complaint of the proper and authorized representative of the government body offended. In any action under this section, all rights guaranteed by the United States Constitution will be guaranteed for the benefit of the accused. Acts under this statute shall be confined to personal conduct which affects official governmental proceedings, and matters of attendance, cooperation, and obedience at those proceedings.

The rights to trial by jury, pardon, due process, counsel, impartial judge, to name only the more obvious constitutional provisions, would safeguard the contemnor from possible abuse of governmental power.

The wrong, call it contempt, must be willful from the standpoint of intention and possibility for alternatives. The obstruction to government must be substantial to the extent that the governmental agency was materially damaged (more than inconvenienced), or that no alternative was available other than to treat the act as a completed offense. Where the individual had a legitimate right to act in the way he did, a constitutional or legally recognized right, his conduct should be protected. (For example, a refusal to testify should not be punished where the testimony would incriminate the witness.)

In the area of congressional contempts, the activity in issue will fall within four categories: *a*) refusal of a witness to appear personally, or *b*) to produce subpoenaed documents, *c*) refusal to testify after appearance, or, finally, *d*) acts of misbehavior. Whether any of the four acts will constitute an offense under the proposed statute will depend upon the nature of the legislative inquiry, and of course upon the cooperation of the prospective witness. Assuming a reluctant witness, an offense would be made out only if there was a valid legislative inquiry which would be frustrated by the act in question. If the legislative end could be as easily reached without the contemnor, his obstruction would be nominal not material, and hence not criminally punishable. This would avoid any tendency toward using the legislative investigatory power as a criminal punishing power. Legislative compulsion would be more selective, though where it is on reasonable ground it would be upheld. It should and would be an offense, for example, for a person to willfully destroy documents sought by the legislature in the course of its proper work. In other words, where there is a proper legislative inquiry, and *a*, *b*, or *c* above would defeat that inquiry, an offense to government is committed.

Example *d*, the misconduct, might also come under the proposed statute. Ordinarily, misconduct before Congress would be covered by some prevailing breach of the peace statute or a facsimile, as well as the proposed misdemeanor to government statute. Instances of this misconduct would probably be rare. An example might be swearing at or attacking a working congressman. Election could then be had between the proposed statute and any other statute which might also cover this situation.

Misdemeanors to government within the judicial sphere could arise in a more numerous variety of ways. These possible situations were discussed earlier in this chapter. They are contempt by the press, misconduct by attorneys or other officers of the court, physical disturbances in the vicinity of the proceeding, disobedience to court orders, and refusal to appear or to produce documents. The exclusiveness of contempt as the answer to problems posed by these examples has been questioned already.

The first three types of contemptuous conduct could, as a general rule, be handled without recourse to the proposed statute, though limited exceptions could undoubtedly arise. The latter three situations could more usually come within the potential application of the statute. The same conditions (described above) which limited the use of the statute to congressional contempts would apply equally to contempts of court. However, a lesser degree of proof should be necessarily required of the government to establish the legitimacy of the proceeding and the materiality of the obstruction. In proper judicial proceedings there should be minimal collateral inquiry into the ultimate obstructiveness of a contempt, since the dependency upon uninterrupted procedure is greater, the abuses have proved to be less, and the procedure is, of course, subject to immediate appellate review.

A corresponding power could be considered here. It might be wise to empower the courts to summarily imprison for a limited time (this should be confined to a day or, at the most, the duration of the trial) where a court order is disobeyed or an act of misconduct is committed during the course of a trial and in the physical presence of the court. Imprisonment should be on the premises of the court. This would be part of the court's plenary power of control, akin to its unquestionable right to eject, ensure proper demeanor, and generally run a trial. It would dispose of frivolous minor delays in cases where the contempt was dilatory or momentary and where neither the contemnor nor the court really wanted a full-scale legal contest on the issue of the contempt. This would undoubtedly avoid the majority of courts contempt problems which, though minor in themselves, might cause undue administrative problems under my proposal. It would leave for trial those disputes which were truly contempts of court, worthy of criminal prosecution.

It is difficult to imagine any but the most unusual situation where executive officials would invoke this prosecutive statute. In all likelihood those situations would be covered already by other statutes. Executive officials could as well be specifically excluded from coverage of this statute, without violating any precedent of contempt practice. However, if only for symmetry, the exceptional case or the official with blended duties, it would be better to write the statute in its broadest terms—"*any government official.*" Discretion and interpretation would no doubt limit executive use of the statute to the minor extent to which these officials now seek the contempt sanction.

Contempt of administrative agencies would also fall within the coverage of the proposed statute. The specific breakdown of these offenses was described in the conclusion to Chapter III. The recommendations made there could readily be molded into the framework of the model statute.

Physical disorders should be excluded, as a general rule, from the coverage of this misdemeanor statute. These offenses to governmental operations are better handled through a summary, plenary power, truly inherent in any legitimate working government body, of physical control and expulsion. The position that a government body should have some means of controlling noise, misbehavior and similar physical obstructions in its presence should require little argument and raise less dispute. Certainly a court or a congressional meeting should not be at the mercy of the obstreperous and uncouth. Still, the issue is how best to meet this problem, and it is suggested that criminal treatment is often too severe—certainly more severe than necessary to solve the problem. An aggravated situation would undoubtedly be covered by prevailing breach of the peace laws. These few extreme situations could as well be misdemeanors to government, under the proposed statute, but then a choice would be forced between that and the breach of the peace statute.

Contempt by officials could be well controlled by ordinary existing departmental methods. Lawyers, marshals, officers of courts and congresses are subject always to official standards of conduct and licensing scrutiny. The need for criminal indictment in cases of contempt arising out of misconduct by such officers as these is rare, and could come within the coverage of the suggested statute without dragging in all the other, more usual acts of misconduct by this class of contemnors, which are now classified as contempts. Such a distinction, beside clinging closer to constitutional law, is better aimed at the end goal of these contempt cases—responsible conduct of agents of government bodies.

The breadth of the penalty provision of this statute is intended to allow discretion in sentencing. A violation of the statute could involve a serious wrong or a relatively minor one. Therefore, the sentencer (be he judge or jury) should have a broad range of fine and imprisonment power with which to blend punishment to both crime, criminal, and circumstances.

Perhaps the proposed statute should be broader and make certain classes of offenses misdemeanors and others felonies. Felonies require grand jury indictments, while misdemeanors do not, so this feature would be added. And, the particular offense under the statute could vary greatly in gravity and warrant variant punitive treatment.

An option providing for dependent sentencing could be added to the punishing provision of this statute. Where the judge decides that the government's interest in coercing cooperation is greater than its interest in punishing the contemnor, he could make the sentence subject to a purge provision. Then, the punished wrong-doer could absolve himself from imprisonment by meeting the condition of his dependent sentence at any time during the course of his imprisonment. Such a provision could be added to the model statute, without changing its general complexion, so long as it was clearly understood that its inclusion was in no way meant to avoid the general procedural protections guaranteed by the statute.

The thought behind dependent sentencing is uniquely appropriate to contempt cases. Here more so than in other cases which come to mind is the motivation to punish one which would change were the contumacious misconduct to change.

A fair and serious concern about this plan is that it could be subjected to dilatory tactics, would clog court calendars with delayed pending proceedings, and would cause great governmental inconvenience by requiring judges or congressmen or other officers to leave their primary work to testify at numerous misdemeanor to government trials on the merits of these cases. Some speedy but fair special handling of these frequent cases would have to be developed. Two procedures might alleviate this problem. One would provide for immediate calendar preference for trial of these cases upon the reasonable request of the government party. The other would allow testimony of government officials involved in these cases to be taken by deposition. This would avoid undue distraction from the official's primary work, as well as the awkward position of subjecting government officials to courtroom attack for their ordinarily privileged public acts.

Legislative draftsmanship is an art. I intended in making these specifications only to draw the contours of a possible statute and to express a policy and a purpose for its substance. A far-reaching revision of so broad an area of the law is perforce one subject to the vagaries of language and imagination, as well as the fallibilities of the author. The exact articulation I leave to others more skilled at the art. However, the policy, purpose, and reasons for my suggestions should by now be clear.

The statute suggested would have certain beauties of intelligent compromise which would satisfy certain of the just though competing interests of the conflicting individual and government official. A fair guide of crime and punishment would prevail. The accused would be treated according to normal procedures —no better or worse than other doers of antisocial deeds. Government work could proceed. Through the intervention of juries, prevailing popular attitudes would be brought to bear upon issues, and this might leaven these harsh clashes of men and officials. Juries might provide that deterrent or guide, for both the individual and the government official, which would narrow to the least number the instances where differences of opinion would have to occasion official power plays. The martyr may appear a maverick when judged unreasonable by his fellow man. So may the government official reason further before he submits his cause to the ultimate decision-makers of his government. The directions of the Bill of Rights would be more closely heeded. The resolution of conflict would be settled by power, but a power more closely directed by reason and fairness.

Notes

1: The History of the Contempt Power

1. For an interesting analysis of contempt as a comparative legal technique, see Pekelis, *Legal Techniques and Political Ideologies: A Comparative Study*, 41 MICH. L. REV. 665, 671 (1943).

2. *Id.* at 674.   3. Watson v. Williams, 36 Miss. 331, 341 (1858).

4. THOMAS, PROBLEMS OF CONTEMPT OF COURT 5 (1934).

5. Shakespeare, *Henry IV*, part 2, act 5, scene 2.

6. 1 CAMPBELL, THE LIVES OF THE CHIEF JUSTICES OF ENGLAND 125–42 (1894).

7. CAMPBELL, *op. cit. supra* note 6, referred to several amusing and in parts contradictory chronicles of this event.

8. For a more extensive and annotated treatment of this incident, see Deutsch, *The United States Versus Major General Andrew Jackson*, 46 A.B.A.J. 966 (1960).

9. *Id.* at 972.

10. Title 3, bk. 1; tit. 7; see PASQUEL, CONTEMPT OF COURT, p. 175.

11. Canon 1640, tit. 3, bk. 4. Canon 1842, tit. 9.

12. *Supra* note 10, PASQUEL, at p. 176.

13. PATTERSON, ON LIBERTY OF SPEECH AND PRESS 18 (1939).

14. In the dissent to Green v. U.S., 356 U.S. 165, 218 (1958), it was suggested that respect and obedience in this country are not engendered by arbitrary and automatic procedures, but that in the end such procedures yield only contempt to the courts and the law.

15. THOMAS, THE LAW OF CONSTRUCTIVE CONTEMPT (1934).

16. SIEBERT, PETERSON, AND SCHRAMM, FOUR THEORIES OF THE PRESS 44–51 (1956).

17. FIGGIS, THE DIVINE RIGHT OF KINGS 38–65 (2d ed. 1922).

18. *Id.* at 19.   19. SCOTT, TWILIGHT OF THE KINGS (1938).

20. FIGGIS, *op. cit. supra* note 17, at 15.   21. *Id.* at 6.

22. Beale, *Contempt of Court, Criminal and Civil*, 21 HARV. L. REV. 161 (1908).

23. AIYER, LAW OF CONTEMPT, ch. 1 at 3.

24. *Supra* note 22, at 162 and 166.

25. LANGDELL, SUMMARY OF EQUITY PLEADING 38 (1877).

26. Fox, *The King v. Almon*, 24 L.Q. REV. 184, 194 (1908). The decision referred to is that by Fletcher, J., in Taaffe v. Downes which is out of print, but reported in 24 L.Q. REV. 194 (1908).

27. Fox, *supra* note 26, at 195.

28. Fox, *The Summary Process to Punish Contempt*, 25 L.Q. REV. 238, 241 (1909).

29. *Supra* note 22, at 167.

30. Fox, *Eccentricities of the Law of Contempt of Court*, 36 L.Q. REV. 394 (1920); Fox, *The King v. Almon*, 24 L.Q. REV. 184, 266 (1908); Fox, *The Nature of Contempt of Court*, 37 L.Q. REV. 191 (1921); Fox, *The Practice in Contempt of Court Cases*, 38 L.Q. REV. 185 (1922); Fox, *The Summary Process to Punish Contempt*, 25 L.Q. REV. 238, 354 (1909); Fox, *The Writ of Attachment*, 40 L.Q. REV. 43 (1924). See also Fox, CONTEMPT OF COURT (1927).

31. Fox, *The Nature of Contempt of Court*, 37 L.Q. REV. 191, 194 (1921).

32. *Id.* at 195.   33. *Id.* at 201.   34. *Id.* at 199.

35. Fox, *supra* note 28, at 244.

36. Solly-Flood, *The Story of Prince Henry of Monmouth and Chief-Justice Gascoigne*, TRANSACTIONS OF THE ROYAL HIST. SOCIETY 47 (1886).

37. THE HABEAS CORPUS ACT, 1640, 16 Car. 1, c. 10.

38. Fox, *The King v. Almon*, 24 L.Q. REV. 266, 273 (1908).

39. Anon. (1631) Dy. 1886; AIYER, *supra* note 23, at 7.

40. Stroudis' Case, 3 How. St. Tr. 267 (1629).

41. Wilmot's Notes (Wilmot ed. 1802).

42. OSWALD, CONTEMPT OF COURT (3d ed. 1910).

43. Frankfurter and Landis, *Power of Congress Over Procedure in Criminal Contempt in "Inferior" Federal Courts—A Study in Separation of Powers*, 37 HARV. L. REV. 1010 (1924).

44. Fox, *The King v. Almon*, 24 L.Q. REV. 184 (1908).

45. Fox, CONTEMPT OF COURT 1 (1927).   46. *Id.* at 5–6.

47. Wilmot's Notes 254, (Wilmot ed. 1802), as cited in Fox, CONTEMPT OF COURT 7–8 (1927). (Emphasis added.)

48. Fox, *op. cit. supra* note 45, at 8–9, citing for opposing argument, CHIEF BARON GILBERT, HISTORY OF THE COMMON PLEAS 20 (1737), where this summary power was traced to the Statute of Westminster II, c. 39, noting however that after attachment the trial was in the ordinary course of law.

49. Wilmot's Notes 255 (Wilmot ed. 1802), as cited in Fox, CONTEMPT OF COURT 9 (1927).

50. See 41 Harv. L. Rev. 51 (1927), *The Story of a Notion in the Law of Criminal Contempt.*

51. Fox, Contempt of Court 16 (1927).

52. Thomas, Problems of Contempt of Court 5 (1934).

53. Judiciary Act of 1789 § 17, 1 Stat. 83.

54. Pa. Acts 1809, P.L. 146, 5 Sm. L. 55.

55. N.Y. Rev. Stat. c. 3, § 10 (1829).

56. Nelles and King, *Contempt by Publication in the United States,* 28 Colum. L. Rev. 410, 422–23 (1928).

57. This incident is thoroughly and urbanely discussed by Nelles and King, *id.* at 423–30.

58. See Frankfurter and Landis, *supra* note 43, at 1025.

59. Rev. Stat. § 725 (1875), 18 U.S.C. § 401 (1948).

60. 18 U.S.C. § 401 defines the power of the United States courts as covering misbehavior of court officers in their official transactions, disobedience of writs, and misbehavior of anyone in the court's presence or so near thereto as to obstruct the administration of justice.

61. See Gompers v. Bucks Stove and Range Co., 221 U.S. 418, 450 (1911); cases cited in 17 C.J.S., Contempt § 43 nn.75–77 (1939); 1 Kent, Commentaries 236 (2d ed. 1832).

62. The Supreme Court prophesied that this would happen in Gompers v. Bucks Stove and Range Co., *supra* note 61.

63. 17 C.J.S. Contempt § 43 nn.75–77 (1939).

64. 17 C.J.S. Contempt § 43 and n.72 (1939).

65. See *Note,* 11 Va. L. Rev. 639 (1925), which questions the necessity rationale.

66. Oswald, *op. cit. supra* note 42, at 8; Rapalje, Contempt § 4 (1890).

67. *Ex Parte* Robinson, 86 U.S. (19 Wall.) 505, 510 (1873).

68. State *ex rel.* Attorney General v. Circuit Court, 97 Wis. 1, 8, 72 N.W. 193, 194–95 (1897).

69. Green v. United States, 356 U.S. 165, 195 (1958) (*dissenting opinion*).

70. See Frankfurter and Landis, *supra* note 43, at 1047.

71. See Green v. U.S., 356 U.S. 165, 202, 203 (1958).

72. See 2 Tenn. L. Rev. 215 (1924).

73. See generally Jane, The Coming of Parliament (1905); McIlwain, High Court of Parliament (1910).

74. Watkins v. U.S., 354 U.S. 178 (1957); Kilbourn v. Thompson, 103 U.S. 168 (1880); Potts, *Power of Legislative Bodies to Punish for Contempt,* 74 U. Pa. L. Rev. 691 (1926).

75. Kilbourn v. Thompson, *id.* at 183.

76. Jurney v. MacCracken, 294 U.S. 125, 129 (1935).

77. Potts, *supra* note 74, at 697.   78. *Id.* at 694.

79. Jurney v. MacCracken, 294 U.S. 125 (1935); Gompers v. Bucks Stove and Range Co., 221 U.S. 418 (1911); Anderson v. Dunn, 19 U.S. (6 Wheat.) 204 (1821); 1 Kent, Commentaries 236 (2d ed. 1832).

80. Marshall v. Gordon, 243 U.S. 521 (1917).

81. Anderson v. Dunn, 19 U.S. (6 Wheat.) 204, 226 (1821).

82. The language that the contempt power is an inherent one, both of courts and Congress, seeped into rationales either through loose language, or a subtle extension of accepted doctrine. It followed naturally from rationales of expediency, then necessity. See, *e.g.*, Quinn v. United States, 349 U.S. 155, 160–61 (1955); McGrain v. Dougherty, 273 U.S. 135, 175 (1927); *In re* Chapman, 166 U.S. 661, 671–72 (1897); *Ex Parte* Robinson, 86 U.S. 505, 510 (1873); Anderson v. Dunn, 6 (Wheat.) 204, 232 (1821).

83. Beck, Contempt of Congress 2 (1959).

84. See Potts, *supra* note 74, at 700–12.

85. Jurney v. MacCracken, 294 U.S. 125 (1935).

86. Potts, *supra* note 74.   87. Beck, *op. cit. supra* note 83 at 3.

88. U.S. Const. art. 1, § 5.

89. Burnham v. Morrissey, 80 Mass. (14 Gray) 226 (1859).

90. Potts, *supra* note 74 at 713.

91. Beck, *op. cit. supra* note 83 at 191.

92. 19 U.S. (6 Wheat.) 204 (1821).   93. *Id.* at 208.

94. Kilbourn v. Thompson, 103 U.S. 168, 196 (1880).

95. Beck, *op. cit. supra* note 83, at 4.

96. Anderson v. Dunn, 19 U.S. (6 Wheat.) 204, 219 (1821).

97. *Id.* at 225.   98. *Id.* at 227.   99. *Id.* at 228.   100. *Id.* at 231.   101. *Id.* at 235.

102. Stewart v. Blaine, 8 D.C. (1 MacArth.) 453 (1874).

103. The only other case at that time was *Ex Parte* Nugent, 18 Fed. Cas. 487 (No. 10375) (C.C.D.C. 1848).

104. Stewart v. Blaine, 8 D.C. (1 MacArth.) 453, 472 (1874).

105. 103 U.S. 168 (1880).

106. *Id.* at 184–85. Several English cases were cited where the power of the legislature was upheld upon its judical character.

107. *Id.* at 189.   108. 4 Moore 63, 13 Eng. Rep. 225 (P.C. 1842).

109. *Id.* at 89–90, 13 Eng. Rep. at 235. (Emphasis added.)

110. 103 U.S. at 191.   111. 37 Harv. L. Rev. 1010, at 1012, 1014.

112. Rapalje, § 12, p. 14.

113. *In re* Atchison, 284 Fed. 604 (S.D. Fla., 1922).

114. *Regulation of Contempt of Court*, 13 Harv. L. Rev. 615 (1890), at 620.

115. *Ex Parte* Grossman, 267 U.S. 87 (1925); see also The Laura, 114 U.S. 413 (1885). Civil contempt not pardonable, *In re* Nevitt, 117 F. 448, 453. Also see Townsend v. U.S., 95 F.2d 352, *cert. denied* 303 U.S. 664 (1938), contempt of Congress *pardoned*.

116. Nelson v. Steiner, 279 F.2d 944 (4th Cir. 1960), at 948.

117. 11 Stat. 155 (1857), 2 U.S.C. § 192 (1958).

118. Supplemental brief of Sol. Gen. Rankin to U.S. Sup. Ct., Watkins v. U.S.

119. 8 App. D.C. 302, 310–11 (1896), *writ error dism'd,* 164 U.S. 436.

120. Hitz, *Criminal Prosecution for Contempt of Congress,* 14 FED. B.J. 139, 144.

121. Rumely v. U.S. Kamp v. U.S.; Fields v. U.S. (cited in Table of Cases).

122. *Ex Parte* Frankfeld, 32 F. Supp. 915 (D.C. Dist. 1940).

123. BECK, *op. cit. supra* note 83, at 6, 7.   124. *Id.* at 7.

125. *In re* Chapman, 166 U.S. 661 (1897).

126. Marshall v. Gordon, 243 U.S. 521, 533 (1917).

127. Watkins v. U.S., 354 U.S. 178 (1957).

128. KEETON, TRIAL BY TRIBUNAL (1960).

129. GALLOWAY, CONGRESS AND PARLIAMENT (1955).

130. TAYLOR, GRAND INQUEST (1955).

131. GALLOWAY, *op. cit. supra* note 129.

132. Maslow, *Fair Procedure in Congressional Investigations: A Proposed Code,* 54 COLUM. L. REV. 839 (1954).

133. CARR, THE HOUSE COMMITTEE ON UN-AMERICAN ACTIVITIES (1952).

134. GELLHORN, AMERICAN RIGHTS 117 (1960).

135. BARTH, GOVERNMENT BY INVESTIGATION (1955); O'BRIEN, NATIONAL SECURITY AND INDIVIDUAL LIBERTY (1955).

II: The Varieties of the Contempt Power

1. Moskovitz, *Contempt of Injunctions, Criminal and Civil,* 43 COLUM. L. REV. 780 (1943).

2. 21 Fed. 761 (Tenn. Cir. Ct.).

3. St. James, Evening Post, 2 Atk. 471 (1742).

4. Volume VI (1897).

5. See Harnon, *Civil and Criminal Contempts of Court,* 25 MOD. L. REV. 179 (1962).

6. HALSBURY'S LAWS OF ENGLAND, 2 ed., v. 7, Contempt of Court.

7. King v. Myers, I Durn. E. 265 (K.B. 1786).

8. Wellesley v. Duke of Beaufont, 39 Eng. Rep. 538 (1831).

9. *Supra* note 6.   10. Halsbury, § 3, p. 24.

11. *Supra* note 8, at 544 and 548.

12. Rapalje, A Treatise on Contempt (1884).

13. Rapalje, § 21, p. 25.   14. Oswald, Contempt of Court (1911).

15. Bessette v. Conkey, 194 U.S. 324 (1903).

16. Gompers v. Bucks Stove and Range Co., 221 U.S. 418 (1911).

17. *Id.* at 441, 442.

18. *In re* Nevitt, 117 Fed. 448, 461 (8th Cir. 1902).

19. 3 L. Raym. 1108; 4 Johns 375 (cited in Nevitt case).

20. U.S. v. United Mine Workers, 330 U.S. 258 (1947).

21. Wyman v. Uphaus, 360 U.S. 72 (1958).

22. *E.g.*, Fed. R. Civ. P., Rule 69, forbids imprisonment for a civil debt.

23. 17 F.R.D. 167; U.S. v. Bittner, 11 Fed. 293 (4th Cir. 1926); Farese v. U.S., 209 Fed. 312 (1st Cir. 1954); Myers v. U.S., 264 U.S. 95 (1923); *In re* Graves, 29 Fed. 60 (E.D. Iowa 1886); Duell v. Duell, 178 F.2d 683 (D.D.C. 1949).

24. Myers v. U.S., 264 U.S. 95 (1923).

25. McCann v. N.Y. Stock Exchange, 80 F.2d 211 (2d Cir. 1935).

26. Wakefield v. Housel, 288 Fed. 712 (8th Cir. 1923).

27. Lamb v. Cramer, 285 U.S. 217 (1932).

28. Mitchell v. Dexter, 244 Fed. 926 (1st Cir. 1917).

29. *In re* Kahn, 204 Fed. 581 (2d Cir. 1913).

30. Denny v. State, 203 Ind. 682, 182 N.E. 313 (1932).

31. 46 Yale L.J. 326, at 329.   32. See note 1.

33. See note 25, at 214, 215.   34. Fed. R. Crim. P., Rule 42.

35. See note 20.

36. Penfield Co. of California v. U.S.E.C., 329 U.S. 706 (*granting certiorari*) (1947).

37. 143 F.2d 746.   38. 330 U.S. 585 (1947).

39. 181 Fed. 217 (C.C.M.D. Ala. 1919); 230 Fed. 120 (6th Cir. 1916); 48 F.2d 216 (S.D. Ga. 1930).

40. Kreplik v. Couch Patents Co., 190 Fed. 565 (1st Cir. 1911).

41. Thomas, Problems in Contempt of Court 3 (1934).

42. U.S. v. Parker, 126 F.2d 370 (1st Cir. 1942); and see 57 Yale L.J. 83, at 103, 104.

43. Encyclopedia of English Laws, v. 3, p. 315; also see Halsbury, 3 ed., v. 8, pp. 2, 3.

44. *Ibid.*; also see Dangel, Contempt (1939) § 199, 212; Rapalje, § 23.

45. Rapalje, § 23.   46. Dangel, § 199, 212.

47. Cushman Co. v. Mackesy, 200 A. 505.

48. 18 A.L.R. 212; 17 Am. Jur. 399.

49. U.S. v. Anonymous, 21 Fed. 761, at 769 (Cir. Tenn. 1884).

50. 21 Harv. L. Rev. 101.

51. Thomas, Problems of Contempt of Court at 3.

52. Ohio v. Local 5760, United Steel Workers of America, 176 Ohio St. 75 (1961).

53. Fed. R. Crim. P., Rule 42.   54. 18 Fed. B.J. 34 (1958).

55. U.S. v. Shipp, 203 U.S. 563 (1906).   56. Blackstone Comm. 285.

57. Goldfarb, *The History of the Contempt Power*, 1961 Wash. U.L.Q. 1.

58. Goldfarb, *Public Information, Criminal Trials, and the Cause Celebre*, 36 N.Y.U.L. Rev. 810 (1961).

59. Story, Constitution of the United States, 4 ed. § 1882.

60. Siebert, Peterson, and Schramm, Four Theories of the Press, ch. I.

61. Duhamel and Smith, Some Pillars of English Law (1959).

62. 24 L.Q. Rev. at 277.   63. Fox, Contempt of Court, ch. 3, p. 16.

64. Maryland v. Baltimore Radio Show, 338 U.S. 912 (1950).

65. Rex v. Clarke, 27 T.L.R. 32 (K.B. 1910).

66. Rex v. Hammond, 30 T.L.R. 491 (K.B. 1914).

67. Rex. v. Evening Standard, 40 T.L.R. 833 (K.B. 1924).

68. Rex v. Daily Herald, 75 Sol. J. 119 (K.B. 1931).

69. Rex v. Surrey Comet, 75 Sol. J. 311 (K.B. 1931).

70. Rex. v. Hutchinson, 2 All E.R. 1514 (K.B. 1936).

71. Rex v. Griffiths, 2 Q.B. 192.   72. See note 79 *infra*.

73. See notes 77 and 82 *infra*.   74. See note 82 *infra*.

75. 24 L.Q. Rev. at 270.   76. 2 A.T.K. 469, see p. 471.

77. 1 K.B. 32 (1906), see p. 35.   78. King v. Parke, 2 K.B. 432 (1903).

79. Regina v. Odham's Press, 3 Weekly L.R. 796 (1956), 1 Q.B. 73 (1957).

80. 20 Mod. L. Rev. 275; 73 L.Q. Rev. 10.   81. 73 L.Q. Rev. at 11.

82. Rex. v. Editor of the New Statesman, 44 T.L.R. 301; also see 47 L.Q. Rev. 315.

83. 47 L.Q. Rev. 315.

84. Goodhart, *Newspapers and Contempt of Court in English Law*, 48 Harv. L. Rev. 885, at 904 (1935).

85. Thomas, Problems of Contempt of Court, pp. 20, 21, 36.

86. Rex v. Griffiths, 2 Q.B. 192 (1957).

87. Emmons v. Pottle, 16 Q.B.D. 354 (1885).

88. McLeod v. St. Aubyn, A.C. 549 (1889); see also 46 Geo. Wash. L. Rev. 347.

89. 8 and 9 Eliz. 2, ch. 65.

90. Donnelly and Goldfarb, *Contempt by Publication in the U.S.*, 24 Mod. L. Rev. 239 (1961).

91. These cases, and the history of early use of the constructive contempt power, were thoroughly and interestingly described by Nelles and King in 28 COLUM. L. REV. 401 *et seq.*

92. JUDICIARY ACT OF 1789, § 17.

93. 28 COLUM. L. REV. 401, 525; also see THOMAS, CONSTRUCTIVE CONTEMPT.

94. 18 U.S.C. § 401.

95. THOMAS, PROBLEMS OF CONTEMPT OF COURT (1904).

96. U.S. v. Toledo Newspaper Co., 220 Fed. 458 (N.D. Ohio, 1915).

97. Francis v. Virgin Islands, 11 F.2d 860 (3d Cir. 1926); Coll v. United States, 8 F.2d 20 (1st Cir. 1925); *In re* Independent Pub. Co., 240 Fed. 849 (9th Cir. 1917); United States v. Sullens, 36 F.2d 230 (S.D. Miss. 1929); United States v. Sanders, 290 Fed. 428 (W.D. Tenn. 1923); United States v. Markewich, 261 Fed. 537 (S.D.N.Y. 1919); United States v. Providence Tribune, 241 Fed. 524 (D.R.I. 1917); McDougall v. Sheridan, 128 Pac. 954 (Idaho Sup. Ct. 1913); State v. Magee Pub. Co., 224 Pac. 1028 (N.M. Sup. Ct. 1924); State v. Shumaker, 163 N.E. 272 (R.I. Dist. Ct. 1917).

98. 313 U.S. 33 (1940).

99. ESSAYS OF BACON, p. 258, *On Judicature.*

100. 28 HARV. L. REV. 605.

101. Bridges v. California, and Times Mirror Co. v. Sup. Ct. of Cal., 314 U.S. 252 (1941).

102. 14 Cal. 2d 464, 15 Cal. 2d 99.

103. Schenk v. U.S., 249 U.S. 47, 52 (1919).

104. Pennekamp v. Florida, 328 U.S. 331 (1946).

105. 331 U.S. 367 (1947).   106. 338 U.S. 912 (1949).

107. 341 U.S. 50 (1941).   108. Irvin v. Dowd, 366 U.S. 717 (1961).

109. *Supra* note 90.

III: The Extensions of the Contempt Power

1. WIGMORE, EVIDENCE, § 2195, p. 81.   2. *Ibid.*, § 2195, (3).

3. *In re* Huron, 48 P. 574 (S.C. Kan. 1897).   4. *Ibid.* at 576.

5. RAPALJE, CONTEMPT OF COURT, § 3; also see 33 N.J.L. 344.

6. BLACK, LAW DICTIONARY, p. 993.

7. *E.g.,* ALA. CODE, tit. 13, § 2, 3 (1940).

8. *But see In re* Clark, 65 Conn. 17, 31 A. 352 (1894).

9. Joslyn v. People, 67 Colo. 297, 184 P. 375 (1919); *In re* Gannon, 69 Cal. 541, 11 P. 240 (1896); *In re* Archer, 134 Mich. 408, 96 N.W. 442 (1903), Gendron v. Burham, 146 Me. 387, 82 A.2d 773 (1951).

10. Brown v. U.S., 359 U.S. 41, 49 (1959).

11. Carlson v. U.S., 209 F.2d 209 (1954); Camarota v. U.S., 111 F.2d 243 (3d Cir. 1940).

12. FEDERAL GRAND JURY HANDBOOK, Section of Judicial Administration of ABA (West 1961).

13. *In re* Oliver, 233 U.S. 257 (1948); 48 COLUM. L. REV. 813 (1948).

14. Levine v. U.S., 362 U.S. 610 (1960); 7 WAYNE L. REV. 366 (1960).

15. *Supra* note 10.

16. *Matter of* Hitson, 177 F. Supp. 834 (N.D. Col. 1959); U.S. v. Curcio, 234 F.2d 470 (2d Cir. 1956).

17. 18 U.S.C. § 401.   18. Rule 42.

19. See dissent in Brown v. U.S., *supra* note 10, at 54. Also see, U.S. v. Rinieri, 308 F.2d 24 (2d Cir. 1962).

20. *Supra* note 14.

21. Carlson v. U.S., 209 F.2d 209, 218 (1st Cir. 1954).

22. BLACK, LAW DICTIONARY 1445 (4th ed. 1951).

23. REMINGTON, BANKRUPTCY, v. 7, cl. 44 § 3032; *e.g.*, see, Glenmark, Inc. v. Carity, N.Y.A.D., 1st Dept. *decided* Oct. 9, 1962.

24. REMINGTON, 6 ed., v. 9, cl. 53, § 2 a (13).   25. *Supra* note 22.

26. *Supra* note 24, at § 41.

27. Boyd v. Glucklich, 116 Fed. 131 (8th Cir. 1902), at 135.

28. *Supra* note 24, § 3544.   29. *Ibid.* at 168.

30. Ohio Valley Bank v. Mack, 163 Fed. 155 (6th Cir. 1906); *Re* Kaplan Bros., 213 Fed. 753 (3d Cir. 1914).

31. *Supra* note 24, § 3548.

32. For a full discussion of these procedures, see REMINGTON, BANKRUPTCY *supra* note 24, § 3524–63.

33. SKINNER, NOTARY MANUAL (Bender, N.Y., 1912).

34. *Ibid.;* also see ANDERSON'S, MANUAL FOR NOTARIES PUBLIC (2 ed. 1950).

35. *Ibid.*, ANDERSON at § 2.11, p. 16.   36. SKINNER, § 12.

37. 8 A.L.R. 1583.

38. See JOHN, AMERICAN NOTARY AND COMMISSIONER OF DEEDS MANUAL (4 ed. 1931); 81 U. PA. L. REV. 996 (1933).

39. *Supra* note 34, ANDERSON.

40. U.S. v. Pratt, 3 Alaska 400 (1907); Burtt v. Pyle, 39 Ind. 398 (1883).

41. Burtt case, *supra* note 40; Haight v. Lucia, 36 Wisc. 355 (1874) (Commissioner); *In re* Mason, 43 Fed. 510 (1890) (Commr.).

42. *In re* Huron, 58 Kan. 152, 48 P. 574 (1897).

43. *Ex Parte* Noell, 317 Mo. 392, 295 S.W. 532 (1927); *Ex Parte* Bevan, 126 Ohio St. 126 (1933); Bevan v. Krieger, 289 U.S. 459 (1933).

44. MacDonald v. Leubischer, 34 A.D. 577, 54 N.Y.S. 869 (1898); Burns v. Superior Court, 140 Cal. 1, 73 P. 597 (1903).

45. *Supra* note 42.

46. Kendall, *Can Authority Be Delegated to Notaries Public to Punish for Contempt*, 56 CENT. L.J. 144 (1903).

47. Dogge v. State, 21 Neb. 272, 31 N.W. 929 (1887); Coleman v. Roberts, 113 Ala. 323, 21 S. 449 (1896).

48. *Ibid.*

49. *Ex Parte* Bevan, 126 Ohio St. 126 (1933), 289 U.S. 459 (1933).

50. *Ex Parte* Johnson, 54 Tex. Crim. 113, 111 S.W. 743 (1908); Harbison v. McMurray, 163 S.W.2d 680 (1942).

51. *Ex Parte* Mallin Krodt, 20 Mo. 493 (1855); *Ex Parte* Schoepf, 74 Ohio St. 1, 77 N.E. 276 (1906); Courtnay v. Knox, 31 Neb. 652, 48 N.W. 763 (1891); Pierce v. Carrington, 5 Utah 531, 17 P. 735 (1888); May v. Stoner, 12 Wyo. 478, 76 P. 584 (1904).

52. *Supra* note 46, at 144.

53. Keller v. Goodrich, 117 Ind. 556, 39 N.E. 196; Taylor v. Thornton, 178 Ky. 463, 199 S.W. 40; *Re* Niday, 15 Idaho 559, 98 P. 845 (1908); Bradley Fertilizer Co. v. Taylor, 112 N.C. 141, 17 S.E. 69 (1893).

54. *E.g.,* see N.Y. CIVIL PRACTICE ACT, § 406.

55. Fed. R. Civ. P., Rule 37; Puterbaugh v. Smith, 131 Ill. 199, 23 N.E. 428; McIntyre v. People, 227 Ill. 26, 81 N.E. 33; People v. Rushworth, 294 Ill. 455, 128 N.E. 555.

56. ANDERSON, *supra* note 34, at § 741, 2; Kuhlman v. Superior Court, 122 Col. 636, 55 P. 589 (1898).

57. *In re* Kerrigan, 33 N.J.L. 344, 346 (N.J.S.C. 1869).

58. *E.g.,* see Kuhlman v. Superior Court, 122 Col. 636, 55 P. 589 (1898) (Coroners); *Re* Sims, 54 Kan. 1, 37 P. 135 (1894) (County Attorney); Llewellyn's case, 13 Pa. County Ct. 126, 2 Pa. Dist. 631 (1893) (Borough Auditor); Martin v. Meyers, 171 La. 313, 131 S. 31 (1930) (Supt. of Police); Plunkett v. Hamilton, 136 Ga. 72, 70 S.E. 781 (1911) (Board of Commissioners); People v. Learned, 5 Hun 626 (N.Y. 1875) (Investigation Commission); Brown v. Davidson, 59 Iowa 461, 13 N.W. 442 (1882) (Insanity Committee).

59. In reality, they are not truly independent because they are always subject to the budgetary control of Congress and the appointment power of the President, see COOPER, THE LAWYER AND ADMINISTRATIVE AGENCIES (1957); SCHWARTZ, THE PROFESSOR AND THE COMMISSIONS (1959).

60. For more elaborate discussions of the general nature and functions of administrative agencies, see: DAVIS, ADMINISTRATIVE LAW; GELLHORN AND BYSE, ADMINISTRATIVE LAW 1–28 (1960); SCHWARTZ, INTRODUCTION TO AMERICAN ADMINISTRATIVE LAW 1–25 (1958).

61. Report of the Attorney General's Commission on Administrative Procedure, 77th Cong., 1st Sess. (1951); 69 YALE L.J. 131.

62. *Ibid.*

63. *E.g.,* see ARK. STAT. ANN. § 19-1310 (Civil Service Com.).

64. *E.g.,* see 47 U.S.C.A. § 409(m) (F.C.C.).

65. See note 133 *infra.*

66. *E.g.,* see 33 U.S.C.A. § 927 (Workmen's Compensation Com.); Internal Revenue Service, INT. REV. CODE OF 1954, § 7604(b).

67. John F. Camp, 96 N.L.R.B. #7, 1 Ad. L.2d 500 (1951), *rev'd* Camp v. Herzog, 104 F. Supp. 134 (D.D.C. 1952); *Ex Parte* Doll, Fed. Cas. #3, 968 (E.D.Pa. 1870).

68. N.L.R.B. Rules, Regulations, and Statements of Procedure, § 102.35(f), § 102.44(a).

69. Okin v. S.E.C., 137 F.2d 398, 402 (2d Cir. 1943); *Matter of* Electric Bond and Share Co., 73 F. Supp. 426 (S.D.N.Y. 1946).

70. *Supra* note 68, § 102.44(a) and (b).

71. Schwebel v. Orrick, 153 F. Supp. 701 (D.C.D.C. 1957), *aff'd* 251 F.2d 919, *cert. denied* 350 U.S. 920.

72. Weirton Steel Co., 8 N.L.R.B. 581.

73. N.L.R.B. v. Weirton Steel Co., 135 F. 2d 494, 497 (3d Cir. 1943).

74. *Supra* note 68, § 102.44(b), § 102.41.   75. *Supra* note 73.

76. *Supra* note 72.

77. Camp v. Herzog, 104 F. Supp. 134, at 136 (D.C.D.C. 1952).

78. N.L.R.B. Rules, § 102.44.

79. *In re* Rouss, 221 N.Y. 81, 116 N.E. 782 (1917); *In re* Daugherty, 38 S.E.C. 82 (1957).

80. Sometimes, suspension from practice before one commission will automatically disbar before another. See, Survey of Administrative Organizations, Part IIc, 85 Cong., 1st Sess., P. 1819 (1955) (see note 81 *infra*).

81. N.L.R.B. Rules, § 102.44. The NLRB has recently expressed this thought as follows: "The Board believes that because of the serious nature of the sanction involved, it is only fair that an attorney charged with misconduct is accorded a full hearing." Survey and Study of Administrative Organization, Proceedings and Practice in the Federal Agencies by the Committee on Government Operations, Part IIc, 85 Cong., 1st Sess., P. 1819 (1955).

82. The APA provides for judicial review of all final orders of administrative agencies—§ 10(d). Suggested legislation on the question of disciplinary proceedings of agencies' practitioners has included provisions for judicial review. See, Practice Before Government Agencies, Subcommittee 2 of the Committee on the Judiciary (H.R.), 80 Cong., Sess. 1 and 2.

83. *E.g.,* ALA. CODE, tit. 17, § 261 (Election Committee); ARIZ. CODE, § 4-112 (Supt. Liquor Licenses).

84. *E.g.*, COL. CONST. art. 12, § 22 (R.R. Com.); LA. CONST. art. 6 (Pub. Serv. Com.); OKLA. CONST., art. 9, § 19 (Corp. Com.); VA. CONST. XII, § 156(c) (Corp. Com.).

85. *In re* Sanford, 236 Mo. 665, 139 S.W. 376 (1911) (Bd. Equalization); see 40 ILL. L. REV. 344 (1946).

86. *In re* Hayes, 200 N.C. 133, 156 S.E. 791 (1931) (Indus. Com.).

87. People v. Learned, 5 Hun 626 (12 Sup. Ct., 3 dept. 1875) (Investigating Commission).

88. *E.g.*, Haas v. Jennings, 120 Ohio St. 370, 166 N.E. 357 (1929) (Investigating Commission); Garrigus v. State, 93 Ind. 239 (1884); Martin v. Meyers, 171 La. 313, 131 S. 31 (1930) (Supt. of Police); Noyes v. Byxbee, 45 Conn. 382 (1877) (Ins. Com.); *Matter of* Blue, 46 Mich. 268, 9 N.W. 441 (1881) (Bd. Supervisors).

89. Parker, 40 ILL. L. REV. 344 (1946); also see Brown v. Davidson, 59 Iowa 461, 13 N.W. 442 (1882).

90. People v. Swena, 88 Colo. 337, 296 Pac. 271 (1931); Langenberg v. Decker, 131 Ind. 471, 31 N.E. 190 (1892); Roberts v. Hackney, 109 Ky. 265, 58 S.W. 810 (1900); *In re* Sims, 54 Kan. 1, 37 Pac. 135 (1894); State v. Ryan, 182 Mo. 349, 81 S.W. 435 (1905), *but see* note 85 *supra* (Mo. case upholding the state).

91. *E.g.*, see KY. REV. STAT. ANN., § 417.030 (1944); TENN. CODE ANN. § 5408 (1936); TEX. STAT. art. 6024 (1936), *but see*, 173 Tenn. 308, 318 117 S.W.2d 4, 8 (*approving* Tenn. statute) (1937); 121 Tenn. 420, 117 S.W. 508 (1908).

92. *Supra* note 84.

93. *E.g.*, see ALA. CODE, tit. 17, § 261 (direct power); tit. 55, § 48 (misdemeanor); tit. 55, § 49 (direct court action); tit. 48, § 78 (application for court enforcement order).

94. *But see* Garrigus v. State, 93 Ind. 239 (1884).

95. ICC v. Brimson, 154 U.S. 447 (1894), *dissenting opinion* at 155 U.S. 1.

96. U.S. CONST., art. III.

97. *Supra* note 95, at 488, 489.

98. *Ibid.* at 485.

99. Whitcomb's case, 120 Mass. 118 (1876); Langenberg v. Decker, 131 Ind. 471, 31 N.E. 190 (1892).

100. Langenberg, *supra* note 99, at 31 N.E. 195.

101. SCHWARTZ, INTRODUCTION TO AMERICAN ADMINISTRATIVE LAW 101 (1958).

102. Lloyd Sabudo Societa v. Elting, 287 U.S. 329 (1932); Oceanic Steam Navigation Co. v. Stranahan, 214 U.S. 320 (1909); Helvering v. Mitchell, 303 U.S. 391 (1938).

103. 1952 Annual Survey of N.Y. Law 928, 9; GELLHORN AND BYSE, ADMINISTRATIVE LAW 163 (1960).

104. Annual Survey, *ibid.*

105. GELLHORN AND BYSE, *supra* note 103.

106. Wong Wing v. U.S., 163 U.S. 228 (1896); Abel v. U.S., 362 U.S. 217 (1960); 36 N.Y.U.L. REV. 89–92 (1961).

107. 69 YALE L.J. 131 (1960).   108. *Supra* note 106.

109. *Supra* note 103.

110. 71 HARV. L. REV. 1541, at 1553.

111. Dreyer v. Illinois, 187 U.S. 71, at 84 (1902).

112. Ritholz v. Indiana State Board of Regents, 45 F. Supp. 423 (1937).

113. *In re* Groban, 352 U.S. 330 (1956).

114. Tresolini, *The Use of Summary Contempt Powers by Administrative Agencies,* 54 DICK. L. REV. 395 (1950).

115. Plunkett v. Hamilton, 136 Ga. 72, 70 S.E. 781 (Sup. Ct. 1911).

116. Anderson v. Dunn, 19 U.S. (6 Wheat.) 204, see Chapter I.

117. See Tresolini, *supra* note 114.

118. 35 COLUM. L. REV. 587 (1935); and in COOPER, *supra* note 59; it was opined that agencies are little courts or little legislatures.

119. Anderson v. Dunn, 19 U.S. (6 Wheat.) 204 (1821); Michaelson v. U.S., 266 U.S. 42 (1924).

120. *In re* Clark, 65 Conn. 17, 31 A. 522 (1894).

121. FREUND, ADMINISTRATIVE POWERS OVER PERSONS AND PROPERTY (1928); SWENSON, FEDERAL ADMINISTRATIVE LAW 127 (1952).

122. Albertsworth, 25 A.B.A.J. 954 (1939).

123. SWENSON, *supra* note 121.   124. 71 HARV. L. REV. 1541 (1958).

125. Penfield Oil v. SEC, 330 U.S. 585, 603 (1947).

126. 35 COLUM. L. REV. 578, 579 (1935).

127. Pekelis, *Administrative Discretion and the Rule of Law,* 10 SOCIAL RESEARCH 22 (Feb. 1943); COOPER, *supra* note 59.

128. *Ibid.,* Pekelis at p. 24.

129. SCHWARTZ, THE PROFESSOR AND THE COMMISSIONS (1958).

130. Report of the House Special Subcommittee on Legislative Oversight, N.Y. *Times,* Dec. 31, 1958; Landis, Presidential Task Force Report, Dec. 1960.

131. Tresolini, *supra* note 114; also see COOPER, note 59.

132. 47 U.S.C.A. § 409(m) (F.C.C.). See, 1 DAVIS, ADMINISTRATIVE LAW 3.11.

133. See *e.g.,* 7 U.S.C.A. § 499m(c) (Dept. Agric.); 15 U.S.C.A. § 49 (F.T.C.); 15 U.S.C.A. § 78u (S.E.C.); 19 U.S.C.A. § 1333(b) (Tariff Commission); 29 U.S.C.A. § 161(2) (N.L.R.B.); 42 U.S.C.A. § 2281 (A.E.C.); 45 U.S.C.A. § 362(b) (R.R. Unemploy. Ins. Bd.); 47 U.S.C.A.

§ 409(g) (F.C.C.); 49 U.S.C.A. § 12(2) (I.C.C.); 50 U.S.C.A. § 792(c); 819(d)(2) Internal Security Bd., ARIZ. REV. STAT. ANN. § 23–677 (Employment Service Commission); § 27–519 (Oil and Gas Commission); ARK. STAT. ANN. § 853–113(b) (Oil and Gas Commission).

134. See 61 A.L.R.2d 1090.   135. 5 U.S.C.A. § 1005(c).

136. ADMIN. PROC. ACT, § 12.

137. FPC v. Metropolitan Edison Co., 304 U.S. 375, 386 (1938).

138. I.C.C. ACT OF 1887, § 12.

139. *In re* Pacific Ry. Comm., 32 Fed. 241 (C.C.N.D. Col. 1887); *In re* McLean, 37 Fed. 648 (E.D. N.Y. 1888).

140. 53 Fed. 476 (N.D. Ill. 1892).   141. *Supra* note 95, at 476–77.

142. *Ibid.* at 485–87.   143. *Id.* at 476.   144. 155 U.S. 7, 8.

145. 18 U.S.C. § 401 (1952).

146. *E.g.*, see Endicott Johnson Corp. v. Perkins, 317 U.S. 501, 510 (1943) where dissent described this "rubber stamp" process.

147. U.S. v. Morton Salt Co., 338 U.S. 632 (1950); also *infra* note 154.

148. 353 U.S. 322 (1957).   149. *Ibid.*   150. *Supra* note 146.

151. NLRB v. Giannasca, 119 F.2d 756 (2d Cir. 1941).

152. NLRB v. Retail Clerk's International Assn., 203 F.2d 165 (9th Cir. 1953); N.Y.S. Labor Relations Bd. v. Wheeler, Inc., 177 Misc. 945, 31 N.Y.S.2d 785 (1941).

153. JAFFE, ADMINISTRATIVE LAW 481–85 (1953).

154. *Supra* note 152 (NLRB case).

155. *Supra* note 152 (Wheeler case).   156. 350 U.S. (1955).

157. *Supra* note 125.

158. *E.g.*, see 5 U.S.C.A. § 773(c); 33 U.S.C.A. § 927; ARK. STAT. ANN. § 81–1331, 81–116 (1947).

159. 5 U.S.C.A. § 773(c).

160. Haughey v. Ryan, 182 Mo. 349, 81 S.W. 435 (1904); Chidsey v. Mallen, 360 Pa. 606, 63 A.2d 49 (1949).

161. Puterbaugh v. Smith, 131 Ill. 199, at 203, 23 N.E. 428 (1890).

162. Brody v. U.S., 243 F.2d 378 (1st Cir. 1956), *cert. denied* 345 U.S. 923 (1957).

163. Chidsey v. Mallen, 63 A.2d 49, 360 Pa. 606 (1949).

IV: Limitations of the Contempt Power

1. The detailed account and citations for the facts in this summary are presented in earlier chapters. See Goldfarb, *The History of the Contempt Power*, 1961 WASH. U.L.Q. 1, 1961.

2. 18 U.S.C. § 401 (1958).

3. 18 U.S.C.A. § 3691 (formerly 28 U.S.C. § 386, 389).

4. SWAYZEE, CONTEMPT OF COURT IN LABOR INJUNCTION CASES (Col. U. Press, 1935), see ch. V, Legislative Steps toward Revision, p. 105 *et seq.*

5. NORRIS LAGUARDIA ACT, Public Law 64 11 and 12–72d Congress, March 23, 1932, 18 U.S.C. § 3692 (1958).

6. Michaelson v. U.S., 266 U.S. 42 (1924).

7. 71 Stat. 637, 42 U.S.C. § 1971(e), 1975(g), 1971.

8. 43 CORNELL L.Q. 622, at 676.

9. Causal interpretation of this phrase in 131 U.S. 267, Savin case; 131 U.S. 280, Cuddy case; Toledo case, 247 U.S. 402; Craig v. Hecht, 263 U.S. 255; Froelich v. U.S., 33 F.2d 660 (8th Cir. 1929). Physical interpretation in NYE v. U.S., 313 U.S. 33 (1940).

10. Cammer v. U.S., 350 U.S. 399 (1956); Farese v. U.S., 209 F.2d 312 (1st Cir. 1954); Schmidt v. U.S., 124 F.2d 177 (6th Cir. 1941).

11. Green v. U.S., 356 U.S. 165 (1957).

12. Dennis v. U.S., 341 U.S. 494 (1960).

13. Justice Black's dissent in the Green case will be frequently cited throughout this chapter. Rather than citing each separate thought, I will refer to the dissent in general. It appears from pp. 193–219.

14. 356 U.S. at 189.   15. *Ibid.* at 193.

16. Frankfurter and Landis, *Power to Regulate Contempts*, 37 HARV. L. REV. 1010, at 1054 (1924).

17. See also Black's dissent in Sacher v. U.S., 343 U.S. 1, at 20 (1952).

18. LESSER, HISTORY OF THE JURY SYSTEM; 1 JOURNALS OF THE CONTINENTAL CONGRESS 1778–79, at 69 (Ford ed. 1904).

19. Green at 207.   20. See 57 MICH. L. REV. 258, at 262 (1958).

21. U.S. v. Ballantyne, 237 F.2d 657, at 667 (5th Cir. 1956).

22. See RAPALJE, § 10; Fox, CONTEMPT OF COURT, at 2, 3.

23. *Ex Parte* Wilson, 114 U.S. 417 (1884).

24. U.S. v. Moreland, 258 U.S. 433 (1922); U.S. v. Lindsey Wells, 186 Fed. 248 (W.D. Tenn. 1910).

25. 18 U.S.C. § 1(l) (1958).

26. Justice Holmes, in the Gompers Case, 233 U.S. 604, at 610 (1913).

27. Eilenbecker v. District Court of Plymouth County, 134 U.S. 31, at 36 (1890).

28. Bessett v. Conkey, 194 U.S. 324 (1904).

29. U.S. v. Goldman, 277 U.S. 229 (1928).   30. *Supra* note 21.

31. Fisher v. Pace, 336 U.S. 155 (1948).

32. Farese v. U.S., 209 F.2d 312, at 315 (1st Cir. 1954).

33. 1 LIVINGSTON, COMPLETE WORKS ON CRIMINAL PROCEDURE 258–67 (1873).

34. *Ibid.* at 264.

35. Toledo Newspaper Co. v. U.S., 247 U.S. 402, at 425, 426 (1918).

36. New Orleans v. Steamship Co., 87 U.S. (20 Wall.) 387, at 392 (1874).

37. Creekmore v. U.S., 237 Fed. 743 (8th Cir. 1916).

38. 343 U.S. at 20 (1951).

39. For example, see *In re* Steiner, 195 Fed. 299 (S.D.N.Y. 1912); U.S. v. Appel, 211 Fed. 495 (2d Cir. 1913).

40. Black's dissent in Green, at 193, 194.   41. U.S. CONST., amend. I.

42. Stansbury v. Marks, 2 Dall (U.S.) 213 (1793).

43. Cited in RAPALJE, § 23; 2 Gall. 364.

44. Lynch v. Uhlenhopp, 78 N.W.2d 491, 248 Iowa 68 (1956).

45. For review of the decision see 34 N.C.L. REV. 509; and 42 IOWA L. REV. 617.

46. Prince v. Massachusetts, 321 U.S. 167 (1943); Pierce v. Society of Sisters, 268 U.S. 510 (1925).

47. 10 LAW AND CONTEMPORARY PROBLEMS 721, 731 (1953).

48. 29 HARV. L. REV. 485, 492; 50 YALE L.J. 1286.

49. Shelley v. Kraemer, 334 U.S. 1 (1947).

50. Pierce v. Society of Sisters, 266 U.S. 510 (1925).

51. *E.g.,* State v. Dunn, 229 N.C. 734, 51 S.E.2d 179, *appeal dismissed,* 336 U.S. 942 (1949) (use of snakes in religious ceremonies); Reynolds v. Utah, 98 U.S. 145, 163 (1878); Church of Jesus Christ v. Utah, 136 U.S. 1, 49 (1889) (polygamy).

52. See Oriel v. Russel, 278 U.S. 358, at 364–65 (1928).

53. See Chapter II for detailed analysis of this doctrine.

54. Goldfarb, *Public Information, Criminal Trials and the Cause Celebre,* 36 N.Y.U.L. REV. 810 (1961).

55. Goldfarb and Donnelly, 24 MOD. L. REV. 239 (1961).

56. Toledo case, 247 U.S. 402 (1918).

57. Nye case, 313 U.S. 33 (1940).   58. 24 MOD. L. REV. at 241.

59. Schenck v. U.S., 249 U.S. 47 (1919).

60. Bridges and Times Mirror cases, 314 U.S. 252 (1941).

61. *Ibid.*   62. *Id.*   63. 24 MOD. L. REV. at 243.

64. Dennis v. U.S., 341 U.S. 494, 510 (1951).

65. Fisher v. Pace, 336 U.S. 155 (1949).   66. *Ibid.* at 165–66.

67. Stone v. Wyoming 77 Wyo. 1, 53, 305 P.2d 777 (S.C. Wyo., 1957), *cert. denied* 352 U.S. 1026 (1957).

68. People v. Goss, 10 Ill.2d 533, 141 N.E.2d 385 (1957).

69. Reviewed on other grounds, see 24 BROOKLYN L. REV. 123 (1957).

70. *Ex Parte* Ewell, 71 Cal. App. 744, 236 P. 205 (1925).

71. Hendrix v. Consolidated Van Lines, Inc., 176 Kan. 101, 110, 269 P.2d 435, 442 (1954).

72. Kaspar v. Brittain, 245 F.2d 92 (6th Cir., 1957), *cert. denied* 355 U.S. 834 (1957).

73. 370 U.S. 230 (1962).   74. 369 U.S. 689 (1962).

75. 369 U.S. 749 (1962), *included* Shelton, Whitman, Liveright, Price, and Gojack v. U.S.

76. Whitney v. California, 274 U.S. 357 (1927).

77. This remark was made by Chief Justice Warren in his opinion in the Watkins case, 354 U.S. 178, at 215.

78. See BECK, CONTEMPT OF CONGRESS; TAYLOR, GRAND INQUEST; CARR, HOUSE UN-AMERICAN ACTIVITIES; CARR, THE CONSTITUTION AND CONGRESSIONAL INVESTIGATING COMMITTEES.

79. GELLHORN, AMERICAN RIGHTS; BECK, CONTEMPT OF CONGRESS.

80. See appendices to BECK's book cited above.   81. BECK at 181.

82. Finer, *The British System*, 18 U. CHI. L. REV. at 523.

83. BECK at 186.

84. Landis, *Congressional Power of Investigation*, 40 HARV. L. REV. 213.

85. McGrain v. Dougherty, 273 U.S. 135 (1926).

86. CARR, THE CONSTITUTION AND CONGRESSIONAL INVESTIGATING COMMITTEES 19–25 (1954).

87. BARTH, GOVERNMENT BY INVESTIGATION 11 (1955).

88. Opinion of Judge Clark, Josephson v. U.S., 165 F.2d 82, at 95 (2d Cir. 1957).

89. 68 Sup. Ct. 609.

90. Barskey v. U.S., 167 F.2d 241 (D.C. Cir. 1948).

91. Wilkinson v. U.S., 81 Sup. Ct. at 579.

92. Black, *The Bill of Rights*, 35 N.Y.U.L. REV. 865, 867.

93. *Supra* note 91, at 576.   94. Barenblatt v. U.S., 360 U.S. 109, at 143.

95. *Supra* note 91, at 580.   96. 103 U.S. 163 (1880).

97. *Ibid.* at 190.

98. These decisions are summarized in BECK, chs. III, VI, and VII.

99. Marshall v. Gordon, 243 U.S. 521, 542 (1916).

100. 18 U.S.C.A. § 201.

101. Sinclair v. U.S., 279 U.S. 263, at 291 (1929); McGrain v. Dougherty, 273 U.S. 135, 173 (1926).

102. Bowers v. U.S., 202 F.2d 447, at 448 (D.C. Cir. 1953).

103. Watkins v. U.S., 354 U.S. 178, at 195 (1956).   104. *Ibid.*

105. Sweezy v. New Hampshire, 354 U.S. 234, 245 (1956).

106. GELLHORN, AMERICAN RIGHTS, at 123.

107. Barenblatt v. U.S., 360 U.S. 109 (1959).

108. Braden v. U.S., 365 U.S. 431 (1960), *rehearing denied* 365 U.S. 890.

109. Wilkinson v. U.S., 365 U.S. 399 (1960), *rehearing denied* 365 U.S. 890.

110. 291 S.W.2d 843.

111. 1959 H.U.A.C. annual report, ch. 7 lists pending cases.

112. See McKay, *Speaking up for Silence*, ACLU News, No. Cal., Jan. 1961.

113. Talley v. California, 362 U.S. 60 (1959).

114. Bates v. Little Rock, 361 U.S. 516 (1960).

115. Barsky v. U.S., 167 F.2d 241, at 254 (D.C. Cir. 1948).

116. Bates v. Little Rock, *supra* note 114; NAACP v. Alabama, 357 U.S. 449 (1958).

117. NAACP v. Alabama, *ibid.*

118. Quinn v. U.S., 349 U.S. 155 (1955).

119. *E.g.*, see Barsky case at p. 256, footnote 19; also, Mr. Dies has publicly stated this.

120. Musser v. Utah, 333 U.S. 95 (1947).   121. *Supra* note 115, at 259.

122. Warran and Brandeis, *The Right to Privacy*, 4 Harv. L. Rev. 193 (1890).

123. *Ibid.* at 198.   124. *E.g.*, see N.Y. Civ. Rts. L. § 50.51.

125. Coudert, *Congressional Inquisition v. Individual Liberty*, 15 Va. L. Rev. 537 (1929). See also, Shapiro, *The Supreme Court's Supervision of Congressional Investigations*, 15 Vand. L. Rev. 535 (1962).

126. Marsh v. Alabama, 326 U.S. 501 (1946).

127. U.S. Const., art. 1, § 10.

128. See Black's dissent in Barenblatt, 360 U.S. at 153 *et seq.*

129. *Supra* note 115, at 260; also discussed in Barenblatt v. U.S. (*dissent*), *supra.*

130. Lovett v. U.S., 328 U.S. 303 (1945).

131. Sky, *Judicial Review of Congressional Investigations*, 31 Geo. Wash. L. Rev. 399.

132. Carr, House Committee on Un-American Activities (1952).

133. Coudert, 15 Va. L. Rev. 537.

134. Maslow, 54 Colum. L. Rev. 839 (1954).

135. Carr, *supra* note 86, at p. 49 *et seq.*

136. U.S. Const., amend. IV.

137. Jones v. U.S., 131 F.2d 539 (10th Cir. 1942); State v. Frye, 120 P.2d 793, 58 Ariz. 409 (1942).

138. U.S. v. O'Dowd, 272 Fed. 600 (N.D. Ohio 1921).

139. Nueslein, 115 F.2d 690 (D.C. 1940); State v. Nelson, 300 N.W. 685, 231 Iowa 177 (1941).

140. Grau v. U.S., 287 U.S. 124 (1932); U.S. v. Zager, 14 F. Supp. 23 (Md. D.C. 1936), aff'd mem. 84 F.2d 1023 (4th Cir.), cert. denied 299 U.S. 558 (1936).

141. U.S. v. 1013 Crates of Empty Old Smuggler Whiskey Bottles, 52 F.2d 49 (2d Cir. 1931).

142. *In re* Chapman, 166 U.S. 661, at 671 (1897).

143. People v. Montesano, 12 N.E.2d 915, 293 Ill. App. 630 (1938).

144. *In re* Estes, 87 F. Supp. 461 (N.D. Tex. 1949), *cert. denied,* 340 U.S. 920 (1951).

145. Nelson v. U.S., 208 F.2d 505 (D.C. Cir. 1953), see pp. 512, 513, 514, 520; *cert. denied* 346 U.S. 827 (1953).

146. Schwimmer v. U.S., 232 F.2d 855 (8th Cir. 1960).

147. *Ibid.* at 861.

148. State v. James, 36 Wash.2d 882, 221 P.2d 482, *cert. denied,* 341 U.S. 911, *rehearing denied* 341 U.S. 937.

149. Sinclair v. U.S. 279 U.S. 263, at 294 (1928).

150. Fed. R. Civ. P., 45(f); Fed. R. Crim. P., 17(g).

151. McMann v. Engel, 16 F. Supp. 446 (S.D.N.Y. 1936); Precision Casting Co. v. Boland, 13 F. Supp. 877 (S.D.N.Y. 1936), *aff'd* 85 F.2d 15.

152. Josephson v. U.S., 165 F.2d 82, at 88 (2d Cir. 1948).

153. Landis, *The Congressional Power of Investigation,* 40 HARV. L. REV. 153, at 219 (1926).

154. U.S. CONST., amend. V.

155. U.S. v. Central Supply Association, 34 F. Supp. 241 (Ohio D.C. 1940).

156. *Ex Parte* Wilson, 114 U.S. 417 (1884).   157. *Ibid.* at 423.

158. *Id.* at 426.   159. Hurtado v. California, 110 U.S. 516 (1884).

160. For example, courts-martial.

161. Conley v. U.S., 59 F.2d 929 (8th Cir. 1932); U.S. v. Seidmon, 154 F.2d 228, 230 (7th Cir. 1946).

162. Fanning v. U.S., 72 F.2d 929 (4th Cir. 1934).

163. Smith v. U.S., 360 U.S. 1 (1958).

164. Jurney v. McCracken, 294 U.S. 125 (1935).   165. *Ibid.* at 151.

166. *In re* Chapman, 166 U.S. 661 (1897).   167. *Ibid.* at 672.

168. DANGEL, CONTEMPT OF COURT, § 170.

169. U.S. v. United Mine Workers, 330 U.S. 258 (1947).

170. Rex Trailer Co. v. U.S., 350 U.S. 148, 150–51 (1956).

171. *Ibid.,* citing Helvering v. Mitchell, 303 U.S. 391, 399 (1937).

172. See Bartkus v. Illinois, 359 U.S. 121 (1959), where Supreme Court approved this practice.

173. Clayton Act *supra,* and Civil Rights Act of 1960, 74 STAT. 90, 42 U.S.C. § 1971(f).

174. Yates v. U.S., 225 F.2d 146 (9th Cir. 1955), *rev'd* 354 U.S. 298 (1957).

175. 9 Syracuse L. Rev. 328; 104 U. Pa. L. Rev. 998.

176. 78 Sup. Ct. 128 (1957).

177. *Compare* People v. Amarante, 100 N.Y.S.2d 677, 682 (Sup. Ct. 1950); Fawick Airflex Co. v. United Elec. Workers, 92 N.E.2d 431, 436 (Ohio Ct. App. 1950) *with In re* Ward, 295 Mich. 742, 745, 295 N.W. 483, 485 (1940), *and In re* Amato, 204 Misc. 454, 456, 124 N.Y.S.2d 726, 728 (Sup. Ct. 1953).

178. Following the Yates rule, U.S. v. Costello, 198 F.2d 200 (2d Cir. 1952); U.S. v. Abe, 95 F. Supp. 991 (How. 1950); U.S. v. Orman, 207 F.2d 148 (3d Cir. 1948) and *contra*, see Trumbo v. U.S., 176 F.2d 49 (D.C. Cir. 1949), Lawson v. U.S., 176 F.2d 49 (D.C. Cir. 1949).

179. Wyman v. Uphaus, 360 U.S. 72 (1959).

180. *Matter of* Cirello (N.Y. Ct. App. Jan. 1963).

181. U.S. Const., amend. V.

182. Kroner, *Self-Incrimination: The External Reaches of the Privilege*, 60 Colum. L. Rev. 816 (1960).

183. *E.g.*, Dilucia v. U.S., 256 F.2d 493 (7th Cir. 1958).

184. 8 Wigmore, Evidence, v. 8, p. 336, at 341 § 2257.

185. Killpatrick v. Superior Court, 314 P.2 164, 153 Cal. App.2d 146 (D.C. App. 1957).

186. *Ibid.* at 166.   187. 221 U.S. 418, 441 (1911).

188. Counselman v. Hitchcock, 142 U.S. 547 (1891).

189. Merrick, *The Privilege of Self-Incrimination as to Charges of Contempt*, 14 Ill. L. Rev. 181, at 187.

190. U.S. v. Costello, 198 F.2d 200 (2d Cir. 1952) *cert. denied* 344 U.S. 874 (1952) (Senate); Hoffman v. U.S., 341 U.S. 479 (1950); Blau v. U.S., 340 U.S. 332 (1950) (court).

191. See Beck, Contempt of Congress, chs. 4 and 5.

192. Beck at 89, 90.

193. U.S. v. Cohn, 101 F. Supp. 906 (N.D. Cal. 1952); Regan v. N.Y., 349 U.S. 58 (1955).

194. U.S. v. Hoffman, 341 U.S. 479, 488–89 (1951).

195. U.S. v. Coffey, 198 F.2d 438 (3d Cir. 1952); Greenberg v. U.S., 343 U.S. 918 (1951), *reviewing* 187 F.2d 35, 192 F.2d 301 (3d Cir. 1951); Singleton v. U.S., 343 U.S. 944 (1951), *reviewing* 193 F.2d 464 (3d Cir. 1952); Hoffman v. U.S., 341 U.S. 479 (1951); *but see* Duffy v. Brody, 147 F. Supp. 897 *aff'd* 243 F.2d 378, U.S. v. Coffey, 198 F.2d 438 (3d Cir. 1952); Greenberg v. U.S., 341 U.S. 944 (Per. Cur.).

196. Emspak v. U.S., 349 U.S. 190, 195 (1955).

197. U.S. v. Bart, 349 U.S. 219, 223 (1955).

198. Counselman v. Hitchcock, 142 U.S. 547 (1892).

199. *Ibid.* at 562.   200. *Id.* at 585.   201. *Id.* at 586.

202. Graham v. U.S., 99 F.2d 746, at 750 (9th Cir. 1938).

203. *Supra* note 182, at 838.   204. 68 STAT. 748.

205. See BECK at 119.   206. U.S. v. Reina, 364 U.S. 507 (1960).

207. 170 F. Supp. 592 (S.D.N.Y. 1959).

208. 273 F.2d 234 (2d Cir. 1959).

209. Murdock v. U.S., 284 U.S. 141 (1931).

210. The Supreme Court compared and cited, U.S. v. Ullman, 350 U.S. 422 (1955); Adams v. Maryland, 347 U.S. 179 (1953); Brown v. Walker, 161 U.S. 591 (1895).

211. Knapp v. Schweitzer, 357 U.S. 371 (1958), see p. 385.

212. U.S. v. Di Carlo, 102 F. Supp. 597, at 606 (N.D. Ohio 1952).

213. U.S. v. Licavoli, 102 F. Supp. 607 (N.D. Ohio 1952); U.S. v. Aiuppa, 102 F. Supp. 609 (N.D. Ohio), *rev'd* 201 F.2d 287 (6th Cir. 1952); Marcello v. U.S., 196 F.2d 437 (5th Cir. 1952).

214. Oct. Term, May 1962.

215. Sacher v. U.S., 343 U.S. 1, at 36—Justice Frankfurter's dissent.

216. 267 U.S. 517 (1925).

217. *Ibid.* at 537; *followed* in *Matter of* Los Angeles County Pioneer Society, 217 F.2d 190 (9th Cir. 1954).

218. Rule 42 B.

219. Oriel v. Russell, 278 U.S. 358, at 362 (1928).

220. Nilva v. U.S., 227 F.2d 75, at 80 (8th Cir. 1955), *aff'd in part and sentence vacated,* 352 U.S. 385 (1957).

221. Fox v. Capitol Co., 96 F.2d 684, at 686 (3d Cir. 1938).

222. McPhaul v. U.S., 364 U.S. 372, 383 (1960).   223. *Ibid.* at 383.

224. *Cert. granted* 362 U.S. 917 (1959).

225. U.S. v. Bryan, 339 U.S. 323 (1950); Bevan v. Krieger, 289 U.S. 459 (1933). Also see, U.S. v. Fleischman, 339 U.S. 349 (1950).

226. Rogers v. U.S., 340 U.S. 367, 372 (1951).

227. At 4016 (29 L.W.).

228. Patterson v. U.S., 219 F.2d 659 (2d Cir. 1955).

229. *Ibid.* at 662.   230. *Supra* note 222.

231. U.S. v. Jose, 63 Fed. 951, at 954 (C.C.N.D. Wash. 1894).

232. U.S. v. Bowles, 50 F.2d 848 (4th Cir. 1931).   233. *Ibid.* at 852.

234. *In re* Murchison, 349 U.S. 133, at 136 (1955).

235. *In re* Oliver, 333 U.S. 257 (1948), see concurring opinion of Justice Rutledge at p. 280.

236. Green v. U.S., 356 U.S., at 199.

237. Rule 42B, Fed. R. Crim. P.

238. Cooke v. U.S., 267 U.S. 517, at 539 (1925).

239. *Ex Parte* Grossman, 267 U.S. 87, at 122 (1925).

240. Goldfarb, *Public Information, Criminal Trials, and the Cause Celebre*, 36 N.Y.U.L. REV. 810 (1961).

241. Offutt v. U.S., 348 U.S. 11, at 14 (1954).

242. See ANATOMY OF FREEDOM, by MEDINA for his side of the affair (1959).

243. Sacher v. U.S., 343 U.S. 1, at 30 (1952).

244. Also see, Hallinan v. U.S., 182 F.2d 880, 887–88 (9th Cir. 1950); MacInnis v. U.S., 191 F.2d 157, 161 (9th Cir. 1951).

245. Tumey v. Ohio, 273 U.S. 510, 522 (1927).

246. 44 CALIF. L. REV. 428; 91 Eng. Rep. 343, 344 (K.B. 1699); and see Frank, *Disqualification of Judges*, 56 YALE L.J. 605, at 611 (1947).

247. Conference on Constitutional Review, N.Y.U. Law School, November 1960.

248. See dissent by Justice Douglas in Fisher v. Pace, 336 U.S. 155, at 167 (1949).

249. *In re* Murchison, 349 U.S. 133 (1955).

250. 348 U.S. 11, 14 (1954).

251. See dissent of Justices Minton, Reed, and Burton in U.S. v. Murchison, 349 U.S. 133, at 139. Also see Nilva v. U.S., 352 U.S. 385 (1957).

252. Fisher v. Pace, 336 U.S. 155 (1948).   253. *Ibid.* at 161.

254. U.S. CONST., amend. VI.

255. Myers v. U.S., 264 U.S. 95 (1924).

256. Dunham v. U.S., 289 Fed. 376 (5th Cir. 1923); Sullivan v. U.S., 4 F.2d 100 (8th Cir. 1925); McCourtney v. U.S., 291 Fed. 497 (8th Cir.), *cert. denied*, 263 U.S. 714 (1923).

257. See Steers v. U.S., 297 Fed. 116.

258. 18 U.S.C.A., F.R.C.P., Rule 18.

259. 28 U.S.C.A. § 1391(b) (1958).

260. Sullivan v. U.S., 4 F.2d 100, 101 (8th Cir. 1925); Binkley v. U.S., 282 Fed. 244 (8th Cir. 1922).

261. 289 Fed. 376, at 378 (5th Cir. 1923).

262. 233 U.S. 604 (1914).   263. *Ibid.* at 610.   264. *Id.* at 612.

265. *Id.* at 613.   266. Pendergast v. U.S., 317 U.S. 412 (1943).

267. 18 U.S.C.A. § 3282 (1958).   268. 18 U.S.C.A. § 3285 (1958).

269. Parker v. U.S., 126 F.2d 370 (1st Cir. 1942).   270. *Ibid.* at 380.

271. Odell v. Bausch and Lomb, 91 F.2d 359, at 361 (7th Cir.), *cert. denied* 302 U.S. 756 (1937).

272. Savin, 131 U.S. 267 (1889).

273. *Ex Parte* Terry, 128 U.S. 289, at 307 (1888).   274. *Ibid.* at 313.

275. Savin, 131 U.S. 267 (1889).   276. *Ibid.* at 277.   277. *Id.* at 279.

278. *Ibid.*   279. Cooke v. U.S., 267 U.S. 517 (1925).

280. *Ibid.* at 537.   281. *In re* Oliver, 333 U.S. 257 (1947).

282. See opinions of Justices Frankfurter and Rutledge in the Oliver case, 333 U.S. 257 (1947), at 273–76.

283. U.S. CONST., amend. VIII.

284. Green v. U.S., 356 U.S., at 200 (1957).   285. *Ibid.* at 208.

286. See note in April 1961, 36 N.Y.U.L. REV. 841, where this whole subject was thoroughly discussed.

287. Politano v. Politano, 146 Misc. 792, 262 N.Y.S. 802 (S.C. 1933).

288. *Id.* at 794.   289. 21 Q.B.D. 236 (1868).

290. 330 U.S. 258, at 377 (1947).

291. *E.g.,* see, Wyman v. Uphaus, 360 U.S. 72 (1959).

292. U.S. v. Thompson, 214 F.2d 545, 546 (2d Cir. 1954), *cert. denied* 348 U.S. 841 (1954).

293. Commonwealth v. French, 114 S.W. 255 (1908).

294. 97 S.W. 433; 97 S.W. 427.

295. See 73 HARV. L. REV. 353, at 358 (1959).

296. 220 Fed. 458, 515 (N.D. Ohio 1915), *aff'd* 237 Fed. 986 (6th Cir. 1916), *aff'd* 247 U.S. 407 (1918). *Overruled in* Nye v. U.S., 313 U.S. 33 (1941).

297. 330 U.S. 258 (1946).

298. *In re* Kemmler, 136 U.S. 436, at 477 (1890).

299. Kaspar v. Brittain, 245 F.2d 92 (6th Cir. 1957), *cert. denied* 355 U.S. 834 (1957).

300. *Ex Parte* Pickens, 101 F. Supp. 285, 288 (D. Alaska 1951).

301. 342 U.S. 165, 172 (1952).

302. DiSimone v. U.S., 267 F.2d 741 (2d Cir. 1959), *cert. denied* 361 U.S. 827 (1959).

303. Weems v. U.S., 217 U.S. 349 (1909); U.S. v. Rosenberg, 195 F.2d 583.

304. Weber v. Commonwealth, 196 S.W.2d 465, 303 Ky. 56.

305. Brown v. U.S., 247 F.2d 332 (2d Cir. 1957) *aff'd* 359 U.S. 41 (1959).

306. Lopiparo v. U.S., 216 F.2d 87 (8th Cir. 1954), *cert. denied* 348 U.S. 916 (1955).

307. U.S. v. Green, 241 F.2d 631 (2d Cir. 1957), *aff'd* 356 U.S. 165 (1958); U.S. v. Thompson, 214 F.2d 545 (2d Cir.), *cert. denied* 348 U.S. 841 (1954); U.S. v. Hall, 198 F.2d 726 (2d Cir. 1952), *cert. denied* 345 U.S. 905 (1953)

308. 122 F.2d 641.

309. Rhode Island, Vermont, and New Hampshire.

310. 104 U. PA. L. REV. 998, at 1000 (1956).

311. McCulloch v. Maryland, 17 U.S. (4 Wheat.) 316 (1819).

312. 96 Fed. 552 (D. Ky. 1899), *aff'd sub. nom.* Boske v. Comingore, 177 U.S. 459 (1900).

313. *Id.* at 559.

314. *Id.* at 561. See also Hopkins Savings Assn. v. Cleary, 296 U.S. 315 (1935).

315. U.S. v. Owlett, 15 F. Supp. 736 (M.D. Pa. 1936).

316. U.S. v. Tobin, 195 F. Supp. 588 (D.D.C. 1961), *rev'd* 306 F.2d 270 (D.C. Cir.), *cert. denied* 31 U.S.L. WEEK 3165 (Nov. 13, 1962).

317. 70 YALE L.J. 812, 817 (1961).

318. *In re* Wallace, 170 F. Supp. 63 (M.D. Ala. 1959).

319. Tobin v. U.S., D.C. Cir., June 7, 1962, no. 16,604.

320. *Id.* at 9, 10.

321. *Supra* note 131.

V: Conclusion

1. Anderson v. Dunn, 19 U.S. (6 Wheat.) 204, 231 (1821).

2. Newman, *Federal Agency Investigations*, 60 MICH. L. REV. 182, 183 (1961).

3. This phrase is attributed to Justice Douglas's *We the Judges*, in KENNEDY, THE ENEMY WITHIN 293 (1960).

4. TRILLING, FREUD AND THE CRISIS OF OUR CULTURE 42–44 (1955), quoting A Statement Formulated by the Committee on Social Issues of the Group for the Advancement of Psychiatry, G.A.P. Symposium, no. 1, Topeka, Kansas, 1954.

5. TRILLING, *op. cit.*, at 44.   6. DOUGLAS, AMERICA CHALLENGED 15.

7. KENNEDY, THE ENEMY WITHIN 160 (1960).

8. Goldfarb, *Public Information, Criminal Trials, and the Cause Celebre*, 36 N.Y.U.L. REV. 810 (1961).

9. March, *Contempt by Publication in the United States*, 24 MOD. L. REV. 239 (1961). This article was coauthored with Professor Donnelly, Yale Law School.

10. Lanzetta v. New Jersey, 306 U.S. 451 (1938).

The Barnett Case

The recent contempt case concerning Governor Ross R. Barnett, of Mississippi, raises a particular question which I did not answer in this book. The case arose after the manuscript was out of my hands. It raises a very specific and profound problem which this book did not explore. I hope to do this at another time. For now, I should like to make only a passing note of the issue.

If rights guaranteed by the Bill of Rights command preferred treatment, and they conflict with another interest which is not so constitutionally protected, one can be guided in his decision by the policy commanding preferment. But what happens where two civil rights collide? How does a decision-maker resolve a conflict between two civil liberties?

The conflict between competing civil rights or civil liberties (for example, between claims for equal protection and due process of law and claims for the right to trial by jury) creates what is at the same time the most difficult and most important constitutional issue. This kind of issue involves considerations other than the typical jury question in contempt cases; it is an issue which I have not directly answered here.

How can the federal government enforce its court decrees relating to civil rights in the South if violators of these court orders are tried by Southern juries? These juries have demonstrated their aversion to civil rights cases. Aside from the more noble qualities of jury trials, what about the inequities or injustices they promote? Society protects the unpopular defendant; how does it protect itself from the popular one? And, how does it protect the unpopular complainant? Laws can be passed, but they cannot always be applied on a majority rule basis. National interests must be protected at local levels. Yet, when they are not, how can we make exceptions to the Constitution's dictates. Who has the right to say that if juries will not convict in some class of cases we will try those cases summarily? If this right exists, it too could be abused.

This will be the very difficult and unusual problem which the Supreme Court will face in the *Barnett* case—a problem to which either answer will be perplexing.

Statutes and Cases

Statutes

U.S. Const. art. I, § 5, ch. 1, 312*n*88; art. I, § 10, ch. 4, 326*n*127; art. III, ch. 3, 320*n*96; amend. I, ch. 4, 324*n*41; amend. IV, ch. 4, 326 *n*136; amend. V, ch. 4, 327*n*154, 328*n*181; amend. VI, ch. 4, 330 *n*254; amend. VIII, ch. 4, 331*n*283

Admin. Proc. Act, ch. 3, 319*n*82; 322*n*136

Ala. Code, tit. 13, §§ 2, 3 (1940), ch. 3, 316*n*7; tit. 17, § 261, ch. 3, 319*n*83, 320*n*93; tit. 48, § 78, ch. 3, 320*n*93; tit. 55, §§ 48, 49, ch. 3, 320*n*93

Ariz. Code, § 4–112, ch. 3, 319*n*83

Ariz. Rev. Stat. Ann. § 23-677, ch. 3, 322*n*133

Ark. Stat. Ann. § 19-1310, ch. 3, 319*n*63; § 853-113, ch. 3, 322*n*133; § 81-1331, ch. 3, 322*n*158; § 81-116, ch. 3, 322*n*158

Canons Rom. 4.3.1640; 9.1842, ch. 1, 309*n*11

Clayton Act, ch. 4, 327*n*173

Colo. Const., art. XII, § 22, ch. 3, 320*n*84

8 & 9 Eliz. 2, c. 65, ch. 2, 315*n*89

Fed. R. Civ. P., Rule 37, ch. 3, 318*n*55; Rule 45F, ch. 4, 327*n*150; Rule 69, ch. 2, 314*n*22

Fed. R. Crim. P., Rule 17 (g), ch. 4, 327*n*150; Rule 18, ch. 4, 330 *n*258; Rule 42, ch. 2, 314*n*34, 315*n*53, ch. 3, 317*n*18, ch. 4, 329*nn*218, 237

The Habeas Corpus Act, 1640, 16 Car. 1, c. 10, ch. 1, 310*n*37

I.C.C. Act (1887) § 12, ch. 3, 322*n*138

Int. Rev. Code of 1954, § 7604 (b), ch. 3, 319*n*66

Judiciary Act of 1789, § 17, 1 Stat. 83, ch. 1, 311*n*53; ch. 2, 316*n*92

Ky. Rev. Stat. Ann., § 417.030 (1944), ch. 3, 320*n*91

La. Const., art. VI, ch. 3, 320*n*84

N.Y. Civil Practice Act, § 406, ch. 3, 318*n*54

Cases

Tumey v. Ohio, 273 U.S. 510 (1927), ch. 4, 330*n*245
U.S. v. Abe, 95 F. Supp. 991 (1950), ch. 4, 328*n*178
U.S. v. Aiuppa, 102 F. Supp. 609 (N.D. Ohio), *rev'd* 201 F.2d 287 (6th Cir. 1952), ch. 4, 329*n*213
U.S. v. Anonymous, 21 Fed. 761 (Cir. Tenn., 1884), ch. 2, 313*n*2; 314*n*49
U.S. v. Appel, 211 Fed. 495 (2d Cir. 1913), ch. 4, 324*n*39
U.S. v. Ballantyne, 237 F.2d 657 (5th Cir. 1956), ch. 4, 323*nn*21, 30
U.S. v. Bart, 349 U.S. 219 (1955), ch. 4, 328*n*197
U.S. v. Bittner, 11 Fed. 293 (4th Cir. 1926), ch. 2, 314*n*23
U.S. v. Bowles, 50 F.2d 848 (4th Cir. 1931), ch. 4, 329*nn*232, 233
U.S. v. Bryan, 339 U.S. 323 (1950), ch. 4, 329*n*225
U.S. v. Central Supply Association, 34 F. Supp. 241 (Ohio D.C. 1940), ch. 4, 327*n*155
U.S. v. Coffey, 198 F.2d 438 (3d Cir. 1952), ch. 4, 328*n*195
U.S. v. Cohn, 101 F. Supp. 906 (N.D. Cal. 1952), ch. 4, 328*n*193
U.S. v. Costello, 198 F.2d 200 (2d Cir. 1952), *cert. denied* 344 U.S. 874 (1952), ch. 4, 328*nn*178, 190
U.S. v. 1013 Crates of Empty Old Smuggler Whiskey Bottles, 52 F.2d 49 (2d Cir. 1931), ch. 4, 327*n*141
U.S. v. Curcio, 234 F.2d 470 (2d Cir. 1956), ch. 3, 317*n*16
U.S. v. Di Carlo, 102 F. Supp. 597 (N.D. Ohio 1952), ch. 4, 329*n*212
U.S. v. Fleischman, 339 U.S. 349 (1950), ch. 4, 329*n*225
U.S. v. Goldman, 277 U.S. 229 (1928), ch. 4, 323*n*29
U.S. v. Hall, 198 F.2d 726 (2d Cir. 1952), *cert. denied* 345 U.S. 905 (1953), ch. 4, 331*n*307
U.S. v. Hoffman, 341 U.S. 479 (1950), ch. 4, 328*nn*190, 194, 195
U.S. v. Jose, 63 Fed. 951 (C.C.N.D. Wash. 1894), ch. 4, 329*n*231
U.S. v. Licavoli, 102 F. Supp. 607 (N.D. Ohio 1952), ch. 4, 329*n*213
U.S. v. Lindsey Wells, 186 Fed. 248 (W.D. Tenn. 1910), ch. 4, 323*n*24
U.S. v. Markewich, 261 Fed. 537 (S.D.N.Y. 1919), ch. 2, 316*n*97
U.S. v. Moreland, 258 U.S. 433 (1922), ch. 4, 323*n*24
U.S. v. Morton Salt Co., 338 U.S. 632 (1950), ch. 3, 322*n*147
U.S. v. O'Dowd, 272 Fed. 600 (N.D. Ohio 1921), ch. 4, 326*n*138
U.S. v. Orman, 207 F.2d 148 (3d Cir. 1948), ch. 4, 328*n*178
U.S. v. Owlett, 15 F. Supp. 736 (M.D. Pa. 1936), ch. 4, 332*n*315
U.S. v. Parker, 126 F.2d 370 (1st Cir. 1942), ch. 2, 314*n*42

Checklist of Works Cited

ABA, FEDERAL GRAND JURY HANDBOOK (West 1961)
AIYER, LAW OF CONTEMPT OF COURT (1949)
Albertsworth, *Administrative Contempt Powers: A Problem in Technique,* 25 A.B.A.J. 954 (1939)
AMERICAN JURISPRUDENCE, Vol. 17
ANDERSON, MANUAL FOR NOTARIES PUBLIC (2d ed. 1950)
Annual Survey of New York Law (1952) N.Y.U.L. REV.
BACON, ESSAYS (1959)
BARTH, GOVERNMENT BY INVESTIGATION (1955)
Beale, *Contempt of Court, Civil and Criminal,* 21 HARV. L. REV. 161 (1908)
BECK, CONTEMPT OF CONGRESS (1959)
Black, *The Bill of Rights,* 35 N.Y.U.L. REV. 865
—— LAW DICTIONARY (4th ed. 1951)
BLACKSTONE, COMMENTARIES (1765)
Browdy and Saltzman, *The Effectiveness of the Eighth Amendment: An Appraisal of Cruel and Unusual Punishment,* 36 N.Y.U.L. REV. 846 (1961)
CAMPBELL, THE LIVES OF THE CHIEF JUSTICES OF ENGLAND (1894)
CARR, THE CONSTITUTION AND CONGRESSIONAL INVESTIGATING COMMITTEES (1954)
—— THE HOUSE UN-AMERICAN ACTIVITIES COMMITTEE (1952)
Civil and Criminal Contempt in the Federal Courts, 57 YALE L.J. 83 (1947)
C.K.K., *Contempt of Court,* TENN. L. REV. 215 (1924)
Clark, *Developments in Federal Administrative Law,* 44 CALIF. L. REV. 321 (1956)
Congress and the Port of N.Y. Authority: Federal Supervision of Interstate Compacts, 70 YALE L.J. 812 (1961)

Contempt, Enforcing a Divorce Decree, 42 Iowa L. Rev. 617 (1957)

Contempt Power of Notary, U. Pa. L. Rev. 996 (1933)

Contempt, Right to Trial by Jury in Criminal Case, 11 Va. L. Rev. 639 (1925)

Cooper, The Lawyer and Administrative Agencies (1957)

Corpus Juris Secundum, Vol. 17

Coudert, *Congressional Inquisition vs. Individual Liberty*, 15 U.Va. L. Rev. 537 (1929)

Curtis and Curtis, Jr., *The Story of a Notion in the Law of Criminal Contempt*, 41 Harv. L. Rev. 51 (1927)

Dangel, Contempt (1939)

I Davis, Administrative Law (1960)

Deutsch, *The United States Versus Major General Andrew Jackson*, 46 A.B.A.J. 966 (1960)

Donnelly and Goldfarb, *Contempt by Publication in the U.S.*, 24 Mod. L. Rev. 239 (1961)

Douglas, America Challenged (1960)

—— We the Judges (1956)

Duhamel and Smith, Some Pillars of English Law (1959)

Encyclopedia of English Laws, Vol. 5

Enforceability of Antinuptial Contracts in Mixed Marriages, 50 Yale L.J. 1286 (1941)

Federal Rules of Civil Procedure

Federal Rules of Criminal Procedure

Figgis, The Divine Rights of Kings (2d ed. 1922)

Finer, *Congressional Investigations: The British System*, 18 U. Chi. L. Rev. 523 (1951)

Fox, Contempt of Court (1927)

—— *Eccentricities of the Law of Contempt of Court*, 36 L.Q. Rev. 394 (1920)

—— *The King v. Almon*, 24 L.Q. Rev. 184 (1908)

—— *The Nature of Contempt of Court*, 37 L.Q. Rev. 191 (1921)

—— *The Practice in Contempt of Court Cases*, 38 L.Q. Rev. 185 (1922)

—— *The Summary Process to Punish Contempt*, 25 L.Q. Rev. 238 (1909)

—— *The Writ of Attachment*, 25 L.Q. Rev. 238 (1909)

Frank, *Disqualification of Judges*, 56 Yale L.J. 605 (1947)

Frankfurter and Landis, *Power of Congress over Procedure in Criminal Contempt in Inferior Federal Courts—a Study in Separation of Powers*, 37 HARV. L. REV. 1010 (1924)

FREUND, ADMINISTRATIVE POWERS OVER PERSONS AND PROPERTY (1928)

GALLOWAY, CONGRESS AND PARLIAMENT (1955)

GELLHORN, AMERICAN RIGHTS (1960)

GELLHORN AND BYSE, ADMINISTRATIVE LAW (1960)

GILBERT, HISTORY OF THE COMMON PLEAS (1737)

Goldfarb, *The History of the Contempt Power*, 1961 WASH. U.L.Q. 1 (1961)

—— *Public Information, Criminal Trials, and the Cause Celebre*, 36 N.Y.U.L. REV. 810 (1961)

Goodhart, *Newspapers and Contempt of Court in English Law*, 48 HARV. L. REV. 885 (1935)

Gualtieri, *Contempt Power of Federal Court to Summarily Punish in Closed Court*, 7 WAYNE L. REV. 366 (1960)

HALSBURY, LAWS OF ENGLAND (2d ed. 1931)

Harmon, *Civil and Criminal Contempts of Court*, 25 MOD. L. REV. 179 (1962)

Hitz, *Criminal Prosecution for Contempt of Congress*, 14 FED. B.J. 139

H.J.A., *Contempt of Court, Freedom of Speech*, 24 BROOKLYN L. REV. 123 (1957)

HOUSE UN-AMERICAN ACTIVITIES COMMITTEE, ANNUAL REPORT (1959)

JAFFE, ADMINISTRATIVE LAW (1953)

JANE, THE COMING OF PARLIAMENT (1905)

JOHN, AMERICAN NOTARY AND COMMISSIONER OF DEEDS MANUAL, (4th ed. 1931)

JOURNAL OF THE CONTINENTAL CONGRESS 1778–79 (Ford ed. 1904)

KEETON, TRIAL BY TRIBUNAL (1960)

Kendall, *Can Authority be Delegated to Notaries Public to Punish for Contempt*, 56 CENT. L.J. 144 (1903)

KENNEDY, THE ENEMY WITHIN (1960)

I KENT, COMMENTARIES (2d ed. 1832)

Kroner, *Self-Incrimination: The External Reaches of the Privilege*, 60 COLUM. L. REV. 816 (1960)

Landis, *Constitutional Limitations on the Congressional Power of Investigation*, 40 HARV. L. REV. 153 (1926)

—— REPORT OF THE HOUSE SUBCOMMITTEE ON LEGISLATIVE OVERSIGHT (1958)

LANGDELL, SUMMARY OF EQUITY PLEADING (1877)

Larremore, *Constitutional Regulation of Contempt of Court*, 13 HARV. L. REV. 615 (1890)

LESSER, HISTORY OF THE JURY SYSTEM

LIVINGSTON, COMPLETE WORKS ON CRIMINAL PROCEDURE (1873)

McILWAIN, HIGH COURT OF PARLIAMENT (1910)

McKay, *Speaking Up for Silence*, A.C.L.U. NEWS, No. Cal., Jan. 1961

Maslow, *Fair Procedure in Congressional Investigations: A Proposed Code*, 54 COLUM. L. REV. 839 (1954)

MEDINA, ANATOMY OF FREEDOM (1959)

Merrick, *The Privilege of Self-Incrimination as to Charges of Contempt*, 14 ILL. L. REV. 181

Moskovitz, *Contempt of Injunctions, Criminal and Civil*, 43 COLUM. L. REV. 780 (1943)

Murphy, *The Contempt Power of the Federal Courts*, 18 FED. B.J. 34 (1958)

Nelles and King, *Contempt by Publication in the U.S.*, 28 COLUM. L. REV. 401, 525 (1928)

Newman, *Federal Agency Investigations: Procedural Rights of the Subpoenaed Witness*, 60 MICH. L. REV. 169 (1961)

N.L.R.B. RULES, REGULATIONS, AND STATEMENTS OF PROCEDURE

Notes, 47 L.Q. REV. 315 (1931)

Notes, 73 L.Q. REV. 8 (1957)

O'BRIEN, NATIONAL SECURITY AND INDIVIDUAL LIBERTY (1955)

OSWALD, CONTEMPT OF COURT (3d ed. 1910)

PASQUEL, CONTEMPT OF COURT

PATTERSON, ON LIBERTY OF SPEECH AND PRESS (1939)

Pekeles, *Administrative Discretion and the Rule of Law*, 10 SOCIAL RESEARCH 22 (1943)

—— *Legal Techniques and Political Ideologies, A Comparative Study*, 41 MICH. L. REV. 665 (1943)

Potts, *Power of Legislative Bodies to Punish for Contempt*, 74 U. PA. L. REV. 691 (1926)

The Power of Administrative Agencies to Commit for Contempt, 35 COLUM. L. REV. 578 (1935)

Procedures for Trying Contempts in the Federal Courts, 73 HARV. L. REV. 353 (1959)

Prosecutor Cannot Multiply Contempts by Repeated Questioning Within the Same Area of Refusal, 9 SYRACUSE L. REV. 328

RAPALJE, CONTEMPT (1890)

—— A TREATISE ON CONTEMPT (1884)

Regulation of Contempt of Court, 13 HARV. L. REV. 615 (1890)

REMINGTON, BANKRUPTCY (6ed.)

REPORT OF THE ATTORNEY GENERAL'S COMMISSION ON ADMINISTRATIVE PROCEDURE (1951)

Resisting Enforcement of Administrative Subpoenas Duces Tecum: Another Look at CAB v. Hermann, 69 YALE L.J. 131 (1960)

Right to Jury Trial in Criminal Contempt, 11 U. VA. L. REV. 639 (1925)

Schneider, *The Civil Rights Act of 1957 and Contempt of Court*, 43 CORNELL L.Q. 661 (1958)

Schwartz, *Administrative Law*, 36 N.Y.U.L. REV. 88 (1961)

—— INTRODUCTION TO AMERICAN ADMINISTRATIVE LAW (1958)

—— THE PROFESSOR AND THE COMMISSIONS (1959)

SCOTT, TWILIGHT OF THE KINGS (1938)

Separability of Successive Contempts, 104 U. PA. L. REV. 998 (1956)

Shapiro, *The Supreme Court's Supervision of Congressional Investigations*, 15 VAND. L. REV. 535 (1962)

SIEBERT, PETERSON, AND SCHRAMM, FOUR THEORIES OF THE PRESS (1956)

SKINNER, NOTARY MANUAL (1912)

Sky, *Judicial Review of Congressional Investigations*, 31 GEO. WASH. L. REV. 399 (1963)

Solly-Flood, *The Story of Prince Henry of Monmouth and Chief-Justice Gascoigne*, TRANSACTIONS OF THE ROYAL HIST. SOCIETY (1886)

STORY, CONSTITUTION OF THE UNITED STATES (4 ed.)

Summary Punishment for Contempt of One-Man Grand Jury a Denial of Due Process, 48 COLUM. L. REV. 813 (1948)

SURVEY OF ADMINISTRATIVE ORGANIZATIONS, 85 Cong., 1 Sess. (1955)

SWAYZEE, CONTEMPT OF COURT IN LABOR INJUNCTION CASES (1935)

SWENSON, FEDERAL ADMINISTRATIVE LAW (1952)

TAYLOR, GRAND INQUEST (1955)

THOMAS, THE LAW OF CONSTRUCTIVE CONTEMPT (1934)

THOMAS, PROBLEMS OF CONTEMPT OF COURT (1934)

Tresolini, *The Use of Summary Contempt Power by Administrative Agencies,* 54 DICK. L. REV. 395 (1950)

Trial By Newspaper, 28 HARV. L. REV. 605 (1915)

TRILLING, FREUD AND THE CRISIS OF OUR CULTURE (1955)

Warran and Brandeis, *The Right to Privacy,* 4 HARV. L. REV. 193 (1890)

Weinman, *The Trial Judge Awards Custody,* 10 LAW & CONTEMP. PROB. 721 (1953)

WIGMORE, EVIDENCE (3d ed. 1940)

Williams, *Unintentional Contempt of Court,* 20 MOD. L. REV. 275 (1957)

WILMOT'S NOTES (Wilmot ed. 1802)

Use of Contempt Power to Enforce Subpoenas and Orders of Administrative Agencies, 71 HARV. L. REV. 1541 (1958)

Index

Administration of justice, obstruction of: direct contempts, 68, 71; indirect contempts, 68-69, 70, 71-72; constructive contempts, 77, 188-89; legislation to prevent, 91-92; *1821* statute, 165

Administrative agencies, 121-61; rise to prominence of, 101; questions concerning exercise of contempt power by, 128-43; right to impose civil fines, 130-31; powers to detain, 131-33; quasi-judicial nature of, 138; quality of personnel of, 141-42; administrative contempt as statutory crime, 143-44; indirect and direct court enforcement of orders of, 144-51, 156-58; subpoenas by, 151-56; alleged violation of Fourth Amendment by, 229; self-incrimination clause in testimony before, 248; suggestions regarding use of contempt power by, 285-87, 300, 305

Administrative nature of contempt power, 138

Administrative officers, 37, 131-32

Aliens, administrative agencies' powers regarding, 131, 132-33

American colonial assemblies, contempt power and, 29

Anderson, John, 30

Appeal, right to, in direct contempt, 75-76

Appellate courts, contempt power of, 291; *see also* Judicial revue

Association, freedom of, 195, 215, 216, 221

Attachment, 295-96

Attorneys: exclusion from hearings of federal administrative agencies, 125-26; as "officers of the court,"

168; conduct of, in course of trials, 191, 298-99; misconduct by, under proposed statute defining misdemeanor to government, 304

Bail, Eighth Amendment provision, 264

Bankruptcy courts, 115

Barnett, Governor Ross R., 8, 278-79, 333

Beck, Professor Carl, 197, 198, 244

Bills of attainder, 222-23

Black, Justice Hugo La Fayette: nature of contempt power, 24-25; free speech and fair trials, 94; summary procedure, 171-72, 173, 174, 175; necessity of contempt power, 181; jury trial in criminal contempt cases, 184; freedom of the press problem, 188-89, 190; national security and congressional investigations, 201-2, 205; congressional contempt power, 212, 213; First Amendment freedoms, 221; bills of attainder, 223; proof of contempt requirement, 252; role of judge, 254; criticism of sentencing procedure, 264-65

Blackstone, Sir William, 16, 19

Books and records, examination of, 40, 145, 303

Braden, Carl, 210-13

Brandeis, Justice Louis D., 91-92, 194-95, 219, 236

Breach of the peace statute, proposal for, 303

Brennan, Justice William J., Jr., 252

Brewer, Justice David J., 146, 148-50

Bribing jurors, as indirect contempt, 69